HUMAN SEXUALITY AND ETHICS

EDITED BY
JOHN H. PIET
AND
AYODHYA PRASAD

COSMO PUBLICATIONS
2000 INDIA

HUMAN SEXUALITY AND ETHICS

First COSMO Print 2000

ISBN 81-7755-013-6

*This indipendent and complete volume has been derived from the set - **Encyclopaedia of ETHICS AND LOGIC***

Published by
MRS. RANI KAPOOR
for COSMO PUBLICATIONS Div. of
GENESIS PUBLISHING PVT. LTD.
24-B, Ansari Road,
Darya Ganj,
New Delhi-110 002, INDIA

Composed at
Cosmo Publications

Printed at
Mehra Offset Press

CONTENTS

Chapter-1

Sex Ethics.
Sex Life and Sexuality

Chapter 1

Current Definition of Sexual Phenomena — By sexual phenomena we understand, in current language, the manifestations of that imperious propensity which leads an animal to seek sexual pleasure — generally by approaching a member of the opposite sex—and which may result in reproduction. It must be clearly understood that this definition, so far as it claims to be one, is not altogether satisfactory. It groups together phenomena that are in reality distinct, and it perpetuates confusions, to remove which is the very purpose of our present study. Therefore we can only adopt this definition in an entirely provisional way, merely as a basis for discussion.

The Specific and Imperious Nature of Sexual Acts — Before inquiring into the general position of sexual phenomena in physiology, it is well to call to mind their extraordinarily specific and imperious character — a process which itself will provide us with some interesting matter for reflexion.

It seems unnecessary to insist upon this point, clear as it must surely be even to the least observant. It is especially under the name of "love"—by which is understood the exclusive predilection, more or less prolonged, of one human being for another of the opposite sex—that sexuality has been exalted, studied, praised by poets, and regarded favourably, even by law and religion, as a stimulus which is essential for the perpetuation of the race. There is in existence a whole literature ,of love, which, already enormous, is continuously undergoing addition and renewal, and which (as we should add, for the sake of completeness) is supported by the productions of the other arts : painting, sculpture, etc. This literature is of every kind: scientific, technical, romantic, poetic, dramatic, prohibitionistic, or obscene, according to the tendencies of the writer and his public. It enjoys, moreover, a continuous success.

Psychology—scientific or literary—has had every opportunity to apply itself indefatigably to the study of erotic manifestations. In spite of all the cases, general and particular, which it has so minutely described, erotic psychology still flourishes and never fails to arouse our interest, so long as it brings a little ingenuity to bear on its material. It has contributed, no less than history, a mass of documentary evidence, which should help to enlighten us on love in all its forms, and enable us to distinguish its different categories: from the simple passing fancy to the grand passion which death alone can end.

Sexual *psychology*, however, has shown the existence of other phenomena, which are utterly incompatible with the views of those for whom love is the sole and sufficient domain of sexual need. From earliest antiquity, these other phenomena reveal themselves as no less important than love itself. Neither Onan, nor Sodom and Gomorrah, belong to our own day. These names, which have taken on the valure of symbols, are applicable to all civilizations and to all ages. They call our attention to the possibility of sexual pleasures which are independent of love between the sexes and of its psychology.

Thus, sexuality, in whatever dress it is clothed, and by whatever name it is called, dominates and fills the life of human beings; more so perhaps in the case of man than in that of other animals, because man has applied to it all the good will, persipicacity and subtlety of his intelligence. It is, as Sterne says, "An all-consuming fire," "The Good Thing,"[1] "The Great Thing of Life."[2]

Different Views of Sexual Acts — Sexuality has known every variety of fortune. It has been exalted and apotheosized by both individuals and societies. The phallic religions have made it the master of their civilizations. It has been vituperated and combated by religious and philosophic sects; it has been despised and persecuted by prohibitionistic societies. To it, more than to anything else, we may apply Aesop's fable of the tongue, that organ which is at once the best and the most evil thing; so much so that, to-day in the twentieth century, sexual theory is among the most confused of all aspects of human knowledge, pulled as it is in opposite directions by those who glorify sexual pleasure and those who are hostile to it. Our intelligence is here faced with the most lamentable incoherencies and contradictions. Praise alternaties with blame; law varies with time and place; private life is subjected to a quite intolerable degree of interference; social and individual rights are continually confused; we are surprised, moreover, to find sexuality reacting upon everything — philosophy, religion, law, hygiene, art, literature, politics — and exhibiting every-where the same contradictions.

More than this, sexuality has become the secret, but constant, master of all history. It is the hidden influence of woman on man, and man on woman, which is at the bottom of all marriage and concubinage. Royal marriages; royal mistresses, feminine hatred at work behind the warrior and the poisoner; women dominating national leaders (women who are themselves dominated by the crafty exponents of superstitions and supernatural fears); further, the creation of masterpieces in the light of sexual exaltation, and on the other hand, the lamentable abortion of genius by women who are little better than vampires; all this, together with battles, treaties, invasions, tyrannies, assassinations, glory or defeat — explained almost always by the fact that such and such a male has encountered such and such a female and has become her mate.(What would have happened, for instance, "if Cleopatra had had a shorter nose"?) How can we deny this, when, looking back upon our own feeble lives, we see that it has been directed at certain turnings by the hazard of a sexual encounter?

Thus sexuality is of direct interest to the social group. Sometimes the group is hostile to it, sometimes friendly; it can never be indifferent. The reproduction of the species underlies the very life of the species. Even those metaphysical systems which, like Judaism or Christianity, have been hypnotized by the idea of purity, could not condemn it utterly, since a system which did so would be pronouncing its own death sentence.

Neither the final aim of Buddhism towards Nirvana as the outcome of successive reincarnations, nor the pessimism of Schopenhauer, have prevented the Buddhists from reproducing themselves, nor excluded a love interest from the life of Schopenhauer.

Sexuality is no less influential in determining the general form and details of our daily life. It is our conception of sexuality which is responsible for our social group, the milieu in which we live. Marriage or celibacy, free union, the role (overt or covert, sometimes religious and sacred) of the courtesan, monogamy and polygamy; influence of parents on children, and of children on parents; dramas of passion—all these are nothing but the social physiognomy and the collective consequence of sexuality, which overflows everywhere, and invades everything, and in its victorious progress lays hands even on those who would deny its power. And the happiness or unhappiness of each of us—often the happiness or unhappiness of whole peoples—depends upon the manner in which we have conceived and directed our sexual lives, dealt with its various forms, and submitted its manifestations, voluntarily or involuntarily, to some social principle or philosophic system.

The *imperious* nature of the sexual urge (so imperious that in spite of repression crimes are committed in order to satisfy it) explains why it so completely dominates the human mind. We must agree with François de Curel that, even in the most refined civilizations, men and women have remained like the stags and hinds of the forests, with every sense alert for the approach of the other sex...... And if we decide that this ought not to be, we must have recourse to the rule that was observed in the Abbey of St. Victor, where the monks were bled five times a year to strengthen them in the virtue of continence.

The Profoundly Individual Nature of Sexuality — There can be no doubt about the intensity of our sexual life; it is perhaps the most vital of our functions. While most regions of our bodies are more or less indifferent and seldom occupy our attention, our esstential activity seems concentrated in two centres: the head, which is the seat of our intelligence, and the sexual centres, which have an intimate and special life of their own.

It has been rightly said[3] that "not all parts of our body are equally parts of ourselves." The authors adds: "My limbs are less intimately a part of me than my head or my trunk." If there are any organs of which this reflexion is true, they are certainly the male and female sexual organs. Of them it may be said that they have a sort of personality, and by no means an insignificant one. They have, in all languages, their very special names, with all the luxury of a double or triple vocabulary: scientific, vulgar, and intimate. In the case of both male and female, our sexual slang treats them familiarly, as though they were individual persons with wills of their own. They play a very imposing role in all the relations, gestures, conversations and memories of lovers. They have their histories. For sexual epicures they are always to some extent individualized, as appears clearly in the pet names[4] that are given them, we can, indeed, safely say that, in those in whom sensuality has undergone a really strong development, they are a subject of constant preoccupation, a centre of powerful and imperious vitality. And there can be no doubt that it is much the same with those who look upon them as enemies, and who, by their hostility, show that they regard these organs as the most redoubtable of foes.

No one—unless he is of those who voluntarily cover their eyes with the bandage of anti-sexual prejudice — can deny this peculiar fascination of the sexual organs; everyone could easily call to mind examples from his own life or from that of his friends and acquaintances. This attraction, which can only be explained on the basis of an imperious law of nature—a law which is perhaps rendered still more imperious by the effects of our social prohibitions—is the secret essence of what we call love, as soon as this latter attempts to realize itself. It explains why, in the face of current disapproval, the popular jargon of the love-novel is apt to use such euphemisms as "charms" and "treasures" to indicate those very organs which our anti-sexual morality bans,and forbids us to look at, or even to name. Mysterious infatuation, incomparable, dazzling, and all-powerful, which is with us from infancy to death. A political theory that was genuinely concerned with the prosperity and happiness of mankind would use it as a potent weapon, instead of vainly trying to shut out its radiance. For the cult og the Lingam and the Yoni has not disappeared; it is merely confined to the alcove. It may no longer display itself proudly in processions and no altars, but its manifestations in lovers' intimacies continue to be legion. In comparison with this most essential and vital of human activities, all else appears lifeless, foreign and inert; more especially that clumsy organ, the heart, which has played such an exaggerated role in our mental economy, and has only too often usurped the functions of our brain.

Co-operation of the other Senses — The sexual sense, tyrannous enough in itself, is very skilfuly at enlisting the co-operation of the other senses: in particular, vision, touch, taste, and smell are ready, whenever necessary, to put themselves at its disposal.

Smell plays a role of considerable importance in the sexual life of all the animals. We know that the female body and its organs generally possess a special odour, which excites the male, and urges him to copulation. "If", says Buchner, "we place a female moth in our window, we shall find that the males, even though, as often happens, they may be an hour's flight distant from the house, will soon begin to arrive in crowds. Nay, more than this, if we keep the female in a closed room, the males, guided by their sense of smell, will finally succeed in finding their way down the chimney." Such examples from insect life are familiar enough. Among mammals the influence of smell upon the sexual sense is equally apparent. In the human species the famous *odor di femina* is, for many lovers, neither a paradox nor an object of disgust. Shakespeare, who understood such matters, make Othello hesitate at the mere perfume of Desdemona. The well-known preferences of Henri IV are too common to be considered exceptional. Some individuals are at once excited by the mere odour of a woman, but are disappointed if it is too faint: a young man once told us that certain Oriental women did not interest him, "because they have no smell."[5]

The Spontaneous Character of Sexuality—The influence and fascination of the sexual sense and its organs can be further explained by the following considerations: the human being has no need to be taught how to use his sexual organs for their immediate purpose, *which is that of giving pleasure.* Put together a young man and a young woman, whom we will suppose to be totally ignorant of all the sexual processes; imagine them left to themselves for a certain time, with every opportunity for indulgence, free from all moral constraint and sartorial obstructions: Adam and Eve in a tropical paradise. No one will deny that, without other teaching than the imperious urge of nature, their instincts will lead them to accomplish the sexual acts, which nevertheless is in itself not such a simple thing. It will be with them as with all other animals, who get on well enough without any theoretical initiation, and who proceed, without unnecessary and irrelevant preliminaries, to the essential act.

Perhaps it will be said that a completely ignorant couple is nowhere to be found. But there can be no doubt that such couples have existed; the convential prohibitions attaching to sexuality must sometimes have succeeded in bringing about a meeting between individuals who are entirely ignorant. And in any case there is another fact which no one will attempt to deny, a fact both more frequent in occurrence and easier to submit tc scientific control. We refer to solitary onanism.This individual exercise of the sexual functions is scarcely ever learnt; in the great majority of cases it is practised by the individual as a personal discovery, which often enough he keeps entirely to himself; it is, indeed, the final outcome, one might almost say the crowning achievement, of the fascination exercised by the sexual organs. This fascination is at first more or less diffused, but before very long it becomes definitely associated with a particular act that is found to give a greater satisfaction than all others.

Psychology of Human Sexual Desire — If there is an international language, it is that of sexual desire. Whatever may be the race or culture of the individuals concerned—a gaze, a wink, an attitude, a gesture, have everywhere the same meaning; they are grasped intuitively, and never fail to bring about an immediate understanding between a man and a woman who are bent on mutual sexual satisfaction. All travellers of experience who have not contented themselves with studying the geological characteristics or commercial possibilities of the different countries they have visited, but who have tried to understand the intimate social life of their peoples — an attempt in which our common sexual nature is of more assistance than anything else—are in agreement on this point. There may be prolonged misunderstanding and suspicion between a white visitor and a group of native Papuans. But this same white man and a Papuan girl will immediately understand one another with no more help than that afforded by glance, a touch, or a significant gesture, which is all that they require to make clear to one another their mutual desire and to arrive at a mutual understanding, unnoticed perhaps by others but completely intelligible to themselves. Thus the traveller, in whatsoever country he may be, find it easy to carry out quite extensive and conclusive sexual studies, in sipte of the barriers of language.

If this facility of understanding for purposes of sex is so great as to bridge the gulf between the most distant races, how much greater still is it within any one society! It is a commonplace that social functions, the theatre[6] (think of Stendhal and the Scala at Milan!), lectures, holidays, dances, are, in every social class— in spite of differences in external trappings and social conventions—but so many convenient pretexts for bringing the sexes together and helping them to arrive at an understanding. There is no need to explore this well-known field; we can refer the reader to the novelists and the writers on psychology.On the other hand we shall lay all the greater emphasis on certain manifestations of courtship, which are less often described, because less often observed, but which are rich in lessons for our own particular study.

(*a*) A crowd affords a happy hunting-ground for sexual pursuits, since it provides a variety of favourable circumstances; the very number of those present, the anonymity that it generally ensures, the ease of contact when individuals are pressed close together, the excitement which is always an element of the crowd mind, the greater opportunity of speaking without previous acquaintance. These conditions are of great assistance to men and women who are on the alert for opportunities of sexual enjoyment. Such people habitually seek crowds, just as others seek solitude. Hence the attraction of balls, of travelling fairs, of carnivals (with or without disguises), and the varied gatherings that are to be found in all big towns. Crowded public buildings are likewise favourable for this purpose. In the archives of the *Parquet de la Seine* the reader will find some investigations that were made at the beginning of the century with regard to the various practices of "sexual touching" and of onanism that were to be observed among the public herded together in the Hotel des Ventes.[6]

(b) Travel also facilitates sexual adventure, and for the following reasons: the traveller is no longer among those who know him; consequently he is anonymous; he is in close proximity with others in the same compartment, in which it is an easy matter to start a conversation; there are the same delays at given places; there are the manifold possibilities of hotel life, together with a certain general spirit of adventure which induces in all travellers a state of mild excitement or intoxication. Men who are constantly *en route* enjoy numerous occasions for sexual encounter with women, who in their turn are much more accessible than they would be if they were at home. A gesture, a look, a touch, and there is at once an understanding. In the larger towns there have been prostitutes who have exercised their profession in the numerous suburban trains which are running all day long, showing thus their understanding of the psychology of travel and their ability to profit by it.

(c) We may take this opportunity of stressing the hitherto unduly neglected factor of a certain feeling of guilt shared in common, a feeling which plays a considerable role in love. This sense of conspiracy or common guilt constitutes a tie, by preference a secret and carefully hidden one, between the two individuals concerned, and unites them against the rest of humanity. It may be superficial or profound; it may confine itself to the knowledge of some common tastes or predilections, or it may go as far as crime. Bergson has justly observed that laughter establishes a common bond between the laughers, and derives an added value from this fact. It is in sexual acts however that such a common bond is most fully developed; a circumstance which is partly due to our prohibitionistic attitude, which treats some of these acts as illegal, criminal and punishable offences, and thus *ipso facto* introduces into sexual life an element of genuine guilt. But it is not these last cases that we wish to speak of here. It is this very cloak of immorality, with which our prohibitions have eveloped the sexual act, that allows us to understand how deep is the idea of common guilt between a man and a woman who deliberately arrive at an understanding and unite to experience a forbidden pleasure. The awareness of this guilt constitutes an additional bond between the parties concerned. It makes them stand together against the rest of the world, which is ignorant of their secrets, which menaces their happiness, and is hostile to their little comedy. In fact it produces a general exaltation of their reciprocal desires. This fact draws attention, once again, to the incoherent nature of our system of taboos, which always ends in strengthening just those tastes and manifestations which it seeks to combat. Certain loves may even, in a sense, be kept alive by the mere fact that they are secret; in such cases, lovers who may have adored one another in a difficult situation, such as free love or adultery, soon become cool when circumstances permit of "regularizing" their union, and of their living together openly and legally. Havelock Ellis has published a psycho-analytic document, "The Confessions of a South Russian," to which he justly attributes great importance as a detailed analysis of certain erotic facts.[7] We find here a description of the feelings aroused by a "guilty" situation, which has rarely been equalled as regards detail and completeness, and from which we may be permitted to quote: "When I am in bed with a respectable woman, what excites me most is the idea that something very strange and improbable is happening: here is a woman, who considers it a terrible thing to show certain parts of her body; she hides them from everybody, especially from men; she looks upon them as *shameful,* she does not dare even to name them.... And yet this same woman is now showing them to a man, the very one moreover to whom she ought to be most careful not to show them; for it is her lover, i.e. the man who arouses in her the greatest emotion and anxiety — the man who, more than any other, is conscious of her charms, and who is now gloating on the with lascivious gaze, who, not content with looking at these parts, feels them, manipulates them and excites them by his touch; and he touches them not only with his hands, but with a part of his own body which is equally *shameful* in the eyes of the woman; who, on her part, is usually afraid, not only of touching, but of seeing or even mentioning them, who *ought* indeed never to think about them (for such at least is the convention). This contact, moreover, is not merely superficial; the man introduces his most shameful part into the most shameful part of the woman.....And this violation of modesty is all the more piquant in that it is purely temporary. An hour earlier, or an hour later, the woman has been, or will be, dressed, will carefully conceal nearly every part of her body, and will blush at the very mention of the thing which has given her so much pleasure..... How much would sexual pleasure lose, without all this convention of feminine modesty—absurd as it may seem!"

It will be our task to try to enumerate and trace the origin of the absurdities of our sexual ethics, absurdities which are even greater than the author of this striking description imagines. But for the moment we will confine ourselves to the remark that the emotion which figures in this analysis made by a man is, for analogous reasons, felt also—and in all its vividness—by the woman. It is this emotion, too, which explains why many men feel no desire for professional prostitutes; most of the feelings analysed above are weakened or annihilated as soon as it is known that, through habit or profession, the woman is incapable of experiencing those subtleties and intensities of passion which are associated with the possession of a guilty secret.

(*d*) We must note, finally, that an intensive development of sexual needs may often coincide with a high degree of intellect. This is explained by the fact that individuals who are willing to accept ready-made ideas, without criticism and without sufficient intellectual energy to think for themselves, are equally disposed to accept without opposition those conventional restrictions which limit their sexual activities to a narrow field, or canalize them in a fixed direction (e.g. marriage). Artists, intellectuals and other active minds have difficulty in feeling this same respect for the conventions, and often find themselves compelled to circumvent them. Freud has also drawn attention to the fact that "sexua lprecocity frequently goes with intellectual precocity, and as such is often to be found in the childhood of the most able individuals."

This same relationship doubtless exists in the race as well as in the individual. Puritanism is a characteristic product of the Anglo-Saxon mind; whereas the Latin races, who enjoy an atmosphere of greater freedom of discussion, particularly in matters of religion, are for the most part much more liberal and easy-going in all affairs of sex.

Maeder's Classification—It is obvious that sexual desires are not equally obsessive in all persons. There are some, both men and women, who live only for sex, to which everything else in their existence is subordinated; even if they devote themselves with considerable energy and perseverance to the quest of fame and wealth, it is always with the *arrière pensée* of ultimately making use of these for sexual purposes. Others seem relatively indifferent, both to the variety and to the quality of their sexual pleasures, and content themselves with a more monotonous and scanty ration. In this matter there are the same differences of degree as exist between the gourmet (or the gourmand) and the man who is indifferent to the pleasures of the table and is satisfied with a permanent menu of boiled beef and potatoes. Do these differences depend ultimately upon physiological differences of temperament?

On this question, as on so many others, the classifications made by the psycho-analysts have thrown much light. "Maeder has furnished an example of the process of character-formation as psycho-analysis understands it; according to him, it is possible to recognize two fundamental types among Western women: the uterine or maternal type, and the clitorid or sexual type."[8] We can see at once how easily these two terms can be applied; all those who have studied women have made similar classification, which permits them to place all the women whom they know, and often too those whom they just casually observe, in one category or another.

The woman of the uterine type seeks a situation that is tranquil or assured; in general, she is content with a single man for her whole life; marriage, or (if necessary) a free union of a frankly bourgeois kind, seems to her the natural solution for her problems; deprived of these, she becomes an old maid and, with increasing age, soon loses all appetite for love. Such a woman will, if possible, have children, will be zealously concerned with household matters, and will find sufficient distraction in her own home and the social relations that this brings.....People will write on her tombstone, "a good mother and a good wife." But we should not forget the gratitude we owe to her uterus for these good qualities.

A woman of the clitorid type loves a man for his own sake.

From her first love onwards, she knows no satisfaction greater than sexual enjoyment, i.e. "love," as it is called. She seeks and attracts the attention of males, arrives at an understanding with them with the help of a glance or a gesture, is ready to play her part in sexual intrigue, and is quick to reach the stage of sexual abandon. She lavishes care and attention on her body, always with a view to the "grande affaire," as Stendahl called it, the "love" which is her life. She is always on the look-out for amorous adventure; everything else is of secondary importance. She seeks, or at any rate allows, the most intimate relations with the opposite sex, and looks upon this as a state of affairs that is obvious and natural, regarding it in the light of a passing pleasure, soon to be renewed, rather than as the poem or romance of her life. She is generally broadminded and of a lively intelligence, her love of liberty, individual and social, being strongly opposed to the doctrines of resignation and asceticism. Family life, on the other hand, has but few attractions for her.

Men who understand women seldom make mistakes in this matter: they have only to watch a woman's gait or bearing, to hear her voice or her laugh, to exchange a deep look, to shake her hand—and their opinion is formed. Appearances count for little. "Uterines" may be found in a "clitorid" environment, and *vice versa* ; but the disguise is a simple one, which will not mislead for long, and which a good psychologist will see through without difficulty. It is true that the disguise may be attempted in all good faith, but in such cases the actors inevitably suffer for having to play a role for which they are not fitted. Sometimes they will suddenly abandon the pretence, and then there occurs what in society is called a scandal. The princess elopes with a gipsy, or the courtesan buries herself in a provincial marriage: but in both cases there had been a false start, one that was really in contradiction with the woman's temperament. There also exist, of course, intermediate degrees of these two types-due generally to the exigencies of social life. Thus a married woman may have the habits of a courtesan, although she may find it to her advantage to retain the nominal status of a wife;

another, who is a partner in some irregular union, may, like Juliette Drouet, Victor Hugo's mistress, lead a life that is strictly conjugal in everything except the absence of official sanction.

We have dwelt on this twofold classification of Maeder's because it shows itself so useful in everyday life; also, because it reveals the injustice of indulging in indiscriminate blame or criticism, without reference to the physiological constitution of the woman in question; and lastly, because it reveals the fundamental opposition between the reproductive function, so clearly dominant in the uterine type, and the sexual function, which as obviously takes first place in the clitorid type. We must add, however, that there is no *raison d'etre* for Maeder's restriction of these two types to Occidental women (who merely happen to be the objects of his study). Both types are to be found, not only in the white race, but in all races. The present writer has been able to make thousands of observations which confirm this statement.

Which is the more numerous of these two classes? Maeder and Laumonier, who ask this question, decide in favour of the uterine type. But it is difficult to be sure; such categories are dangerously at the mercy of subjective factors. We have good reason to believe that there are many members of the clitorid type, who, by mediocre observers, might be classed among the uterines. There are married women whom one may put into this latter class, just because of their title of wife, and in spite of the fact that they are notorious clitorids. If we go back to psychic origins and in particular to the period of infancy, which has so much to teach us, it might well be that we should find that clitorids predominated; whereas, later on, many of them are more difficult to recognize, in virtue of that repression of the sexual instinct, with which we shall have to deal in subsequent chapters.

Addition to Maeder's Classification—If Maeder's classification is correct, should it not be applicable to men also? The question has not been asked, doubtless because the sexual acts of men attract less attention than those of women. Women moreover, we must admit, are more discreet, and less ready than are men to compromise their partners. But as soon as we pierce below the surface, and carefully observe the male members of our environment in the light of a little psychological experience, it is easy to divide them also into two large categories, which we propose to call the orchitic and the phallic respectively.

The orchitic type corresponds to the uterine type; to make a good marriage we must bring together members of these two types. The orchitic has no complicated sexual desires : he is dominated by sexuality, like everybody else, but his aim is the expulsion of the seminal fluid, which causes him discomfort when present in excess. But, this desire satisfied, he is generally content to wait in patience till his need recurs. He seeks no unnecessary complications outside of normal coitus. Such excitement as can be obtained from change of partner attracts him but little; in any case he feels no strong need for variation; his sexual appetite can be adequately satisfied in marriage. If a married man, he is unlikely to want a mistress; or at most he will content himself with a very fleeting and occasional affair. If a bachelor, he will develop regular and periodic habits; though, if of a timid disposition, he may, all his life, remain a moderate onanist. He is fond of family life, of the fireside and of children. He often displays greater intelligence than the uterine woman, but he has little artistic ability and is generally conservative; he belongs to the type of good administrator, of the perfect Civil Servant, of the good husband.

The phallic type has the qualities and the defects of the clitorid — indeed there is a perfect understanding between them; they recognize one another in a moment, by their general bearing, if not indeed by their very odour. The typical member of the phallic type is completely dominated by "La Femme",; the *odor di femina* is his daily bread. Except perhaps when very young, he does not so much love any particular woman as all women. He would like to possess them all, if he had sufficient potency. Scarcely has he gained possession of one than he begins to dream of winning another. In fact he is obsessed by the thought of women. He is generally intelligent and brilliant (except when his desires are inhibited, in which case he may be gloomy and reserved), he is often artistic. He is perfectly capable of achieving success, of gaining and occupying the highest posts. But he will always exhibit a certain kind of laziness, or, more strictly speaking, a desire to get through with social obligations, so as to be free to devote himself (as though it were a deliverance and a recompense) to amorous adventure. If he is not too much occupied by this profession, and is more or less free to dispose of his time according to his fancy, he will devote most of it to the search for sexual stimulation, to the society and the embraces of women. The monotonous regime of marriage appals him; or at the very least he feels the need of constantly escaping from its trammels. If married to some quiet and faithful woman of the uterine type, he will make a martyr of her; he may himself be in despair at the suffering he causes, but he will remain none the less incapable of living without change and without sexual liberty. Towards children he is more or less indifferent. Even when he occupies a very prominent position, he will be unable to contemplate an existence without sexual pleasure, and he will run the risk of scandal rather than leave his desires unsatisfied.

It goes without saying that, with men as with women, there are transitional types, exhibiting these characteristics in various degrees. But when (by psycho-analysis or other means) you have once removed the mask of outer convention, you will be able to place any given man without much difficulty in one or other of these classes. Let us as, moreover, that there is neither merit nor disgrace in belonging to one class or the other. Nature is the determining factor, and the individual himself has no more say in the matter than he has in deciding whether he shall be fat or thin.

Constant Influence of the Sexual Concept — The pshycoanalytic studies of Professor Freud have very rightly drawn attention to the continuously active nature of the sexual obsessions which underline the neuroses. It would seem that, after a period of preliminary resistance on the part of the psychologists and psychiatrists, who were at first very startled by Freud's statements, the fact itself is now scarcely any longer contested. But we can go further than this. We can say that, not only nervous patients, but all human beings, are, if not obsessed (for this is a clinical term, and as such reserved for cases of definite neurosis), at least constantly and generally preoccupied with sexual matters.

This sexual preoccupation is clearly evident with those individuals who belong to the phallic and clitorid types; and Freud has shown that it is operative in all children. What he has told us of the symbolism of dreams (and there are many points in his interpretations which are beyond all question) emphasizes once again the constant urge of sexual ideas, which during sleep are continuously manifesting themselves in an indirect fashion,more or less cunningly disguised so as to evade the watchfulness of a half-waking censor.

We would maintain further that, however veiled or hidden in its manifestations, sexuality is continuously active in the case of all individuals without exception. Marriage, both at the early stages of love and later on when it has become a simple thing of habit, is an institution which itself betrays the continuous necessity, both for male and female, of achieving sexual union. Christian doctrine does not hesitate to declare that husband and wife are two halves of a single human being; marriage is therefore a permanent sexual connexion, a sort of second nature. It satisfies the needs of sex in the sense that, both practically and theoretically, it allows them to be constantly and continuously relieved; thus creating,as it were, a permanently sexualized condition of the individual concerned.

The constant nature of our sexual preoccupations is no less evident when we contemplate the structure and content of human thought. Even among those who are commonly held to be absorbed by ambition and to be always hungering after honours and distinctions, the desire to dazzle and impress the female, in order to possess her the more surely, is seldom absent. If wealth is coveted, this is because it is a means of procuring the favours of women and can often make up for deficiencies in youth and manly beauty.Our ordinary conversation frequently reveals an *arrière pensée* of a sexual kind, though sometimes shown only by a *double entendre,* an allusion or a smile. The attraction exercised by one sex on the other may even manifest itself, independently of any *arrière pensée,* in the most ultimate family relationships; the father prefers his daughters, the mother her sons; and many a father, accustomed to a free sexual life, which implies the habit of paying court to women, automatically sets out to win the affections of his daughter, without any sexual intention, but nevertheless with a certain care and coquetry which he would never employ in his relations with a son.

But, above all, we have to realize that this sexual preoccupation does not confine its manifestations to any particular sphere; it is always present, depending as it does upon the physiological centres of sex, which have a more potent appeal than any other organs; in brief, we can truly say that, by its very nature, it is associated with all our acts, almost as strongly as is our very sense of self, in virtue of which we know at every moment that we exist, and who we are. As regards concepts of this kind, it matters little, *so far as practical results are concerned,* whether they are definitely conscious or at least preconscious, or whether they emanate from the distant caverns of the unconscious and merely surround our psychic activity as a light and omnipresent aura; what we have to bear in mind is their permanence, and as a consequence of this, the immense influence which they exert upon our whole behaviour. Of certain individuals, and probably indeed of all (though in some cases this is difficult to show unless we have favourable opportunities of observation), we may say that all the social activities, which have become so absorbing in modern times, were in their origin only in the nature of accessories—

accessories, too, which were not particularly welcome, and were accepted only in virtue of stern necessity; and that the human race has always sought to free itself from them as soon as possible, in order to revert to its essential and dominant occupation, which is sexual. We have all known — and history gives us further numerous examples — energetic, eminent and illustrious persons who, after having dealt in masterly fashion with their task, even if this were the governing of empires, were wont to seek relief and refuge in those sexual satisfactions, of which they had been compelled temporarily to deprive themselves.

Domination of the Sexual Prohibitionists by the Sexual Concept.—If, as we have seen, sexuality exercises an overwhelming mastery over many persons, there are others with whom sexual prohibitions, directed either against themselves, or (if they are active preachers or propagandists) against others, have degenerated into an almost maniacal obsession. Sometimes, under the mastery of this obession, they will adopt utterly indefensible positions; as is the case, for example, with those ardent sexual prohibitionists who are opposed to the prevention of syphilis, or who are alarmed at the prospect of an efficient remedy for this disease, for fear lest this should bring about a greater freedom of sexual relations.

But this state of mind itself implies that the individuals concerned are obsessed by their sexual thoughts. Others may think of sexuality only in order to discover the necessary means of satisfaction; the fanatics of sexual prohibitionism on their part are no less haunted by desire; the only difference is that they pretend to combat it. This itself seems to give a measure of the great power which their sexual thoughts have over them; the strength of these thoughts is revealed by the very necessity for ostracizing them. There would be no need for such elaborate defences if the citadel were not seriously in danger.

In reality, these people experience an all-compelling attraction for the sexual. They surround themselves with it, they are penetrated by it. But, since it meets with energetic opposition from their powerful repressions, which are usually religious in origin, they solve their difficulties by an act of unconscious hypocrisy, which hides their obsession by a noisy and turbulent resistance; not unlike the priest who enjoys the recital of carnal sins when listening to confession. We must not forget that there is operative also the tendency (so little flattering to human nature) to prohibit others from enjoying those pleasures in which we will not, or cannot, ourselves indulge; many of the more ruthlesss systems of morality are based upon such a misconception, conscious or unconscious, of the relativity of needs.

This violent and pugnacious prohibition of sex is itself evidence for the all-powerfulness of sexual ideas; it is a *sauve qui peut* of frightened wills, in constant combat with a formidable enemy; so formidable indeed, that, if the sexual prohibitionists happen to possess religious sentiments of a somewhat archaic kind, they will attribute their obsession to Satan or the Spirit of Evil, in brief, to a sort of exterior power which is endeavouring to "tempt" them. All this, it has been well said, is nothing but a "defence reaction." In his story, *Rain,* Mr. Somerset Maugham gave us a description of this state of mind, which at the time aroused widespread interest.

Chapter-2

Adhesion to Freud's Gerneral Principles—Concordant Evidence From Infantile and Primitive Sexuality

Chapter 2

The Sexual Postulates of Psycho-analysis. – We shall assume, here as elsewhere, that the reader has some knowledge of the now famous researches and conclusions of Professor Freud. We need only remind him in a general way that the outcome of these researches was to demonstrate the extremely important role played by sexual factors in individual and social psychology, a role which had hitherto received too scant attention. We may summarize as follows the essentials of Freudian teaching, so far as its sexual postulates are concerned, reserving for ourselves the task of returning in another chapter to the strictly pathological and medical part of psycho-analytic doctrine:

(a) The sexual emotions and desires plan an important and continuous role in the individual mind.

(b) This is true even in the case of children.

(c) The institution of the "Censor", which represses these sexual desires, and drives back into the unconscious all ideas associated with them (ideas which our modern morals regard as wicked and shameful), is due ultimately to the anti-sexual bias imparted to the growing mind by our social system.

(d) Repression is a condition which is responsible for the formation of the symptoms which reveal the presence of a neurosis due to the non-satisfaction of sexual needs; these symptoms are in the nature of a *pis-aller* or a defence; "human beings become neurotic when they are prevented from satisfying their libido".

(e) When the watchfulness which an individual exercises on himself is relaxed for any reason, the repressed sexual manifestations begin to appear and reveal their importance in a more or less coherent manner (i.e. dreams, delirium, and anxiety).

Value of Psycho-analysis.— This very brief resume will be sufficient to remind us that the welcome accorded to Freud's discoveries has been a very curious one. In Germany and the Anglo-Saxon countries they eventually triumphed over the initial resistances, but in the Latin countries professional psychologists have continued to treat them with a marked reserve. It would seem that the latter attitude has, unfortunately, been determined much more by emotional reactions than by any genuinely critical considerations. There has been a strong tendency to judge the Freudian system according to the standards of conventional morality, rather than to revise this morality in the light of Freud's discoveries.

In other words, our moral traditions have been shocked by the disproof of the conventional view concerning the purity of childhood, and this has led to the fear that an acceptance of the Freudian position may lead to a general overthrow of the conventions of our official sexual morality. In this way our critics, in virtue of their own emotions, have judged psycho-analysis less on its own merits than on its consequences; a very unfortunate state of mind in which to examine a scientific system. It is a resuscitation of the old manoeuver adopted by Kant, when he wrote his *Critique of Practical Reason* to water down the logical consequences of his own *Critique of Pure Reason*.

But there is probably another reason why psycho-analysis has had but little success in the Latin countries, namely, that it raised smaller hopes here than elsewhere. When *Rain*, the dramatic adaptation of S. Maugham's novel, was given in Paris (1927), it had only a half-hearted reception; the critics very rightly said that the character of the anti-sexual and prohibitionistic clergyman, fanatic to the point of cruelty, was incomprehensible to the French public, which has no experience of such extremists. Sexual liberty, less victimized by a pitiless ostracism in Latin Europe than in Anglo-Saxon countries, did not find in psycho-analysis the sudden revelation of the truth, together with the hope of sexual relief and deliverance from a hard and tyrannous regime, which Freud's work brought to these races which were suffering more cruelly from a narrow prohibitionism. For if psycho-analysis, together with its ethical corollaries, must in the end bring about a liberal revolution in our morals, this revolution is in the latter countries already half accomplished.

It goes without saying that a strictly rational criticism would waste no time in dealing with the purely sentimental objections that have been raised against Freud's conclusions, however justifiable these may be from their own standpoint. It would not allow us to overlook or underestimate the value of scientific observations for fear of offending an established doctrine. When such a doctrine, as in the case of our present sexual morality, abounds in contradictions, absurdities, and illogicalities, there is really not much sense in being afraid of the possibility of having to modify or transform it. Indeed, it is rather our efforts to defend it that will in the long run be superfluous; illogical conventions have never permanently prevailed against the teachings of experience. It is astonishing how quickly they change, in spite of the efforts of their old-fashioned defenders; such is the strength of truth.

Far from asking ourselves, therefore, whether we should fear lest Freudian conclusions may necessitate a modification of our sexual morals, we shall not even stop to consider such a useless question. We propose, on the contrary, to start from these conclusions, after having corroborated them, as we think, by certain further observations of our own; and then, with the help of a fuller and more humanistic psychology, to examine what should be our ethical attitude towards sexual acts — a task in which we must not allow ourselves to be blinded by any tendency to regulate these acts in accordance with the moral presupposition that sex is in itself an evil thing.

Difficulties Encountered by Psycho-analytic Observations.—In the first place we must note that in the Western countries where Freud and his fellow-workers have for the most part carried out their studies, especially those concerning the spontaneous manifestations of infantile sexuality, the conditions of observation have been deplorably difficult. It has been maintained that sexual relations attract more attention in German-speaking countries than in others, and that this was the reason for the premature sexual initiation of children so often found in the former countries. But, even if there is a real difference of this kind between Berlin or Vienna on the one hand and Paris on the other, which itself is very doubtful, it nevertheless remains true that the whole psycho-pathology of Western nations is twisted and distorted by the artificial character that has been imposed on sexuality. What dominates Western societies and the civilizations based on Judeo-Christian principles is the idea of sin, an idea which has become intimately associated with the sexual act. We know the import of that doctrine of "original sin" on which the whole of Christianity is built, including the advent of the Messiah Himself. We know that, as a consequence, sexuality dominates the whole logic and ethics of Christianity; and, indeed, one of the most striking proofs of the ever-present force of sexual preoccupations lies just in this fact, that they appear with so much force in a doctrine which has itself exercised so profound an influence upon the human mind.

Now the Judeo-Christian system, in conformity with its presuppositions, has for nearly twenty centuries carried on a bitter warfare against the manifestations of sex. This hostility has found expression in catechisms and in sermons, in sumptuary laws, in the confessional. The sexual act is the *bette noire* and the scape-goat on which the dominant religions of the West hurl their anathemas. It has been looked upon as an example of all that is wicked and shameful, and has long been removed from the field of calm, logical and scientific study.

The result is that Western man, on whom the Freudian observations have been made, is, from the sexual point of view, an artificial being, who has been cut off from nature and lives in a world of conventions.Repression is, in fact, a consequence of the theory of sin. Through the medium of both inheritance and education, it distorts human nature, and interferes with normal behaviour. If repression is absent or is but little evident, we are so surprised at such an exception to the general rule, that we are inclined to regard the person concerned as pathological or unbalanced: the imperious call of nature is immediately looked upon as an infirmity or an anomaly.To pierce this artificial covering has been the task of psycho-analysis; but our primitive nature has been so thickly enveloped by this covering, that artificial beings are to-day in the majority, and therefore give the impression of being normal – to the great confusion of psycho-analysis itself, as we shall presently try to show.

A special effort is therefore needed if we are to rediscover the natural individual, exhibiting the free and primitive co-operation of his senses and his functions, before he has tamely acquiesced in the conventional dictates of morality. And this, doubtless, is one of the reasons why all the observers who have made this effort have naturally turned their attention to childhood, where they could much more easily find a being who was not yet artificialized.

Erroneous Limitations of Sexual Manifestations. — One of the most persistent errors of our general sexual ignorance, an error which has resisted all the teachings of the ancient world and of those civilizations which have escaped the dogma of sin, consists in thinking that sexuality is confined to that period of life which commences at puberty.

Puberty is the moment when, in both male and female, there appear those anatomical and physiological conditions which are needed for procreation. Puberty is indeed a very interesting event. But it is a phenomenon connected with the reproductive function. It indicates that the individual is ripe for reproduction, is fertile, and can carry out the necessary preliminary actions (Lipschutz, Ferenczi, Freud). But sexual life, in so far as it fosters the desire for gratification (though not perhaps in its full measure), has been in existence long before this. Puberty endows this life with new possibilities; it does not call it into being.

Persistence of Sexual Desire among the Impotent. – This fact should perhaps have been brought home to us by the study of those individuals in whom the reproductive functions have ceased to play a part; those who, in virtue of their age, are impotent and sterile. In their case, sexual phenomena may continue to manifest themselves quite strongly, sometimes indeed as strongly as at puberty, and, as is well known, the same is true in the case of professional eunuchs.

According to J.J. Brousson, Anatole France once made the remark: "We laugh at amorous old men, but we are fools to do so." These are the words of an experienced psychologist. In certain persons, no doubt, desire diminishes or disappears with age. But in many others it remains alive, one may even say youthful, in spite of a possible weakening of reproductive power. Here, therefore, we see that the organic functions of reproduction and of sexual pleasure are clearly separated. The need for sensual gratification may be as strong as ever: naturally, the relations between such old men and their partners are determined by the capacities which they retain, but, allowance being made for this, they are not lacking in ingenuity or variety. Beyond a doubt, we have to do here with a persistence of that imperious attraction of sex, in its own right and for its own purposes, which we shall presently show to be operative also in the pre-adolescent.

Elderly women are no less apt to retain the need for sexual pleasure. But the circumstances of their life, their environment, their failing attractions, and their fear of ridicule, compel them to a prudent but unwilling restraint. The facilities available in large towns provide certain possibilities of satisfaction for those who are unable to resign themselves, especially if they are wealthy. But they rarely allow this to be discovered, differing as they do from elderly men in their greater care to keep the matter secret. Occasionally an unexpected incident betrays them. "The murder of a woman in a furnished flat twenty years ago," Colette tells us, "revealed the age and honourable name of the victim., an octogenarian seducer. Notwithstanding her advanced age, she consistently and deliberately led a double life, run on two completely independent lines, which were only brought together by the indiscretion of her death. A stubborn-willed Ninon of Montmartre, she also maintained an unblemished reputation as an indulgent grandmother, and she never confused the two roles."

It is clear that, with certain individuals, the sexual instinct, far from weakening with age, has, on the contrary, a tendency to become more imperious and urgent in its demands. If we may judge from the somewhat reticent explanations furnished by the persons concerned, the reasons for this would appear to be as follows:

(a) Among subjects who have withstood the tendency to repression, the approach of old age, and the fear lest the opportunities for sexual enjoyment should become less easy and less frequent, may cause them to seek such opportunities. In one case we have known, a woman who had been married for thirty-five years burst into tears at the thought that her sexual adventures were perhaps coming to an end.

(b) Among those who have obediently followed the dictates of repression, it sometimes happens that the experience of life eventually brings about a greater scepticism, the various sexual prohibitions, which had at first been accepted without question, no longer arousing such unshakable convictions as they did before; such persons, fearing that they may have been duped during the greater and better part of their lives, may then, with an unexpected haste which is very disconcerting to their relatives, seek to procure the sexual pleasures which they had not allowed themselves in earlier years.

(c) In both these cases it may happen that the better financial position so often enjoyed by elderly persons enables them to be more lavish in expenditure (a thing which is never harmful from the point of view of sexual success), and thus to enjoy pleasures which were formerly impossible. In polygamous countries the number of a man" wives is usually proportionate to the wealth he can devote to their maintenance. In monogamous countries the same rule holds, except that the difference receives no legal recognition.

Thus Anatole France was right. Notwithstanding a complete reversal of circumstances, the elderly person is in much the same position as the child; like the child, but for opposite reasons, he is admonished, criticized and persecuted, whenever he seeks to satisfy his sexual desires. His sexual acts arouse the same scandalized astonishment. This is because the same error is at work in both cases; because the reproductive function is non-existent, we ignore the force and ethical justification of sexual desire, which is not confined to the middle period of life but accompanies the whole of it, childhood and old age included.

The important matter for the sexual psychologist is the fact that *desire* remains just as imperious, just as urgent, just as well defined as in earlier life. And if we grant this, it is easy to foresee that, if, on the one hand, sexuality persists when the reproductive powers have disappeared, there is, on the other hand, equally no reason why it should not ante-date the reproductive functions.

Infantile Sexuality: its Prolonged Neglect.— The recent studies of Professor Freud have drawn widespread attention to the numerous sexual activities which can be observed in children. One of the greatest merits of the Viennese investigator assuredly lies in this first scientific formulation of the doctrine of infantile sexuality, and in the manner in which he has brought forward observations in support of it.

The scientific observation of children is very new. "We may say that the human mind has only just become aware of the existence of children," wrote Gilbert Robin in 1927. Before this time, psychologically speaking, children were regarded as completely negligible quantities; they aroused but little interest, and were all placed without examination in one and the same category.Even in comparatively recent times Comte was led to protest that psychology was wrong in devoting its attention exclusively to adults.And in truth it was neglecting a whole vast territory, from which the students of infantile, feminine and pathological psychology have subsequently reaped such rich harvests.

It is therefore only very recently that we have had any suspicion of the fact that grown-up people knew little or nothing, about children, excluded as they were from all the intimate life of the young.The great gulf which separates the two groups has now been made clear, and, in view of the obstinate vanity of grown-ups, it has been possible to write: "all children are youthful martyrs." Jules Renard had already given expression to the melancholy reflection of Poil de Carotte to the effect that "it is not possible for everyone to be an orphan."

The complete ignorance on the part of grown-up persons of the sexual life of children is doubtless to a large extent responsible for this great lack of sympathy between successive generations, especially in so far as it concerns the relations between parents and children. It is indeed incredible how far some parents can misunderstand their offspring; they believe that the child is indifferent to sexual situations and allusions, and incapable of understanding them, that it is ignorant concerning reproduction and sexual satisfaction. They are blind, for behind their backs there is all the time being enacted a sexual life that is intense and ardent, though secret and concealed. The children who live this life are talking about sex, dreaming about sex, and so far as it is possible for them, tasting its excitements and its pleasures; and thus their intimate life is more hidden from their parents than from many strangers. Indeed, these latter persons, if their powers of observation can penetrate the barriers of reserve, can often verify the fact of infantile sexuality; and it is relatively easy for them to obtain the confidence of the young persons who are so totally misunderstood by their near relatives.

Thus it comes about that the anti-sexual moralists have

formed entirely false ideas concerning children. They see them in an artificial guise, which they have themselves imposed upon the children in order to confirm their own presuppositions; these presuppositions have so successfully ousted direct observation that they have fostered a complete ignorance concerning the immense influence of sexuality in the intimate life of children. With the present work in mind, I have observed, examined and questioned young people of all ages and of all races for a period of thirty years, and I have arrived at the conclusion that Freud's theory of infantile sexuality is profoundly right, and is in harmony with the facts.

Psycho-analysis and Infantile Sexuality.— As is well known, the celebrated Viennese professor has called in question the traditional idea of the purity of children, as contrasted with the open sexual interests of the adolescent. His critical considerations, which have been conducted in a strictly scientific spirit and have been of the greatest value to psychology, have led him to the conclusion that, contrary to what is usually supposed, there exists in earliest childhood, that is to say up to the sixty or eighth year, a highly developed sexual life that has its own well-marked characteristics. Under the influence of teaching and admonishment, exercised by a social environment that is definitely biased against sexuality, the early sexual tendencies, meeting as they do with continual obstacles both from persons and from outer circumstances, gradually succumb to repression. When this process of repression is completed, we have the finished article, i.e. the civilized man according to our modern formula; an individual who has acquired either the desired degree of artificiality or else a neurosis.

Before we proceed, it is well to call to mind the general criticism that has been raised against the psycho-analytic theory of infantile sexuality. Psycho-analysis, it is said, is so bent on finding explanations in accordance with its own theory, even when working in perfect good faith, it is inevitably led to interpret all its observations in terms of sex. Now it is true that this general criticism can be justly made against all those who study their facts with a view to the verification of some general principle or system, and to that extent account must be taken of it in the present case.But it must be equally borne in mind in considering the claims of Freud's opponents when they deal with this question of infantile libido; these latter are themselves too often victims of an opposite prejudice; the traditional view of the "purity" of young children appears to them so unquestionable that they are inclined to reject a *priori* all evidence to the contrary, and, in their turn, tend to minimize the significance of certain observations, or to shut their eyes to their true scientific value.

We must, here as elsewhere, make every effort to prevent our observations being coloured by our desires. But, first of all, we must understand the real nature of infantile libido, and its imperious character.It has been said, for example: The little boy and little girl play at being husband and wife. They kiss and embrace one another, repeating actions which they have seen, but it is impossible to know whether their actions correspond to the feelings experienced by their father and mother in the same circumstances." True, but we must realize that the infantile libido has little or nothing to do with these games. It is a very different thing. It relates to actions and desires of a much more imperious kind, as we shall have occasion to show.

In other words, the study of children, as the psycho-analyst understands it, is a very different matter from a superficial examination; it goes without saying that, as Freud reminds us, "if it were generally true that the simple observation of children were sufficient, psycho-analysis would be unnecessary."

The Child and its Early Memories. —We are entirely in accord with Professor-Freud when he says: "the child devotes to the solution of sexual problems an energy with which we should hardly credit him, and we may even go so far as to say that it is these very problems which awaken his intelligence."

As is well know, psycho-analysts have put forward the very interesting view that, owing to the repression which occurs about the age of six or eight, there is brought about a half-voluntary, half-unconscious, forgetting of the impressions of earliest childhood, which are overcome in their struggle against the superior forces of (so-called civilizing) education; and which, as is usual with the vanquished, must submit to being banished, and therefore forgotten.

We believe, however, that it is not really so difficult as is often thought to recover the sexual memories of infancy, even without the aid of psycho-analysis; though in this case, perhaps even more than elsewhere, we have to overcome that strong tendency to reserve and concealment, often scarcely realized even by the individual himself, that the practitioners of this therapeutic method know so well.

For general purposes (and without reference to exceptional cases) we may define childhood as that period of life which ends at puberty. To write, as is sometimes done, with exaggerated moral emphasis, of "a child of eighteen years" is pure nonsense.Such a phrase can only come from a gerontomaniac. And we may say that even the law has gone too far in its tendency to extend the duration of minority to the twentieth or twenty-first year. For this amounts to putting human beings in tutelage for a third of their whole existence, although, as a matter of fact, they would probably be more capable of directing their own lives if we did not take such care to ward off every occasion which would be useful in providing them with real experience.

If, following a more reasonable rule, we take childhood to be the period that ends at puberty, it still covers some eleven or twelve years, with variations according to climate and personality.But very little observation is required to show that this period itself is not uniform, but must be subdivided.

It is generally admitted that there exist a first and a second period of childhood. According to this view, the first period lasts until about the seventh or eighth year, while the second extends from then onwards to the age of puberty. It is remarkable that these observations are in harmony with certain distinctions which had already been made in some of the ancient civilizations of Europe and Asia. In Rome, especially, such a distinction was admitted by law, and from the age of seven years a child had the right to carry out himself such acts as he thought might be to his advantage.

The first period of childhood is one which is naturally devoted primarily to the education of the more automatic functions; the child directs his attention to the working and the mastery of his various organs; he learns useful or conventional rules which help him to the proper control of equilibrium and gait, the positions suitable for sleep and rest and the nutritive and excretory functions, the easier and simpler associations of ideas, the use of memory for purposes of classification, the steps to be taken to avoid danger, the methods of acquiring desirable objects. In the beginning, associative memory appears to work under somewhat unfavourable conditions, and will only later on reveal itself in its true value. Indeed, the memories of the first seven years are usually vague, *blurred* and confused; for the first months they are non-existent.

The second period of infancy is characterized by much greater clarity and precision of memory. This difference is so great that it must strike even the least skilful observer; hence the rule established by the ancients, though they did not enjoy the help of scientific psychology. The difference corresponds perhaps to some physiological maturation of which we are still ignorant. But, whatever be the reason, this period, supported as it is by an already perfect memory(often indeed more perfect than at a riper age), is a period of psychic education. The intelligence is, as we say awakened.The child can learn, retain, investigate, and make use of, the more difficult relations between ideas. The social importance of conventions begins to make itself felt. The individual learns, more and more, how hopeless is his fight against the community. Hypocrisy is one result of this; while another consequence is to be found (in terms of Freudian psychology) in the half-voluntary, half-instinctive rejection by the unconscious of much that the first period of childhood, guided as it was only by nature, had admitted—of much, too, that is better to forget, if we are to abandon the useless fight against convention.

Taking this distinction for granted, we will now consider what is its importance for sexual development.

Psycho-analysts in general believe that the sexual memories of the first period of childhood are almost entirely forgotten, or at any rate are concealed by a screen of later memories. We do not believe that this statement is altogether true: on the contrary, there is reason to believe that, in the general poverty and confusion of the memories of first childhood, it is just the sexual memories that stand out and dominate the others by, virtue of their remarkable clearness and precision. The difficulty lies in obtaining sincere statements on this point. It is incredible how far dissimulation can be carried in these subjects, and the psycho-analysts themselves are, if we may be allowed the expression, "taken in" nine times out of ten, even when they imagine that they have discovered all there is to know about the patient. If it were possible to obtain complete and circumstantial "confessions," it would be easy in a few months to provide a volume of observations (bearing particularly on the subjects of onanism, incest, and homosexuality) which would definitely this question of infantile libido. Let each one delve sincerely in himself, and he will surely agree with this statement.

The best method of obtaining complete data concerning the sexual memories of childhood, especially its first period, is perhaps not that of psycho-analysis. Our hope lies rather in the attainment of sexual liberty, which will make us look upon sexual manifestations as natural physiological acts, which can be freely confessed, since there is no longer any point in hiding them.In the present prohibitionistic conditions, the best method is perhaps that of intimacy, especially erotic intimacy between lovers, who, far from concealing from each other their earliest sexual memories, will, if only they are intimate enough, freely confide in each other and fearlessly communicate even the most starling details. There are no better amateur psychoanalysts than lovers, when they are alone with one another.

Here, at any rate, is a typical case of a memory from early childhood. The subject has only very vague and occasional recollections of the first seven years of his life, and those that he has are separated from each other by wide gaps.It was only in the case of a few rare and important occasions that there was left behind an isolated memory, an image rising like an island from a confused sea, and having no connexion with the circumstances which preceded or followed it. For example, the subject can "see" himself entering the room of his grandmother when she was dead and lying on her bed, but he has forgotten everything about her funeral; he "sees" himself, being ragged by some mischievous little bullies at his boarding school, but he cannot remember the appearance of the school itself, or of the town where it was situated. He has, however, some very clean sexual memories, the chronological order of which is as follows: at four years, exhibitionistic and coprophilic acts in the quadrangle of the school, carried out during playtime with his small comrades, acts which were accompanied by a clear consciousness of doing something that was forbidden, and which were hypocritically denied when the child was questioned on the matter; at the age four and a half, nocturnal excitement ending in a paroxysm, after having been taken to a somewhat *risqué* play where he had seen a young actress "in a red dress," whose appearance caused him to fall violently in love, and to express himself spontanecusly in words of adoration; at the age of six, renewed exhibitionistic acts like the earlier ones, but this time carried out in the classroom. All these memories differ from the others in that they are extremely clear and definite, just as clear in fact as the memories of the second period of childhood; the subject remembers the exact appearance of the actress "in red"; he can still hear the severe tone of voice in which he was questioned, together with his own hypocritical reply, when at the age of four he was surprised in the middle of his as yet uncensored exploits,

The reader will be asked to accept the statement that such cases could be multiplied indefinitely. Those who have studied these questions by means of psycho-analysis would do well to pay attentions to observations of this kind. It is only by experience and frankness that we can obtain adequate evidence concerning the great strength of infantile sexuality. We believe that it is possible to call to mind quite vividly a great number of facts which are not really forgotten, as has been maintained, but which are only concealed or neglected, and are in truth perfectly accessible to consciousness.

Confirmation of Psycho-analytic Observations on Infantile Sexuality.—We must refer the reader to the numerous psycho-analytic works for a proof of infantile sexuality. As is well known, Professor Freud and his followers have endeavoured to reconstruct all the sexual life of children which is misunderstood by the grown-up observer and concealed, by a voluntary or unconscious amnesia, even from the persons actually concerned. By the time we are grown up we no longer possess the natural sexual mentality of our first years, but a conventional sexual mentality, due to our religious, moral, social, pedagogical and family upbringing. And, having lost to view our primitive mentality, by a false interpretation of values, we imagine that our conventional mentality is natural and corresponds to the logical and physiological reality of things. We cannot insist too much upon this fact, for we believe that it affords the true explanation of why there have been raised against psycho-analysis so many objections of a kind which, though proclaimed in perfectly good faith, were based on an all too superficial observation. We shall return to this point later on.

The existence of infantile sexual activity had been noted even before the time of Freud. In one of the comedies of the younger Dumas we find the following words addressed to a young girl: "You know as well as I do (for you yourself were young not so long ago), that from sixteen years onwards, consciously or otherwise, rich or poor alike, all are really interested in one thing only, marriage. That is the great riddle, the great mystery. ." We may accept this as good evidence — if we allow for the euphemistic use of the word "marriage" to indicate sexual pleasure, and for the age indicated, which is inexact and much too high, as we shall see, but which is a good instance of the erroneous belief, so prevalent in the nineteenth century, that sexual manifestations do not appear until relatively late in the course of development.

We must remember, first of all, that some kind of intimacy between the two sexes was formerly considered normal and permissible, even in our own Western countries, at a much earlier age than at present: the limit which was allowed by law and custom was, as a matter of fact, usually that of puberty.

"Religious law, intended for the use of many different races, but adopted in the first place for the Mediterranean peoples, had preserved, and still preserves, the Roman custom which fixed the age of marriage at fourteen years for a boy, and at twelve for a girl. Revolutionary law had only raised these limits to thirteen years and fifteen years."

The French penal code of 1808 reserved punishment for cases of sexual violence; the law of April 28, 1832, fixed the age of consent at eleven years, and it was only in 1863 that this limit was raised to thirteen. England, true to ancient Christian usage, until 1929 retained the marriage age at twelve for girls and fourteen for boys. To mention only the case of girls, the age for marriage is fixed at twelve years in the Argentine, Mexico, Spain, Kentucky, Louisiana, Virginia, Kansas, Missouri; and at thirteen years in New Hampshire. Sometimes no age is fixed beyond that of puberty (Chili), and the question of fact only is considered. The law of the Koran, very well informed, like all Oriental documents, on the sexual psychology of children, authorized the marriage of girls at nine and of boys at twelve. In India, as is well known, infantile marriage has been customary for many centuries. Statistics relating to the year 1927 show that in the Presidency of Bombay 74,000 children were married before the age of five (among these 3,000 widows); and about 350,000 between the age of five and ten. This Hindu custom seems to be very popular and had never shocked anyone until a few years ago. It is only under the influence of foreign ideas—especially after the publication of a recent book by Miss Mayo, which violently attacked Hindu social customs from the Western point of view, without any attempt to understand the racial differences involved—that certain Hindu politicians hurriedly proposed to suppress the custom of infant marriage.These proposals seemed to be inspired less by local conviction than by the fear of appearing to outrage the sexual code of the West. Finally, we may call to mind that, as a rule, penal law makes the age of consent lower than the age of marriage, as soon as this latter becomes fairly high (France, Italy, Siam, Japan, etc.), thus doing homage to the teachings of nature.

The experience of our fathers was very definite on this point, and it took into account a fact which is supported by all our available data, viz. that the knowledge of matters relating to sex, its mechanism, its significance, the pleasures which it brings, is easily the first to be acquired by the growing human mind, even in cases where ideas on all other matters are elementary and backward. They used to say that love made stupid girls witty; for our part we can only admit the truth of this dictum and attempt to make it more precise: We should then say that sexual phenomena are the first to arouse interest and to provoke experiment even in the least intelligent.

In addition to the evidence from the early age of marriage in former days, biographical writers give numerous instances of the precocity of very young girls and their willingness to indulge in sexual acts, *often even before puberty*. Typical examples can be found in the *memoirs of Casanova.*

Those modern novelists whose work is autobiographical or

based on genuine observations do not hesitate to show us how much our prejudices with regard to the "innocence" of children depend on pure convention, and how precocious in reality are the sexual desires. Thus Rachilde writes: ".....I never believed in any feminine innocence: a girl of fifteen, when she is in love, knows as much as a courtesan." These age limits may be appreciably lowered in certain cases and in certain climates. I have met Chinese or Indo-Chinese girls of ten years or less to whom the above-quoted remark of Rachilde would literally apply. And indeed there is no one who cannot corroborate all this from his own experience, even though it be more or less "repressed" as the result of the anti-sexual prejudices among which we have grown up.

It is only as the outcome of a very artificial custom, a custom due perhaps to the desire of older women to prolong as far as possible their own erotic life *and to protect themselves from the disastrous rivalry of young girls*, that there has come about the gradually increasing postponement of the age of marriage and of the legal age at which a woman is allowed to indulge any wishes she may have for sexual relations outside marriage. To confuse, as certain systems tend to do, this sexual coming-of-age, which implies freedom to dispose of one's own body, with the coming-of-age for purpose of citizenship is at variance with all the principles of physiology and hygiene. A source of unjustifiable interference with private life, this error condemns us either to hypocrisy, to the sexual neuroses the result from the stupid emasculation of our mental life, or to an enforced deprivation of sexual pleasure during just those years when it is most desired and most enjoyable. In general it may be said that every system which arbitrarily attempts to prolong the period of childhood during years in which the individual is adult and perfectly capable of intercourse is in flat contradiction with all the teachings of nature.

Pre-pubertal Onanism.—Even before the time of Freud, physiologists and physicians had of course noticed the unmistakable occurrence of onanism in the pre-adolescent child.

We shall deal a little later on with the conclusions to be drawn from this important fact. For the moment let us confine ourselves to consideration of the available data. Dr. Garnier in his monograph on Onanism reports a large number of observations on such children. Here are some of the most characteristic of them, considered only from the point of view of age, which alone concerns us for the moment.

1. A boy ". . . from the age of six or seven was attracted only to the little *boys* in his school, although this was a co-educational one."

2. A girl of seven, "by means of wheedling allurements and bold embraces, enticed four boys of fifteen to eighteen to handle her, one after another, placing herself between their legs or on their knees, when they were sitting down; when she was alone she would sit astride the edge of a chair to masturbate."

3. A boy of three loses strength because "his nurse had taught him solitary practices."

4. A little girl of one year old "already practiced onanism with great abandon."

5. A little girl of seventeen months practised onanism "not only with her hands, but also with her thighs and her legs, so as to produce the friction necessary for orgasm."

6. A little girl of four years "instinctively abandoned herself to masturbation."

7. A child of seven or eight years was "observed practising masturbation at La Charite."

8. Dr. Garnier's observations on the genital regions of young boys who practised masturbation showed that at nine or ten years there took place the emission of a "thin and imperfect spermatic fluid."

9. A little girl of seven used much ingenuity to practise masturbation in spite of a so-called girdle of chastity.

10. A boy of eighteen months comes back from his wet nurse "with the habit of masturbation."

11. A boy of seventeen years writes that he has practised masturbation for ten years (that is from the age of seven), and particularly during the last four years.

12. A little girl of four years, a patient of Martin in Lyon, practised onanism "by an automatic movement."

13. A girl of five years "handled herself with the greatest excitement, day and night."

14. A girl of eight years is treated by Dr. Morelot for excessive onanism.

15. "From the age of three, a little girl showed the greatest pleasure in masturbation, lying on the hassock, and pushing herself against a piece of furniture."

16. Dr. Lachaise treats a girl of seven years for excessive onanism.

17. The case of a girl of twelve years "addicted to manual practices for several years.

18. Observations by Dr. Garnier on the practices of little girls "who rub themselves with up-and-down movements and crossed legs."

19. A boy of five years, whose right hand had been amputated, practised masturbation by "a peculiar rubbing movement which imitated coitus."

20. The case of two boys between six and seven who were observed in a public walk practising fellatio.

21. It is admitted, in a general way, that the genital organs become capable of erection about the age of three, and that masturbation can take place from this period. (S. Freud.)

Onanism is certainly the most significant manifestation of the sexuality of childhood. In addition to the private cases known to parents and doctors, the fact is well known to the heads of institutions (both of boys and of girls), who are often brought in contact with cases of individual or collective onanism. A very important point for our present purpose, as we shall see later on from its consequences, is here again, the fact that onanism appears *before* puberty.

We must insist upon this fact, because it so clearly reveals the nature of the many errors which have brought such terrible confusion into sexual problems.

Sexual Desire before Adolescence—Before starting on the present work the author collected a large number of observations, both those of others (such as were contained, for instance, in the reports made by the heads of institutions, or in the reports of criminal cases classed as moral offences), and those made by himself (either from personal experience or from confidential accounts he had received, especially those obtained in the course of his residence and travels among many races).

Some of these observations may be added here, in support of those already given

1. La Marquise de Brinvilliers tells us in her confessions that she practised masturbation from the age of five and lost her virginity at the age of seven.

2. Racine wrote a love romance at the age of fourteen.

3. In a boys' school, children of from four to ten met together at each recess, under pretence of some game in an isolated corner of the playground, but really to practise mutual masturbation and exhibition; this being made the subject of a small inquiry by the head of the institution.

4. In another boys' school a pre-adolescent pupil induced his comrades to practise fellatio with him, having smeared himself with some liquor he had brought to tempt the greed of his willing playmates; cases of this, kind though of course with individual variations, are quite numerous.

5. In still another boys' school the young pupils were discovered indulging in mutual exhibitionism at their desks,

and were amusing themselves in "dressing" like a doll the penis which they were using for the purpose.

6. A boy of eight found a substitute for orgasm, of which he had as yet no knowledge, in rubbing his penis against cake or in jam, which he afterwards consumed in a sort of sexual ecstasy.

7. A boy of five was taken by his parents to the theatre to see an erotic play (on the supposition that "he would not understand"): in reality he passed a very disturbed night, crying out to the great stupefaction of his parents—"I love cocottes and mistresses" (*sic*). This boy had no knowledge of the physiological differences between the sexes.

8. There are frequent cases of "childish passion," especially of a little boy for a little girl; the author has noted a case of this kind (a boy of eight), which showed all the phases and sufferings which are found in the loves of adults.

9. On the platform of the station at Khartoum the author observed a naked little body of seven masturbating mechanically with his hand and finishing with a mild orgasm, while walking in full view of the public.

10. In China, at dinners between friends, children of both sexes were sometimes placed under the table and instructed discreetly to masturbate the guests. The use of child (pre-adolescent) courtesans was at one time quite frequent, and still exists, but less openly because of Western criticism.

11. A young Catholic boy of twelve made his first communion; we will say nothing about the sins against chastity of which he may have accused himself in his preliminary confession. Between this confession and the communion itself twenty-four hours elapsed, and, just before the communion, this boy, conscientious and sincere as one is at his age in these matters, told his confessor that he had not ceased to "have dirty thoughts in spite of himself, and just because he knew it was forbidden."The case could be reported because it was outside the confessional. It shows, at one and the same time, the

obessiveness of sexuality, the tendency to neurosis, due to resistance, and the error so frequently made by anti-sexual teachers, who have never understood that prohibition is the best means of stimulating desire.

12. The following observation may be compared to the preceding one, though it applies to an older subject. During some parlour games at a party they were playing: "A lady and a gentleman met one another..." when it came to the question "Where" the only young girl of the company (sixteen years) wrote on her paper, "in a W.C."; but her name was betrayed by her writing....a typical case of sexual obsession.

13. The author has observed numerous cases of preadolescent girls in Egypt, in China, in Indo-China, etc., who are much addicted to sexual manipulations, with all the variations of which they are very well acquainted.

14. The author has also observed that young pre-adolescent Kabyle girls will spontaneously lift their "gandourah" on the high road when a traveller passes, in order to show him their nudity and to obtain some little coin by way of recompense.

15. For details concerning the "child courtesans of the West the reader may consult the already quoted confession of a South Russian for typical observations made in Russia and in Naples. In the course of his own travels the present author has had the opportunity of verifying the facts mentioned in connection with the latter place, for he has himself observed cases analogous to those described.

16. In the case here quoted (13,14, and 15), there is no question of any compulsion on the part of intermediaries. The children in question spontaneously, and with obvious enjoyment, seek occasions of sexual pleasure, even with persons much older than themselves. The South Russian says of a Neapolitan girl of eleven years that her face was "beaming with joy" when he came to her for sexual amusement.

17. In a series of observations made by S. Bell, the earliest appearance of sexual love took place in a child of three; with

this we may compare the love of Alfred de Musset at the age of four for his cousin Clelie.

18. According to the reports of many travellers, in hot countries such as Madagascar, the banks of La Plata, Africa, etc., sexual relations begin between the age of six and seven.

Tragedies of Infantile Sexuality.—From all this we can well understand how it comes about that the prohibition of sexual pleasure brings about many heart-rending dramas in the lives of those whom our ignorant and unobservant anti-sexual moralists insist on treating as "children" (even after puberty),

In most instances, these so-called children, cowed and broken in spirit, true martyrs of our sexual morality, are driven to solitary satisfaction, sternly concealing, meanwhile, the sexual secrets which they cherish in their inmost hearts, and ardently yearning for the greater freedom that will come with age, and the disappearance of those restrictions, which, well meant though they are, in the end arouse the hatred of the victim. Sometimes, when the persection becomes too strong and abstinence is no longer possible, some great drama tragically rends asunder the veil of mystery, stupefying the onlookers, hide-bound as they are in their immovable traditions, and illuminating, as by a flash of lightning, all these hidden secrets; and the price of this is death, in the form of suicide or murder. Cases of suicide of so-called "children" on account of love and "crimes of passion" committed by children could easily be quoted by the hundred.

Parents and neighbours think they have only to do with a child "who ought not to know about these things yet." This is the law of sexual morality. But there is also the law of sexuality itself, i.e. the law of nature. And nature puts into the senses and brain of the so-called child exactly the same ardent desires, the same fierce suffering (since it may even lead to crime), as are to be found in adults, to whom alone convention would allow these feelings. Crime, it is true, is but a rare and startling explosion.The silent martyrdom which testifies, alas, to the tyranny of the family and the obstinacy of society is an everday affair.It arises from the fact that society and the family treat adolescents as responsible individuals when it is a question of sending them to earn their living, of their working and earning money–but suddenly deny them all right of disposing of themselves for sexual purposes, at the very age too when these latter interest them most. How futile, illogical and hypocritical, to deny the right to know that which is in truth already understood and which is desired above all other things...

The societies of the East and Far East, on the other hand, have understood the necessity of allowing adolescent individuals of both sexes to enjoy the pleasures of sex at an early age. They do not condemn their young to sacrifice years in pointlessly delaying the performance of a natural act, just these years too when desire declares itself most frankly, most strongly and most charmingly. In this way they avoid also the gloomy and bloody dramas of the West.They would not even understand such dramas, for if delay of the kind that is customary in the West were proposed to them, they would doubtless reply in words like those of the little Kabyle girl in Elissa Rhais's novel: "Wait for what? Wait till my skin tans and I eat the children in my womb? With us, when the sheep is fat, it is killed for salting, and when the gutter of a girl's house begins to flow, she is ripe for marriage....."

We must leave it to the reader to supplement the cases we have described by others of his own. The most useful observations are always personal ones, and all those who have enjoyed a little experience of life will have some at their disposal. Our present task is to draw from all these lessons such conclusions as we can regarding the true physiological nature of the sexual urge.

Considerations on Infantile Sexuality. — There are, it would seem, a number of individuals in whom the sexual needs are developed so early, that to insist in their case upon a prolonged delay before they are allowed to satisfy them is comparable to the torture which is rapidly growing animal would suffer if it were kept for a long time in the same small cage.

When little girls and boys are not hampered in their development, and thus rendered hypocritical by conventional restrictions, it is astonishing to see how sure and rapid is the growth of their sexual desires. In particular, the appearance of menstruation in girls is by means an indispensable condition, but only indicates the possibility of reproduction. Experience shows that curiosity, desire, pleasure, excitement, satisfaction, and indeed complete sexual relations, can precede menstruation; and it is doubtless just because all this is possible, and is indeed well known, that legislation has thought it necessary to erect so many obstacles calculated to prevent the exercise of the sexual functions in young girls and boys (since the chindren themselves have no personal repulsion in the matter).

Even before all sexual relations, indeed at a time when bodily imaturity renders them as yet impossible, there is nevertheles in many cases an extreme and over-mastering interests in everything sexual; as though it were a period of preparation, during which the individual, by one means or another, gathers information with an ardour which needs no exhortation from a teacher. The present author is acquainted with the case of two girls of ten (of Indo-Chinese descent) who had in this way acquired a more or less complete sexual knowledge; their education having entirely preserved them from all idea of sexual repression as this is understood in the West, they exhibited a surprising accuracy and breadth of understanding, due more to keen observation than to personal experience. Cases of this kind have certainly been very numerous in the societies where children have not been brought up in a directly anti-sexual fashion (Greece, Rome, the East, China, Africa, Polynesia, pre-historic races, etc.).

Freud's Observations on Polymorphous Libido.— Finally, we must refer the reader to the psycho-analysts' explanations of the general sexual pleasure which they believe accompanies even the earliest behaviour of little children. It must suffice to say here that their observations on this subject are at any rate in agreement with that singular and undeniable power of fascination that the sexual organs possess even to the youngest children (and therefore quite independently of any influence on the part of the reproductive functions). It goes without saying that the tendencies to onanism shown in the examples which we have previously given clearly point to the existence of a capacity for pleasure, relatively diffuse and feeble it is true (especially when we compare it with that of puberty), but which always manifests itself in some way or other in the behaviour of the child, and which is easy to interpret in the Freudian sense ("Polymorphous Perversion"). Sexuality is able to function, and does in fact functions, from the earliest years, in the same way as do the other physiological manifestations. In truth, it needed all the power of the conventional hostility to sex to enable us so long to shut our eyes to this, when in reality it was so very clear.

The objection has been raised that such individuals arrive at puberty without having a clear idea as to the real meaning of sex. This objection, however, implies a confusion between *knowledge* and *feeling*. It is true that in sexually prohibitionistic countries, and in cold Western climates where clothes paly an important role, there are some children who do not even know the anatomical differences between the sexes. This may result in their desires being directed indifferently upon beings of their own sex, or even on themselves ("Narcissism"). In one of our above-quoted observations, certain children (in the first period of childhood), who met together to indulge in mutual manipulations and exhibitions, showed in fact that they had not the smallest idea as to the nature of these differences; but the fascination of sex was nevertheless intense and strong enough to overcome all regulations. Since reproduction can play no part here, it follows that reproduction and sexual pleasure are two different things; and after all, in desires which are satisfied mechanically, this question of sexual differences is of minor importance. Although puberty, with its new and more abundant internal secretions, is a great stimulus to sexual activity, sexuality itself has already attained its full scope before this time, and it is clear that a knowledge of the anatomical difference between the masculine and feminine organs is in no sense necessary for the arousal of desires and infantile passions, in which the attraction of the opposite sex makes itself keenly felt. Many little boys who are totally ignorant of these differences are yet in love with women — in the person of their mother, their sisters, their comrades, or an actress (as in observation 7 above).

Confirmation of Psycho-analysis by Observations on non-Europeans. — Here, I think, we may bring some fresh data of a not altogether negligible kind in support of Professor Freud's theories. The Viennese investigator seems, with good reason, to have confined his observations to a milieu which, in its racial characteristics, was essentially Aryan and Western, and in its ethical characteristics Judeo-Christian. This, however, is but a small portion of humanity. His observations would gain in importance if they could be extended to all peoples, especially to those of difference race and creed.

Now, the psychologically minded traveller has many opportunities of proving that the observations made on children or on persons uncontaminated by repression are confirmed by those that can be made among many non-European races.

In the first place, some of these races are still in a mental condition which resembles that of childhood. They are nearer to nature and further from artificiality, just as are young people. They are the children of humanity. Such as they are, however, they enable us to reconstruct those epochs which the Western races themselves passed through thousands of years ago. One of the great benefits which science has reaped from the systematic exploration of all the uninhabited parts of the earth has consisted in showing to the more civilized people of to-day a more or less accurate picture of the stages which they themselves went through in the past. This is especially true of certain tribes of African negroes, of Polynesians, of Australians, of Eskimos, and of the now extinct Tasmanians, who gave us a living picture of human beings of the Palaeolithic period, and who had been isolated from the rest of humanity for twenty thousand years. The nearer a race is to nature, the less artificial, the less influenced by philosophic speculation, the closer its attitude to sexuality approximates to that of children. It required a great effort on the part of missionaries to substitute the theory of sin for the natural, a-moral, and deliberate abandon which existed among the Polynesian peoples; it was necessary to carry out an extensive process of repression, on the lines of the Judeo-Christian ethical system, just as is necessary in the case of young children. Acute minds have indeed asked to what extent this forced and artificial culture may have been, in part at least, responsible for the deadly neuroses which have decimated these races.

On the other hand, we know that in the West, in accordance with the present ethical system, a child is submitted from the earliest age to an intensive moulding influence, which, with the aid of heredity, is responsible for the mechanism of the Censor and repression. Even if, when he is grown up, he abandons the religious beliefs of childhood, he will nevertheless long continue to feel the effect of this influence; and indeed his environment will not easily allow him to forget it. On the other hand, a psychological examination of the races who have not known this culture, who are ignorant of the Christian theory of sin, and who do not hold that the sexual life is necessarily wrong and shameful, should put us in a much better position for seeing sexuality in its true light, freed from all hypocrisy and insincerity; and through such an examination we may hope to acquire a more accurate knowledge of the original nature of man.

This applies particularly to the more civilized of the black, yellow, Hindu and Polynesian races; formerly it would have applied also to the Indian civilizations of the two Americas, if we are to believe the numerous reports of the sixteenth-century travellers. The civilizations of the races which inhabit Asia, from the Arabian peninsula to India and the confines of the Far East, are *different* from those of the white races; they are not *inferior*.The illusion of the whites in this matter has been,if we may so, a mechanical illusion; at a certain moment in their history they found themselves in possession of a number of new inventions, which enabled them to travel more easily to distant countries, to subjugate the races of these countries in unequal combat(thanks to their superior weapons), and to dazzle them by their astonishing applications of steam and electricity. From these economic and mechanical circumstances there emerged what seemed to be a definite and more scientific formula for social organization, one which deeply influenced the structure of the social mechanism.Herein lies the superiority of the whites. But in the domain of pure thought their culture has been infinitely medicore.

We may say, in truth, that this culture has an exaggerated opinion of its own worth, inasmuch as it has entirely misunderstood the value of non-European thought. Alongside of Western civilization and entirely independent of it there exist the striking literatures of Arabia, of Persia and of India, the philosophy and metaphysics of Hindoos, the arts of China, Arabia, Persia, India and Japan; the originality and symmetry so wonderfully blended in the productions of Siam and Cambodia; a whole past, often indeed a whole present, of men who were or are capable administrators, judges, leaders, conquerors. All this is not wiped out by the invention of the steam-engine or the telegraph, wireless or otherwise.

Thus many non-Europeans, especially those of Asia, possessed a culture, a civilization, a morality, which were not at all inferior to those of Europe; Europe merely considered them to be inferior because they were different.It judged them in terms of that intolerant superiority, itself of religious origin, which was divided the world into two parts—Christendom, which was everything, and the rest, which was of no consequence at all. Nothing so much shook the power of

Christianity in Europe as the voyages of the sixteenth and seventeenth centuries, and the discovery of peoples who possessed wise laws, sensible customs and amiable manners, although they did not profess the particular faith of the West.

From the ethical and social points of view, we may say that, generally speaking, there has been more happiness, less neurosis, and less tormenting conflict among the Asiatic, African, and Polynesian races. These races have a better developed sense of the real nature of life, which does not necessarily consist merely in hustle, struggle and speed. They have consequently enjoyed a more serene and contemplative happiness than have the peoples of the West. From this point of view one may even hold that they have been superior in having an ideal that was more practical, and, if we may say so, more easy to attain. To us there seems no doubt that this desirable condition is due in large measure to the fact that sexual neurosis, which has wrought such havoc in the West, has been much less severe among these peoples. The non-existences of the Judeo-Christian system of "sin" has allowed the various non-European cultures and ethical systems to found their ideas of sex on a reasonable, sensible and empirical basis, and has allowed the growth of tolerant laws and sensible customs, which have nothing in common with that fanaticism that fierce narrow mindedness , that disregard of logic, which, in the West, as a consequence of the prohibitionistic view of sexuality, have resulted in so many taboos which have crippled both the individual and society.

The same fact is often revealed by personal observation. The benefits of the culture of these peoples, and of their more reasonable notions on sex, is always the more evident, the more the individuals examined have been uncontaminated by the civilizations and the religions of the West; for example, girls of the peasantry or of the lower classes, who are often illiterate, enjoy a much more open sexual life than those of the richer families, inclined as these are to imitate Western conventions. Among these latter girls themselves the sexual life is much more hidden in the case of those who have been brought up in missionary schools saturated with the anti-sexual system; this is still more the case with students who have returned from Europe or America; only a very deep and thoroughgoing study will here be able to reveal the original mentality,smothered as it is by Aryan ethics (often biased by religion) and much distorted by the natural tendency to imitation. Among the Chinese, in particular, a whole generation is growing up in this way, the female members of which are becoming ardent feminists.

The most interesting observations can, we think, be arranged under four main headings:-

1. Nudity and exposure of the sexual organs is the rule in primitive societies. It arouses no idea of shame, let alone astonishment; and, as has been often shown, it is a habit that ;considerably reduces the mutual interest of the sexes in each other. A part of the neurosis of civilized populations concerning sexual matters comes from clothing; if custom and climate permitted us to go about quite naked, such a practice would doubtless, by a reversal of ideas which is utterly beyond the comprehension of our anti-sexual doctrinaires, become their best ally in the fight for abstinence.

The sixteenth-century travellers who first arrived among the American Indians were seldom tired of repeating how great was their astonishment in seeing the nudity of these latter.Mocquet, describing Brazil in 1616, wrote: "I believe that these Caribous are of all Indian nations the gentlest and most humane...women, girls and children freely boarded our ships, without any trace of shame or embarrassment at their own nakedness"—a striking encounter between repressed and natural humanity.It evidently requires quite a special education to produce that apparently natural and spontaneous horror which Western people experience in all good faith when they see a completely naked body(at least in public).

In Japan, which seems to be the only existing nation of the

world which shows a little common sense in sexual matters, nudity is not shocking, as it is in the West. The two sexes very often bathe together. It was not until the relatively late date when contact was being established with repressed societies, that these questions of nudity began to arouse comment. We have been told that Western missionaries have sometimes raised a shocked protest and have asked the Government to show some sign of disapproval. Orientals have usually shown themselves much more ready to adopt *en bloc* the habits of the West than to discuss critically the reasons for such habits, or to compare them; carefully with their own; if such comparison had been made on exact and scientific lines, would the ethical advantage have lain often with the whites?

It will be well to bear in mind the importance of these considerations for the purpose of studying the sentiment of "modesty", to which we shall have to return later.It goes without saying that we could have added numerous examples from the accounts of every traveller in the many tropical countries where children of both sexes are to be seen going about in a state of complete nudity till a relatively advanced age.

2. Peoples who are not artificially subjected to repression show a great readiness to indulge in sexual acts. We can even say that with them such acts are as normal as the satisfaction of hunger and thirst. Women, especially, abandon themselves with pleasure, and without any long preliminary hesitation; the act accomplished, they would not for a moment adopt that attitude so characteristic of women brought up in the idea of repression, which leads them ;to say to a man after they have given themselves to him: "How you will despise me now....." Such an attitude would indeed seem absurd to both partners. The woman is proud to have given pleasure and to have been appreciated at her true value; she has been the creator of a happiness, transitory perhaps, but very real. The man on his part feels nothing but gratitude towards her. The Chinese and Japanese, for instance, are both kind and courteous in their

dealings with prostitutes. A coolie would blush to treat them with the cruelty and rudeness, not to speak of the violence and deceit, that so-called gentlemen consider quite normal in the West. Well treated as they are, and little tempted, like their Western sisters, to complain of their fallen lot(since they have suffered no such "fall"), the courtesans of these countries are therefore nearly always bright, amiable, considerate, and satisfied with their mode of life.

The readiness of these peoples to enter into sexual relationships has been remarked by a great numbers of travellers.

Among the Battas of Sumatra, a Dutch missionary found it to be generally admitted "that a *tete-a-tete* between a man and a woman must eventually result in an undue intimacy." P.Gauguin says of the women of Tahiti; "They all wish to be taken, taken in Maori manner, without a word and brutally; they all more or less desire to be raped." The present writer has, in many cases, been able to confirm the existence of this sexual freedom, especially in the course of his travels in Indonesia; it is a freedom obviously similar to that reported by the first travellers to reach the Polynesian archipelagoes (Tahiti) or America. The natural rule, if repression does not intervene, is for the sexes to carry out sexual acts as their desires dictate, without hesitation and without any sense of wrongdoing. We should not allow such purely speculative theories as those on which prohibitionism is based to shut our eyes to this essential fact, which is so clear that even the most thoughtless minds must surely find it difficult to believe that human beings in a state of nature actually *prefer* modesty, chastity and abstinence. As to men and women who have enjoyed some intelligent experience in this field, they have no longer any illusions on the matter.

3. A sexual proposal made by a man to a woman is considered as a natural gesture, or, more strictly speaking, as an act of homage.Indeed, a young woman, when she meets a man, usually *expects* to see him manifest sexual desire for her;

if he fails to do so, she is surprised, or even humiliated. Here again we find the contrast due to repression. Occidental ethics has devised and disseminated an elaborate theory, according to which to show desire for a woman is to "insult" her; neither the word, nor its meaning, would be understood by races who are ignorant of sexual prohibition.Thus a man's soliciting gesture to a woman may be interpreted in two exactly opposite ways. In one case it is looked upon as a natural homage, which a woman may, or may not, allow to develop into greater intimacy, but at which she does not take offence.In other case, it is regarded as an attack upon the convention which repression has, after so much difficulty, succeeded in building up, and it is resented on principle, because it is not *comme il faut,* i.e. in accordance with convention.The less hold repression has, the less frequently this interpretation will appear; even in Europe, the farm girl will be almost as sensible to the homage implied in a sexual offer (either by word of mouth or by gesture) as is a girl in a community without repression, she will not feel insulted, but flattered, by it. Indeed, repression is such an artificial thing that the anger shown by a Western woman, unless her nature has become completely distorted by religious fanaticism, is obviously forced and artificial; she is indignant, because she thinks she ought to be indignant; she says the words which the conventional code demands; if necessary, she will make scandal, and, if the laws of her country favour it, will pack the insolent offender off to prison. But what psychologist does not recognize that, behind her pretended irritation, at the bottom of her heart, beyond the reach of censorship and repression, she is flattered by such homage, even when it is so contrary to rule, and is happy to receive it? A terrible form of social hypocrisy, which forces the lips to pronounce words which are very different from those which nature herself would have inspired!

4. Further light can be thrown on the behaviour of peoples in whom repression is very weak or non-existent by a very important observation which I have been able to repeat and corroborate on several thousand occasions; the existence of

the *sexual reflex*

Where repression does not exist, or is but slight, sexual desire will be both natural and permissible, and in consequence always present to the mind in a natural and spontaneous way, like the physiological need of hunger; and not, as among the peoples who have cultivated repression, in the guise of an obsession which is combated and anathematized, and which leads eventually to neurosis.It is benefician, instead of becoming a source of physical and moral torment, and at the same time it is all-powerful. In brief, we know that sexuality is a mighty force in all races and in all individuals; but whereas, in those who have cultivated repression, it may result in pain and disease, where it is not repressed its effects are limited to its own natural development, which appears to be beneficial to the organism

Thus, although sexual desire is always somewhat obsessive in character, the effects of the obsession vary according to whether the mentality of the individual or the race is artificial (i.e. subject to repression) or natural. If there is repression, this obsession must lead to neurosis. If there is no repression, it will manifest itself in reflexes which will not be inhibited or repressed as in the first case (for it is a fact that quite a number of reflexes of a sexual kind are inhibited by repression). In races not subject to repression the sexual reflex manifests as follows; a woman finds herself in the presence of a man(e.g. in the street, in a public vehicle, on a visit, in a shop, or on any other occasion which brings the sexes together); her reflex will consist in directing the eyes instantaneously to two parts of the neighbouring male body, the head and the sexual region. This reflex is, needless to say, automatic. But it functions for a variable period; that is to say, if there is a certain amount of repression, the duration of the reflex will be shortened, it will be merely a fleeting glance. This reflex is the threshold of the full sexual act which follows, or would follow if social circumstances did not prevent it. It must, however, be observed without the knowledge of the woman concerned; for naturally the reflex cannot be elicited if the subject knows that she is being watched with a view to its occurrence. On the other hand, it is possible to provoke the sexual reflex if it fails to appear spontaneously; if the man directs his gaze to the woman's dress in the region of sexual organs, he will in turn provoke the sexual reflex of the woman; but here the reflex is less spontaneous and less interesting, and is probably mixed with the conscious intention of ascertaining whether the man, whose eyes are so inquisitive, is in a state of excitation.

It is obvious that the sexual reflex is much less apparent in societies subject to repression. Nevertheless, it exists here also; it is sometimes manifested by women of erotic temperament. Who are incompletely subjected to repression, and are so to speak, in rebellion against it. But even then it is less frank, more shamefaced and hypocritical. Occidentals excel at seeing an object without *looking at it*; whereas this power, acquired by long practice, is seldom possessed by the races of Africa, Asia and Oceania, who look at an object directly or not at all. The sexual reflex is therefore much less easy to observe in Western women.

Finally, in man, the sexual reflex constantly appears even in the West, but in a form that differs from that of the reflex of the female, a form which renders it at once easier to observe, and less scientifically interesting. When a young and attractive woman comes into the presence of a number of men, the gaze of these latter, especially if she does not see them (if she has her back to them for example), is not directed to the sexual organs themselves, which would be against the rules of repression; it is, however, directed in such a way as to take in the woman as a whole, to make an inventory of her "good points". There are men who are so clever in this respect, that women sometimes feel as if they were "undressed" by such a look.Notice, too, another indication of the sexual reflex in the glances which woman exchange among themselves. When a woman enters a drawing-room, or passes in front of others on a public promenade, those who see her without themselves being seen “undress” her also with their looks, and these looks are directed with a peculiar and spontaneous persistence to the “good points” of the woman (including of course those of sexual importance); in this case, not from desire, but from an impulse to ascertain and evaluate—often not too kindly — what is the strength, and what are the hidden weapons at the disposal of the person concerned in that eternal struggle for the male which is for many women the struggle for life.

The Law of Primitive Phenomena in the Pre-adolescent. —Let us return now to the sexual interests appear very early, in fact almost from the first years of childhood. We can safely say that they are as absorbing as those of the adult, just as liable as these latter to arouse strong passions, joys and pains; capable, too, of eventually bringing about neurosis and other pathological states, when they are opposed or hindered. In a word, they do not authorize us to regard the child as utterly different from the adult in the sexual sphere. They give the lie to all that rather silly and mawkisk sentimentalism about the “purity “ of children and their supposed ignorance of sexual matters. On the contrary, they show that, allowing for natural differences in temperament and constitution, children are just as ready as are adults to interest themselves in sexual phenomena and to take great pleasure in them.

Finally, we may say that sexual phenomena and the pleasure associated with them are the things which most naturally and spontaneously occupy the child’s mind, even at an age when his understanding of other subjects is still rudimentary. The facts connected with this great source of satisfaction inevitably stimulate his interest and arouse his budding intelligence. It is just in this field that we could leave him most easily to his own experience, instead of condemning him to all sorts of unhealthy hypocritical pretences: it is a question of degree and of kind, but not of prohibition.

Such are the facts.We have to draw the necessary conseq-uences, and if possible express their teaching in a scientific formula.

Let us note in the first place that the word "onanism", as used to designate sexual pleasures in children before the age of puberty, appears to be ill chosen. Etymologically it is absurd, since it comes from the act of Onan, who, as is well known, practised it (as we are told in the Bible) in order to let his seed fall upon the earth, so as to avoid having children with Tamar, which was essential if he was to preserve his own family rights. Before the age of puberty there can be no question of a fertile seminal fluid in the male, any more than of that pleasure *sui generis* which accompanies seminal emission. And it is just here that the problem becomes most interesting and involves the most important issues.

In all the above-mentioned observations, there is one fact which emerges time after time, and cannot but strike the attentive student: I refer to the absence of all relation between sexual manifestations and the phenomena of reproduction. Not only is reproduction physiologically impossible in view of the age of the subjects, not only does it constitute a goal which is utterly unrealizable by them, but above all it is something that is completely foreign to the consciousness of the subjects; their behaviour is not prompted by reproductive ends, since they are not yet capable of exercising this function. Indeed, most of them are ignorant of the processes of reproduction and of the differences between the sexes; it is, rather, a sort of naive and primitive homosexuality that they manifest; or else, like Narcissus, they are interested only in themselves.

In these various cases the sexual manifestations are self-sufficient. Often indeed they are not even accompanied by what an adult would consider to be the specific pleasure of sex, or at any rate they provide this pleasure only in an embryonic form. Everything points to the fact that the sexual organs, both male and female, exercise a peculiar fascination and attraction in themselves and in their own right, and this from earliest infancy; so that, even in the absence of specific sensory pleasure, the mere fact of talking about them, looking at them, and touching them, provides a peculiar and highly valued form of satisfaction. The secret nature of these acts is due almost entirely to the fact that they are liable to be punished by father, mother or teacher; though it is probable that this threat, far from diminishing the attraction, actually increases it, in virtue of one of those brilliant pieces of illogicality in which our sexual morals so abound. In any case, if it were not for this threat and for the fact that from its earliest days the child has been continually exhorted to be modest, and to despise its sexual organs(the seats of malodorous secretions), it is probable that its sexual manifestations would be freely exercised without the slightest modesty.

We may summarize all this in the following provisional law: *There exists in the child, from the first years onwards and well before any possibility of copulation or of reproduction, a diffused and attenuated sexual pleasure* sui generis; *and this pleasure is manifested in the overwhelming attraction exercised by the sexual organs, and in the great satisfaction occasioned by their stimulation in any form, either individually or with other persons.*

Later Developments of These Phenomena. — With the gradual extension of knowledge, the attention of one sex is drawn to the other. For some time before puberty the sexual manifestations will, therefore, tend more and more to be directed to, and take as their object, a person of the opposite sex; because the whole of an individual's experience — his reading, his social intercourse, the institution of marriage— soon teaches him that these manifestations must be directed only to that sex. Naturally, this remark only applies to Occidental societies; in tropical countries, where children remain unclothed until a comparatively late age; in communities (such as Japan) where nakedness gives no offence to modesty, or where the sexual act is not made the object of a ridiculous secrecy; in countries like India, where child-marriage is a matter of custom and tradition — here children, who are more natural, and certainly more healthy, become aware at an early age of the final goal of their sexual impulses. But what happens subsequently, at the age of puberty or later? Certainly, the sexual manifestations undergo a profound change at this period; they begin to appear in their full richness and variety, including the possibility of coitus. Nevertheless, it will often happen that sexual pleasure will not be brought about by actual relations between the sexes; especially is this the case in Western communities, where, owing to the accumulation of obstacles in the way of such relations (obstacles which often render them impossible and which reach their climax in the unnatural prohibition of coitus until a late age), adolescents are generally thrown back on the practice of solitary onanism, a practice which we know to be enormously prevalent. But, even in this case, sexual pleasure will acquire a new intensity, and will, in one way or another, take on that new and more developed form which has been so long in preparation.

Persistence of the Primitive Law in Adult and Impotent Persons. — Let us continue our examination. At an earlier or later age, according to the social environment, the sexes at last acquire their freedom, and are henceforward at liberty to copulate. An important point must be made clear at once : beyond a doubt, copulation is one of the most valuable forms of sexual pleasure, *but it is only one form among others*. This act, essential though it is for reproduction, may, for purposes of satisfaction, be replaced by many other procedures (e.g. onanism *a deux*). And this is not all: in the course of those voluntary relationships that occur in love, marriage, and the free exercise of sexual pleasure among adults, we may rediscover all those phenomena which we noted just as now characteristic of the period before puberty.

Indeed, we may say of coitus that it only corresponds to a brief moment in the whole complicated development of the pleasures of love. The various forms of satisfaction that precede it, though doubtless less intense, have such a fascination of their own, that connoisseurs of sexual pleasure willingly prolong them. But these satisfactions, though among adults they may eventually lead to copulation, are of exactly the same nature as those of the pre-adolescent. They consist in erotic talks, in which a special slang is employed, and in which the sexual acts or the sexual organs are the principal objects of interest, or else they are concerned with the arrangements (betrothal) which will permit the two partners to have relations in the near future. They consist in acts of fondling and gazing, which have nothing to do with copulation; indeed, this latter stage may never be reached, since fear of its consequences may lead to a voluntary abstention from the act (as in the case of the *demi-vierge*). We find here the same attraction exercised by the sexual organs (and without doubt also by certain odours and secretions *sui generis*) as in the case of the pre-adolescent. In fact, the feeling are the same — though now more firmly grounded and based on a wider experience. When a man and woman who are in love look at one another, there are awakened many kinds of wonder, admiration, fascination, astonishment and unexpected emotion, all of which occur naturally and spontaneously in both partners, and which are delicious, alike in their arousal and their satisfaction.

Sexual phenomena, then, present all those complications which psychologists have studies at such length. The sexual organs are more easily stimulated than all the others; but they make use of these others to serve their own ends—they demand that vision, touch and smell shall each contribute to the total erotic excitation. The sexual life, which is now so complex, has henceforth its special preferences—preferences which are often difficult to explain, but which determine the direction and the strength of the manifestations in any given individual: thus the arousal of sexuality may come to depend upon such factors as the colour of the hair, a special attraction for a particular part of the body, the influence of certain perfumes, or even the influence of some accessory characteristic of the sexual object (clothes, social class, vocabulary, etc).

Finally, as we have already stated, in old age, when impotence has made copulation impossible, it will be once again the "side shows" of sex which play the chief role, just as in the case of pre-adolescence, except that now they are aided by past experience, which has to compensate for the loss of hope in a love life still to come.

Chapter-3

The Physiology of Sexuality

Chapter 3

The Functions and Senses of Organic Beings.— In general the vital activities of men and the higher animals are manifested through the functions and the senses. Without insisting here on physiological facts which are familiar to every educated person, we must, as a preliminary to our further discussion of sexuality, briefly remind the reader of the exact meaning of these two terms.

In general physiology we understand by "functions" those processes which constitute life itself and which are necessary to its continuance, processes which occur in virtue of their own special mechanisms (the respiratory, circulatory, digestive functions, etc.); by "senses" we understand those peculiar and unique faculties, similarly operating with the help of very specialized organs, in virtue of which the animal is able to experience physical impressions.

These definitions having been stated, it my be understood that the words "function" and "sense" are not indispensable, although they correspond very well to the reality of the facts. There exist mechanisms which are specialized for certain ends; the digestive apparatus for the purposes of nutrition, the auditory apparatus for the perception of sound, etc...; but we must never allow ourselves to forget the facts of correlation, or to abuse these distinctions (however convenient they may be for the physiological study of the organism), by losing sight of the complexity always manifested by the actual working of these mechanisms. Nevertheless, having once isolated and specified these mechanisms and their ends, we might be content with this, and make a complete study of physiology without ever using these convenient terms "function" and "sense." It is the work of scientific classification which has brought these concepts into being; it is, therefore, not astonishing that the specialists who have drawn up the various classifications are not always in agreement as to the total number of vital processes which must be included under the concepts in question, nor upon the category into which this or that particular manifestation should be placed. For example, while there is general agreement as to the digestive and respiratory functions, the cerebral function seems to the materialist to be an adequate explanation of the phenomena of intelligence; as regards the senses, it has often been proposed to extend the conventional list of the five classic categories, and to add new members, such as the sense of direction, or the muscular sense. In striking contrast with this, it is evident to everyone that we cannot add or subtract a muscle or a gland from the anatomical description of an animal body.

Nevertheless, as we said above, the scientific division in question corresponds pretty well to reality. There is nothing inadmissible or arbitrary in thus grouping together everything which concerns such very specialized functions or such very characteristic sensations. All that is necessary is to proceed with caution, not forgetting that we are concerned only with a classification. But, this much understood, the physiological manifestations in question can be easily distinguished, one class from the other. Although function and sense have this much in common, that in both cases we have to do with a specialized mechanism or organ, performing a characteristic and specific task, it is not without reason that a sharp distinction has been drawn between the two categories. Experience forces us to distinguish between processes which have such different and often incompatible characteristics. The distinction corresponds to two separate manifestations of the organism which it is well-nigh impossible to confuse; it is so marked that we may use the following parallel to make clear the essential nature of the difference in question.

Parallelism between Functions and Senses; Organs. — In the first place, we find that in both cases there are groups of specific organs, specialized in virtue either of their function or their sense, and which cannot serve both purposes indifferently. At most there is sometimes quite a subsidiary loan of one of the sense-organs for purposes of function or *vice versa*; but in this case it is easy to see that the loan only occurs in order to facilitate the exercise of the function or the sense in question (in virtue of the general principle of correlation), but is never an indispensable element in the absence of which this exercise could not take place. For example, the tongue is the specific organ of taste, and contains the taste-buds, without which the sense could not exist; nevertheless the tongue subserves also the function of nutrition, in so far as it plays a part in swallowing. But it is not indispensable; we can conceive of organisms (and indeed they actually exist) in whom the taste-buds have disappeared, together with the tongue itself, but which are not thereby debarred from the normal process of nutrition. Everyone is familiar, moreover, with the pathological cases of artificial nutrition. The auditory apparatus, on the other hand, useful as it is, has nothing in common with the general functions of the organism, nor does the respiratory apparatus, so essential for life, require the aid of sensation to carry on its function.

The very important consequence is that – in spite of the occasional cases of loan that we have mentioned — the functions and the senses constitute two different worlds: organic systems on the one side, and neural faculties on the other. There is an absolute independence between them; the functions can work without the senses, and the senses can play their part without help from the functions. The olfactory nerves can be stimulated without causing respiration; we can taste food without swallowing it; we can see, hear and touch without the functions entering into play as a consequence of these sensory manifestations; while the circulatory functions on their part are carried on permanently without the intervention of the senses. For our purpose it is especially important to keep in mind this reciprocal autonomy of function and sense.

Character of Necessity and Revelation. — We must add, however, that the functions are indispensable to organic mechanism, while the senses are not. One cannot put an end to circulation, respiration or nutrition without at the same time putting an end to the organism itself. Each of the classical five senses, on the other hand, can be abolished without causing death, as is shown by the many deaf and blind people whom we constantly meet. The senses are infinitely useful and agreeable, but they are not an absolute necessity.

There follows what may perhaps be regarded as a corollary of this antithesis; it is of the very essence of the functions to carry on their work without the knowledge of the individual. A person who is in good health, that is to say whose functions are working normally, is not aware of the continuous processes connected with the circulation of the blood, with nutrition and respiration; these functions are exercised without revealing themselves, they pass unnoticed. By definition, exactly the opposite is the case with the senses. As the word itself indicates, it is impossible to imagine a sense which does not give rise to sensations. The role of the senses is to give us knowledge of certain things, whose presence we register, more or less consciously as the case, may be, but always effectively; vision itself is subject to this law, and we distinguish naturally, and without the slightest difficulty, between the moments in which we do not see and those in which we do.

Character of Independence or of Subjection.— We can also say that the functions are independent of the individual's will, while the senses, on the other hand, obey the will. This is a result of the necessary character of the functions and the facultative character of the senses. We cannot voluntarily stop the processes of circulation, nutrition or respiration; the most that we can do is to influence them, chiefly in an indirect fashion, by ingestion of appropriate substances calculated to accelerate or retard them; but their complete arrest, except for an extremely brief period, would mean death.On the other hand, we need only make use of our senses when we do desire (and we can quite well imagine their total suppression).We have only to close our eyes and we can exclude the visual sense for just as long as we like; it is easy to interfere with hearing or smelling; touch and taste are, generally speaking, only active when we wish. The senses wait upon the pleasure of the individual, but he in his turn is the fragile plaything of his functions.

Character of Pleasure. — Finally, there exists one other very characteristic difference between the functions and the senses. The functions are not the source of any specific pleasure to the individual (they confine themselves to the infliction of pain, when their mechanism is disordered); in the healthy organism there is no appreciable pleasure in the regular circulation of the blood, in respiration, or in the phenomena of nutrition, anabolism or katabolism. It is the senses which bring us our enjoyments; vision gives us the pleasures of colour and of form; hearing, that of sounds; smell, that of odours; taste, the satisfactions of the table; and touch, finally, brings us those undeniable gratifications of the cutaneous sense in which thermal impressions, no less than those of a mechanical order (friction, pressure of smooth, soft bodies, etc)., play a part of great importance for our happiness.

It would be easy to develop this parallelism at considerable length. But this is not a book on general physiology, and it is sufficient here to emphasize the essential elements. Anyone can supplement the indications here given by numerous further examples.The important thing is to bear in mind these distinctions between the functions and the senses, for this will permit us to discover how far they are to be found in the study of sexuality, and how far they can be used in the classification of sexual phenomena.

Application of the Parallelism to Sexuality. — Let us take up again, therefore, this parallelism, which we have been tracing between the functions and the senses, and ask whether the physiological secret of sexuality, which has caused so much confusion, is not to be found in this neglected distinction between sense and function.

In other words, is not the function of reproduction or of generation to be classed with those of circulation, nutrition, etc.? And, alongside of this, is there not a sense of sexual pleasure comparable in its specificity to the five classic senses, and which should therefore be added to their list?

Organs — First of all, as regards their organs, it is clear that function and sense have each their own.

The function of reproduction is subserved both in man and woman by organs which are self-sufficient. For the organs of generation are just those which are necessary for this function and allow of its existence; in the male, the testicles with their outer coverings and the seminal glands or vesicles (to which must probably be added the prostate and Cowper's glands, if the fertilizing fluid, the semen, results from a mixture of a secretion of all these organs); and, in the female, the womb, the ovaries, and (if we wish to include them also) the Fallopian tubes. These are the specific organs of *reproduction*; they are necessary and indispensable, but sufficient. Certain other organs – which physiology prefers to qualify as "external", in opposition to those already named (the penis in the male, the vagina, the mons Veneris, and the clitoris in the female) – are not organs of the function of reproduction.

So little so, that if necessary this function can take place without them; fecundation, the decisive act of reproduction, is possible without the use of these external organs. For it suffices to bring the male fluid into contact with the ovules of the female to obtain reproduction, and this can occur without intromission of the penis, nay, even without contact of any kind between the male and the female.[1]

Thus the organs which are called external are not organs of a function. We therefore naturally tend to suppose that they are organs of a sense, and that they have the same relation to the generative function as have the organs of taste to the function of nutrition. There can indeed be no doubt that these external organs have exactly the same character as that which distinguishes other sensory organs. As we have already emphasized, they have a sort of personality, one which is well known to lovers, and which is strengthened by the terms used in erotic slang, just as is the case, in a lesser degree, with the tongue, the eye and the ear (whereas neither tradition nor language emphasizes thus decisively the autonomy of the internal organs). They possess an extremely delicate sensibility. They are specialized for the provision of a pleasure which is just as characteristic in its own way as are taste and smell; a pleasure which is as elementary and irreducible as are the satisfactions to be obtained from perfumes or from food, the need of which makes itself so strongly felt as to be designated by the word "lust" and which is sometimes referred to by the simple word "pleasure" without further qualification. These organs have then as clearly marked an individuality as have the classical five senses. Often, too, they unite themselves to these latter, just as happens in the case of the other senses, which often enter into an alliance for the purpose of increasing satisfaction; taste and smell unite in the enjoyment of a delectable dish; in the same way smell and taste assist the sexual sense to increase its intensity and to augment its specific pleasure by the addition of their own specific pleasures (as in the *odor di femina*).

The subsidiary loan of a sense-organ for the purpose of a function is also found in the life of sex. In fact, coitus, which aims at reproduction, also sets into operation the organs of pleasure; just as deglutition, which is normally necessary for nutrition, arouses gustatory sensations. It is the same process in both cases, so long as all the correlations are harmonious and perfect; but, once again, it is possible to conceive of reproduction without participation of the organs of sexual pleasure.

Reciprocal Independence of the Two Systems. — We are therefore in the presence, here also, of two separate worlds; organic system and neutral faculty. Reproduction can be independent of pleasure in many cases; as in artificial injection of the seminal fluid, conception by accidental deposit of spermatozoa on the organs, conception without sexual pleasure on the part of the woman. And as for showing that sexual pleasure is in its turn totally independent of reproduction, this is precisely what is proved by the facts of onanism, and, above all, by the sexual manifestations of the pre-adolescent that we have already studied.[2] In all these cases we see the organs of the sexual sense working for their own (sensory) end, in total independence of organic function.

We realize this even better when we remember that coitus itself does not necessarily, or even usually, result in fecundation. There are individuals who are incapable of impregnating or being impregnated, but who are perfectly able to obtain sexual pleasure through the play of the appropriate organs. Even with individuals capable of reproduction, coitus does not necessarily imply fecundation. Finally, when the female has been impregnated, the uterus being already closed and the ovum in process of evolution, it is evident that subsequent acts of coitus, which are in many cases quite frequent, have nothing to do with the function of reproduction, and that their only purpose is the exercise of the organs of pleasure; such acts can result merely from a desire to continue an habitual form of satisfaction. We may go so far as to say that physical relations between the male and the female, even whey they assume the form of coitus, are, except in certain rather rare cases, inspired only by the hope of a specific enjoyment, and not by any wish to set in action the organic function of reproduction, a function which indeed is often far from being desired.

Necessity. — Continuing our parallel, we may note that the function of reproduction is indispensable, whereas it would be possible to do without the sense of pleasure. Even if we admit that the generative function is not necessary to the individual, since he could continue to live without it, it is none the less true that it is indispensable to the species; if this function were to disappear, the species would be limited to the existing generation —which would be the last. The utility here is one which concerns the species directly, and the individual only through the species, but nevertheless in so decisive a fashion that we find the evidence for its indispensability just as compelling as if it worked directly. We can even go so far as to say that the generative function is the most indispensable of all, since without it the others could have no existence.

The sexual sense, on the other hand, notwithstanding the intense satisfaction it can give, is not necessary and need not be exercised. Indeed, the followers of certain doctrines profess to abstain from its exercise (as is the case with Catholic priests). It is true that the sense is so imperious that, even with such persons, it tends to take its revenge and manifest itself. Nevertheless, it is quite possible to conceive of the sense becoming atrophied; and we can quite well imagine an individual who would correspond in the sphere of the sexual sense to what the deaf and blind are to the senses of hearing and of vision.

Revelation. — There is an obvious corollary to this. We know that functions work without the knowledge of the individual, and that this is true of fecundation, the essential act of reproduction, and the starting-point of the corresponding function.

An act of coitus which results in fecundation is in no way distinguishable from other acts of the kind. The whole pleasure of copulation comes from the stimulation of the organs of the sexual sense. The fact of fecundation adds absolutely nothing to this pleasure, and the subject is as unaware of it as she would be of the healthy working of the functions of circulation and digestion. There is not an atom of serious evidence in contradiction with this fact. After coitus a woman has absolutely no means of knowing whether she has been impregnated or not, and she has to await the subsequent signs of pregnancy before she can be certain; even if she be violated under conditions which have excited her disgust, she may yet be impregnated. As to the male, it is surely unnecessary to show that for him one seminal emission is as good as another, and that in reality his function is limited to the expulsion of semen, without knowledge of, often indeed without interest in, its ultimate fate. Thus the function of reproduction, like the other functions, is known when its effects are observed; it is not felt when it is actually taking place.

Is it necessary to add that, in striking contract to all this, the sexual sense, on its part, makes so deep an impression on the individual that it is responsible for one of the most extreme states of excitation ever experienced by the organism? It may often be provoked by stimuli which are themselves unnoticed (as in the case of dreams and nocturnal emissions); nevertheless, when it occurs, it always makes itself felt, even among those who, in virtue of their doctrine of abstinence, do not wish to feel it.

Will.—All the characteristics that we have been considering show that the will of the individual has no influence on the function of reproduction. This function is not so intermittent as its external manfestations might make us believe.The most important parts of the function, the formation of spermatozoa (spermatogenesis) and of ova (ovogenesis), are continuously active, and cannot be arrested by any act of will. Nor can the will prevent the contact of the one with the other resulting in impregnation; on the contrary, we find,time after time, that a definite desire to avoid conception may be betrayed and frustrated, conception taking place as soon as the partners have brought about the conditions essential for its occurrence. For we have to take into account not only the surgical and mechanical apparatus that may be employed to prevent conception, but also all the varied measures which may be resorted to, during or after copulation, to destroy its effects. When these have done their work, there remains but a caricature of the function, and it would be absurd to suppose that the will could exercise any influence on this. Whereas, as we have already indicated, the will is quite capable of making us refrain from the exercise of the sexual sense and from the specific pleasure associated with it.

Pleasure. — Thus everything confirms the important fact that the function of reproduction can be exercised without the accompaniment of a pleasure *sui generis* (artificial generation by the injection of spermatic fluid, fecundation without pleasure in a frigid woman, or even under conditions which arouse her disgust....); while on the other hand, pleasure is an essential element of the sexual sense, even in its solitary exercise, and even - most striking of all -among children before puberty, who seek gratification when there is still no possibility of generation.

Conclusions Drawn from the Parallelism.— In conclusion, therefore, we find, on the one hand, a function with its own specific organs, one which is essential to the race, and which works automatically, without the awareness of the subject, and without affording him any appreciable pleasure; on the other hand, a mode of sensation of a very specialized kind, which also has its specific organs, which can be used independently, just as is the case with taste or smell, and which impresses itself very forcibly upon the consciousness of the subject as soon as it is set in action. The parallelism with the other senses is so exact that it is impossible to avoid the conclusion that in reality there exist two systems, which are only too often confused with one another; the function of reproduction, and the sexual sense.

We may remind ourselves that, according to the reports of travellers, the native tribes of Australia (the most primitive type of humanity that is known) are still ignorant of the relation between coitus and procreation. Their women believe that they have conceived through the contact of the wind, rain, a tree, etc.[3] This ignorance seems to us extraordinary. But when we reflect upon it, we see that it amounts to no more than this: that there has been a failure to establish a relation between two processes, which, after all, have no resemblance — coitus and child-bearing.But as these aboriginals naturally do not deprive themselves of sexual pleasure, the advantages of which they well appreciate, we are forced to recognize that primitive humanity has, empirically but none the less certainly, achieved that fundamental distinction between reproduction and gratification which in the further course of development has become so unfortunately confused among many of the more advanced races.

Necessity of the Distinction between the Reproductive Function and the Sexual Sense. — Thus we are forced to admit that, as an essential condition of a scientific treatment of the phenomena of sex, we must draw a clear distinction between the function of reproduction and the sexual sense. This sense consists in a mode of pleasure that is specific and *sui generis*. It is localized in special sensory organs, different in the two sexes (whence is derived the name "sexual sense"), and its manifestations are in many cases provoked by proximity (visual, olfactory, gustatory, or tactile) to the organs and secretions of the opposite sex.

Sense of Neural Pleasure. — In view of the importance of correct terminology in this field, it will be better to express ourselves more, exactly and scientifically,and to say that animals, and especially mammals, posses this specific sixth sense, which is a sense of neural pleasure.

We know that smell, "is often diffused over almost all the surface of the organism," especially in molluscs. It is freely admitted to-day that the same holds good of visual sensibility (the so-called dermatoptic receptivity). In brief, though the specific organs of the senses are by their very nature their most direct and essential channels, the whole nervous organism may, if necessary, to some extent put itself at the service of these senses. The extremely important action of the sexual sense, both previous to and subsequent to the function of reproduction, may be due to this character.This is all the more probable in view of the fact that this sense tends to join forces with the other senses-smell, hearing, touch, taste, vision — and to utilize them for its own purpose.We have here a specific nervous mechanism of an absolutely autonomous kind, the full development of which constitutes sexual pleasure, whether this is absolute and localized (as in copulation or mechanical ejaculation), or relative and diffused (as in satisfaction by mutual proximity, by contact, by odour, through caresses, in speech, etc.). The satisfaction developed is less complete in the second case, but it none the less constitutes a highly valued form of pleasure, which is capable, through association of ideas, of giving intense joy, as we see in the case of the pre-adolescent, or of those who are impotent by accident or through old age.

We are now in a position to understand much better that extreme sexual sensitivity which, as we have shown, exists from the earliest years. It is here a question neither of puberty, nor of the internal secretions of the genitals glands, nor even of erection: it is due rather to what has very happily been called a "diffused sexual sensibility...... without any precise anatomical localization."

Indeed, some of the most recent physiological work has provided that the suppression of the internal genital secretions (as the result of disease or operation) sometimes leaves the sexual libido intact, although formerly it was supposed that there existed an essential relation between secretion and pathological abnormality. In the light of our present knowledge all is clear; the study of the early years *before* puberty and that of old *age after* the disappearance of the sexual secretions show that *the sexual sense is not exclusively conditioned by the secretions of the sexual glands.*This sense, like the other senses, exists in its own right, before and after the existence of the secretions. It varies in intensity, but it is always present. This explains why sexual pre-occupations are always so dominant and urgent, why they last throughout life, manifesting themselves in the child and in the old man. As also in those who are impotent by accident or constitution, though these latter individuals, since they cannot find expression in a secretional emission, receive their satisfaction through organs other than those which are specifically sexual (touch, vision, taste, etc).

The term "neural pleasure" permits, finally, of a better understanding of those cases in which, in spite of their definitely sexual character, the sexual organs in the strict sense are — in consequence of some prohibition or of some special taste — not directly utilized (as the kids, anal practices, etc).[4]

Enlightenment Brought by our Distinction. — We can see immediately that the autonomy of the sexual sense, and the nature of its constitution, can explain the peculiarly imperious character of this sense, which is doubtless a consequence of its close relations with the spinal cord and the brain. It is to be noted, too, that, as is also the case with the organs of sense, the *spinal* cord, which plays so important a role in the sensory reactions of sexuality, is strictly ectodermic in its origin. It remains with the physiologists, after having isolated the peripheral receptors and the neural terminations of the sexual sense, to determine the paths by which it is transmitted and its centres.

We are now in a much better position to understand why, even when they are but little concerned with reproduction, human beings are haunted and dominated by the sexual sense, which permeates their whole being; why this so imperious sexual sense is capable of giving one of the most thrilling pleasures of human life; why men, when they are sincere, consider this joy to be of such inestimable worth; why they will sometimes prefer death to impotence; why castration is considered one of the most abominable of crimes; and why the eunuch is everywhere an object of derision.

In Western countries the sexual sense has been dissimulated in certain ways, such as love and marriage, which are held to be legitimate, to the detriment of others; but, though the various forms of gratification may enjoy an unequal measure of praise from the moralist, they are all desired with equal ardour. In Eastern countries, the glory of sexual pleasure has remained relatively untarnished, reminding us of what it was among the Greeks, the Romans, and the peoples of old. Travellers have paid tender eulogies to certain "Earthly Paradises" which they have discovered in distance countries far away from Europe (Tahiti, Bali, Luang-Prabang). Are these eulogies connected with the conditions of work or the standard of living of these countries?Not at all. They are always inspired by the fact that, under a clement sky, sexual life and sexual enjoyment have remained easier and freer, less inhibited than in the West, and that the relations between the sexes take place with an easy spontaneity that is uncorrupted by stern and puritanical laws. For such is the contrariness of human nature, that it is never tired of celebrating the joys of sex, although at the same time it mutilates these joys, or allows them to be mutilated.

Psycho-physiology of the Sexual Sense.— Sense-physiology has been the subject of much study, but the study of the sexual sense has remained in a very backward state, just because of the confusions and inhibitions occasioned by current sexual morality. It is true that the descriptive anatomy, the histology and the description of the physiological mechanism of the sexual organs have, especially on the medical side, been carried as far as those of the ear or the eye. But the physiology of the other senses has, quite rightly, made greater demands; thoroughgoing researches have been made on the relations between the organs and the specific sensations of which they are the seat: retinal impressions and colour appreciation in the case of vision; auditory acuity, pitch discrimination, and reaction to sounds in the case of hearing; the special static sense of the internal ear; the specific functions of the taste-buds and the reactions to tactile stimuli; the various qualities of smell; the roles played by the peripheral organs, and the classification of the senses originating in the skin (contact, pressure, temperature, etc).

But how does it stand with the corresponding study of the relations between the sexual organs and that peculiar pleasure which constitutes their specific manifestations? This line of research has succumbed to sexual prejudice. Such observations as have been made in this field have been largely confined to the pathological sphere, and were undertaken in the hope of discovering a cure for abnormalities; or else they have themselves taken in the hope of discovering a cure for abnormalities; or else they have themselves taken on an erotic tinge, having been pursued with a view to lurid description rather than to scientific exactitude. Methodical experimentation on the nature of sexual pleasure, analogous to that which has been made on the sensation of movement or on sounds, colours, etc., has still to be undertaken. Here we can only attempt a brief sketch of this essential branch of physiology.

The specific organs of sex, like all the other sensory organs, are set into action either by external causes (touch, heat, etc) or by internal causes. Stimulation by external causes follows the same general law as in the other kinds of sensation, when a modification of the peripheral nervous organs is conveyed to the brain. We find, here as elsewhere, that stimulus is followed by excitation. An internal cause, however, appears to be very frequently operative in the case of the sexual manifestations, the internal stimulus consisting perhaps in a condition which modifies the circulation of the blood.

One of the characteristics of the sexual sense is the case with which it can be excited, especially in young persons; not so much perhaps in virtue of a low threshold of excitability (for it may be said that, in a normal subject, the senses of vision or of smell are in an almost constant state of excitation), as in virtue of the multiple forms in which the stimulus may appear. We have already noticed the influence of touch and temperature, which are directly external stimuli. Smell (*odor di femina*), vision (nudity), taste, may also serve as semi-direct stimuli, enabling (through their associations) exterior influences brought to bear upon another sense to take the place of a direct stimulation of the sexual sense itself. Finally, this sense seems more easily affected by memory and imagination than are the others. Here we are dealing with factitious stimuli; but they may be so strong as sometimes to evoke equally factitious sensations. Such sensations may arise in all the sense departments; cases have been cited in which the perception of an individual who was a long way off immediately aroused the illusion of the smell associated with that individual (not necessarily with any sexual connotation), the actual smelling at such a distance being of course in itself a physical impossibility. The hallucinatory smell in such cases was directly due to an association of ideas. In the sexual sense there are innumerable examples of this kind, in which the excitant may be a memory, the receipt of a letter, a ribbon that has been carefully preserved, the reading of an erotic book, or the contemplation of an erotic picture; such an excitant, however, may act so effectively that it produces orgasm. Excitations of this kind go far to explain the minor compensations which are so highly enjoyed in what is called Platonic love.

The increase and decrease of excitation appear to follow the same laws as those that apply to the other senses, but they are physiologically more visible, more easy to observe. It may be noted that the excitation and the sensation persist even after the stimulus has disappeared. They normally culminate in a spasm (often accompanied by a liberation of secretions), after which the excitement abates with staring rapidity.

The great variety of possible stimuli seems to play a very significant role in the prolongation and value of the excitation. There are certain preferences, not always easy to explain, which are important here, though they are often not more inexplicable than the preferences to be met with in some other sensations, such as taste. As a rule we are unable to explain satisfactorily why, for instance, one person likes coffee and another destests it; we are reduced to supposing that there must be some obscure mechanical or chemical reaction responsible for the agreeable or disagreeable quality of the taste. Similar reactions perhaps underlie the undeniable differences in individual preference as a result of which certain men will be especially attracted by women of a particular kind (as regards race, profession, physical proportions, colour of hair, etc.), but will be unmoved by women whom other men consider desirable.

These observations ought, strictly speaking, to be supplemented by methodical research on the organs of the sexual sense, as has been done in the case of the other senses; e.g., the comparative effects of various stimuli, such as contact, temperature, congestion, vision, etc.; the distribution and relative value of the parts affected; specific acuity, the possible combination with olfactory and tactile sensations, electrical effects, etc; but this is a matter for the physiologists, and the book which will give us a completely scientific and experimental physiology of sexual pleasure has still to be written.

Specific Energy of the Sexual Sense.— As is well known, the German scientist J. Muller long ago laid down certain laws regarding the specific energy of the sense-organs. He noticed that the kind of sensation that we experience is a function of the organ of sense, and not of the stimulus. These laws apply without exception to sexual stimuli. For example:

(a) There are no sensations produced by external causes that cannot be produced also by purely internal causes; if internal causes can arouse a sensation of cold or of light, it is evident that they can also arouse a specifically sexual sensation; we have already called to mind a number of such examples (dreams, nocturnal pollutions, etc.).

(b) The same internal cause can produce sensations of various kinds, but in each case the quality of the sensation will depend upon the nature of the sense; the congestion which manifests itself during orgasm and finds expression in its specific pleasure may also at the same time produce certain visual phenomena.

(c) Similarly, the same external cause can produce sensations of various kinds, according to the nature of the sense that is stimulated; rubbing the eyeball will produce luminous phenomena (phosphenes), while the same rubbing on the organs of the sexual sense will bring about the specific sexual pleasure.

(d) Sensations from one and the same nerve may be aroused simultaneously by internal and external causes; sexual orgasm may result from various stimuli, such as touch, temperature, the ingestion of irritating substances, congestion, etc.

(e) A sensation is the conscious correlate of processes in the nerves (and not of processes outside the body); the sexual nerves seem to have their proper energy, just as have the others; when a mechanical cause is at work, it operates without any reference to the nature or quality of the mechanism; hanged men have orgasms and ejaculations, as the result of a condition which is destructive to life. This indifference of the sense to the quality of the mechanism has, as we shall see, a great importance for the proper understanding of the so-called sexual aberrations, and we shall have no difficulty in showing that the role of the stimulus, whatever it may be, consists, in the last resort, of certain movements, i.e. of a self-sufficient mechanical formula.

Finally, there is no reason why we should not apply to this evolution of the sexual sense the stages of differentiation which Wundt has postulated[5] for sensation in general: a period when the whole body is a sense-organ; a period when special organs and senses are beginning to appear; and eventually a period of complete differentiation between these organs and senses.

The Mechanism of Sexual Excitation.— It has for long been well known that repeated excitation diminishes the sensibility of the nervous elements, a fact that has been emphasized, especially by Kiesow, in the case of the gustatory papillae, and which is invariably found in the case of the olfactory cells (as is shown in our inability to perceive those odours that constantly surround us). The same is true of the sexual sense. Given a number of successive acts of coitus, it would be possible to draw a curve of excitation, which would at first rise, then fall; the first act occasions what might be called the normal degree of sensation (varying according to the individual); those that follow indicate an increase of sensitivity, and are preferred by young people who can carry out such repetitions without fatigue; but an excessive number, eight or ten, for example, clearly shows an eventual decrease in the sensitivity of the sexual organs, both as regards their external sensory surfaces and the specific act of ejaculation itself. It is the same with women; professional prostitutes, especially after a busy day, usually end by becoming almost anaesthetic.

The sexual sense is therefore, like the others, liable to the fatigue that follows prolonged excitation. It is possible, too, that the diminution of intensity may, eventually at any rate, depend to some extent upon the quality and density of the emitted secretions. On the other hand, a change in the quality of the stimulus—the substitution of a new partner, for example — may be sufficient to bring back a state of high excitability.

Sexual Pleasure.— May the objection still be raised, however, that sexual pleasure is only a physiological *need*, like hunger, thirst, or sleep? This question deserves to be examined, because, if the objection is justified, it would be superfluous to speak of a special sense. But the essential differences in question are easy enough to see. Hunger, to take this as an example, is the result of local or epigastric pains, peculiar to the alimentary tract and its appendages. It is the translation into consciousness of the organic fact that the function of nutrition is not satisfied and has ceased to function normally; and that is really all. When hunger is in process of being appeased by food, certain associated senses destined to play a part on this occasion (smell and taste) will no doubt be called into play, but only in an accessory role,comparable (with the necessary qualitative reservations) to the role of touch when food is carried to the mouth. This is all there is in hunger, and it is really not a matter of great importance from the physiological point of view; it has been rightly described as a "need", it is the stomach's call of distress, when it is prevented from exercising its specific function and imperiously demands the ministrations of the cook.

A function can, then, give birth to a physiological need. The function of reproduction, when it is not satisfied, is assuredly in the same class. Abstinence leads to an over production of spermatozoa, which eventually becomes embarrassing, and therefore painful (at least in certain individuals or in certain states of prolonged continence, especially if at the same time there has been unsatisfied sexual excitation). There is no doubt that the function of reproduction, like the other functions, is apt to remind us sharply of its requirements, whenever we are tempted to forget them, and that this process gives rise to the physiological need of copulation (nervous states, heaviness of the testicles, tension of the spermatic cords, etc). There will be a reaction on the specific organs, just as in the case of nutrition there is a reaction on the stomach, the pharynx, the palate. But the sexual sense only plays a part as supplementary to the satisfaction of the reproductive need, just as certain other senses are supplementary to the satisfaction of hunger.

If sexual pleasure were only a need, it would always accompany the manifestations that are necessary to the function of reproduction, and would accompany these manifestations only: as hunger always accompanies the calls of nutrition. We cannot conceive of hunger without this latter. But we have seen that sexual pleasure can very well dispense with the manifestations of reproduction; it is autonomous; sometimes, indeed, in the male, the characteristic spasms may occur in such a way as to satisfy and appease the desires, without complete emission; in the woman this is indeed the general rule, since in the immense majority of cases she experiences satisfaction without conception, i.e. without any participation of the reproductive function.

In this point also there is remarkable analogy with the other senses. Even when there is no need of nourishment, when hunger and thirst have been satisfied and are asleep, we can often observe how a stimulus applied to the sense of taste will create a desire which in its turn will make us eat some dainty morsel, though we are not hungry, or drink a glass of good wine, though we are not thirsty.

Physiology of the Fascination Exercised by the Sexual

Organs. — We must here return to that very characteristic fascination exercised by the sexual organs, a fascination the remarkable strength of which we have already had occasion to notice. According to Marcel Le Goff, Anatole France used to say "There is nothing so pretty as a woman's behind"[6] This great and kindly student of human nature has here expressed, with his usual frankly pagan sincerity, the fascination which the sexual organs of one sex exercise upon the members of the other sex (not to speak of homosexuals). Women's appreciation of the male organs is no less acute, and, with regard to this point, the reader will remember the games which were indulged in by the nurses of Gargantua. To these classic cases we must add the fact that the fascination in question begins to manifest itself from a very tender age: psycho-analysts have shown us how strong is its influence in children. But there are as yet few psycho-analytic documents where this appears more clearly than in the sexual confession of a South Russian published as an appendix to Havelock Ellis's *Studies in the Psychology of Sex* (French edition), to which we have already referred. We will not multiply quotations, but will content ourselves with referring the reader to the many other references that he must know, or, better still, to his own personal observations. We must not forget to mention, however, the very marked propensity in persons of both sexes to tell stories which relate to the sexual organs, to buy erotic books, to procure so-called "obscene" pictures or photographs, which latter have a truly intoxicating effect on some people. The evidence, taken as a whole, fully justifies us in drawing up the following general rules concerning this fascination of the sexual organs:

(a) The fascination exercised by the sexual organs is incomparably greater than that exercised by other parts of the body, and it participates in the *sui generis* pleasure which is associated with sexuality; in the case of other charms which enjoy an equal praise (the eyes, the hair, the mouth, the *line* of the body, etc) there is only an impression of beauty, an aesthetic appreciation, but no fascination, unless this fascination is produced in connexion with an erotic state (as in the case of the fascination carried by the glance or the supple movements of the loved person).

(b) The fascination appears to be independent of all aesthetic rules, though these rules themselves, in so far as they relate to the sexual organs in the strict sense, are difficult to state and vary greatly according to individual taste. Nevertheless, the fascination can be diminished or increased by certain accessory conditions, such as size, rigidity, power of secretion, odour, hairiness, etc., though these are all entirely subjective matters.

(c) The sight of the sexual organs is in itself sufficient to produce the fascination; indeed, it often happens that, in the case of "voyeurs: and exhibitionists, no other satisfaction is needed beyond that which is provided by the sense of vision.

(d) The fascination is so powerful that for lovers, or for those of a simply but sensual disposition, to be allowed to see, and then to touch, the sexual organs brings about first aura and then orgasm itself, and thereby produces a state of satisfaction *sui generis*, accompanied, according to the individual concerned, either by satiation or by over excitation.

(e) The fascination is independent of age, of puberty, or of anatomical knowledge; it is just as great in the case of children as in that of adults (a fact which confirms what we have already said about the part played by vision).

(f) The fascination appears to be increased by prohibitionistic rules, the obstacles constituted by clothing, etc.; it tends to diminish in countries where, as a result of custom or of particular conditions (baths in common without costumes, etc.), the sight of the sexual organs is a common one and does not attract special attention, thus furnishing an illustration of the saying that "familiarity breeds contempt"; and, in truth, the fact that the organs seen or touched are well known ones (as is the case in marriage) diminishes the power of fascination that they may have had to begin with; the less familiar the organ the greater is its power.

(g) The fascination has a profound reaction on the whole organism, both bodily and mental; the man who is bored or tired and who is no longer fascinated by the all too familiar organs of his usual partner becomes transformed and regains all his youth and ardour if circumstances provide him with another and hitherto unknown partner. In some cases girls may be morose and anaemic, unable, it would appear, to take an interest in anything life has to offer, for the simple reason that they are indifferent to everything but what is sexual; if we put them in a position to experience the fascination of the sexual organs or to touch them, we shall witness a startling process of reanimation, the zest for life returning the moment that sexual acts become possible; exactly the same applies to the physical transformation so many young girls undergo after marriage.

In the last place, everyday observation shows us that the fascination is not confined to the sight of the sexual organs themselves, but that (in virtue of association) it can be aroused, no less by a gesture or attitude, which, without actually uncovering the sexual organs, calls attention to them or the sexual act.

As our conclusion from these analyses, we may say that the fascination exercised by the sexual organs, is in virtue of a very natural association of ideas, intimately connected with the arousal or the memory of sexual pleasure. And this is true not only of adults but of children, for we know that these latter are capable of a diffused sexual pleasure and may experience orgasm well before the time of puberty. The power exercised by this association of ideas is confirmed by the fact that the fascination diminishes just in those cases where the value of the pleasure is itself depreciated (as in habituation).

From a psycho-physiological point of view, there is nothing so very extraordinary in this mechanism. All the senses become physiologically excited when they are in the presence of the object which will permit them to realize their ends, and this sensory excitation is reinforced from purely mental sources. The sight of some favourite dish, or even the thought of it, makes the mouth water; the probable presence of some perfume makes us sniff the air, etc.It is, no doubt, much the same thing when the presence of the sexual organs bring about a local and general excitation.What is remarkable is, not the mechanism itself, but the intensity with which it works. But sexual pleasure is itself superior to all others; and it is natural, therefore, that the objects which produce it should in turn exercise an unusual degree of fascination; this fascination is only the expression and the consequence of an intense and overwhelming desire.

Theory and Influence of the Sexual Secretions. — No one, of course, will deny that this imperious domination of the sexual sense reaches its climax at puberty and in the immediately succeeding years, at which time the function of reproduction is likewise at its height. In fact, we have here an instance of that association between function and sense, which so frequently occurs in life and which we ourselves experience several times a day, whenever we combine the processes of nutrition with the satisfactions of taste and smell.

The intensive development of the sexual sense is not in any way incompatible with the importance attached by present-day physiology to the influence of the secretions.These secretions, indeed, do not necessarily in every case result from function, there are some which accompany the excitation of the sensory organs, and are peculiar to the latter; the most that we can say is that they are of secondary importance as compared with the generative fluid itself.

The theory of secretions has therefore, here also, its proper place, and, as we know, by no means an unimportant one. The researches on this subject are relatively recent, although in their origins they go back to Claude Bernard and Brown Sequart.[7] Here we must confine ourselves to recalling the main conclusions to be drawn from this work, conclusions which have been accepted for therapeutic purposes, but the ethical importance of which is still far from being adequately recognized. The human body is a permanent laboratory where chemical transformations are constantly taking place; but though this laboratory is organized in more or less the same way in everybody, though it almost invariably contains the same kind of apparatus, nevertheless, it does not follow that the results obtained are the same in every case.

The ultimate causes of these differences are still unknown, though we can say perhaps, in a very general way, that the final results are due to quantitative differences in the various chemical substances of which we are composed. We know how important is the role of the glands in the vital economy, how they break down, build up again, and pour into the circulation a variety of chemical compounds.These products differ from one individual to another. It is becoming more and more probable that these very differences, reacting as they do upon all the psycho-physiological functions, ultimately underlie the psychological differences between individuals. The secretions to a large extent determine our reactions; a particular secretion, which happens to be unusually abundant, may to some degree upset the general equilibrium to its own advantage, and may then direct the whole psycho-physiological activity to its own ends. Apart from medical or surgical intervention, a man has, as a rule, no power to alter the balance of forces in himself. As regards original disposition, at any rate, it is no more his fault if he be calm or irritable, talkative or taciturn, chaste or voluptuous, than it is if he posses a ruddy or a pale complexion (depending on the quantity of iron present in his organism); no more, indeed, than it is the serpent's fault that it possesses a poison which may be deadly for other living creatures.

The Role of this Theory in Sexual Phenomena.— Though the sexual sense both antedates the reproductive powers and survives them, it nevertheless attains its maximum only when working in association with the genital glands, after these have become capable of secreting the sexual fluids. It is, therefore, natural to agree with Brown Sequart in the view that the orchitic fluid exerts a great influence on the genital neuro-muscular system, a view on which he has based a well-known form of therapy.[8]

We readily admit that, during the period when sense and function are both working fully and together, the formation, the abundance and the accumulation of the genital secretions necessarily tend to bring about emission, a process which in itself is perhaps more directly connected with the reproductive function than with the sexual sense, but the occurrence of which implies the operation both of function and of sense. We must admit also that, on the other side, sexual excitation (by means of touch, hearing, smell, etc.) can bring about an increase of the specific sexual secretions, as well as of certain other associated secretions.We have noted that, shortly before orgasm, women will often wipe their eyes, because their condition has been accompanied by slight secretions of the lachrymal glands; and violent sexual desire produces in everybody some degree of secretion from the salivary glands. It goes without saying that these are unconscious glandular reflexes.

Sexual excitation, as we know, may be due to many causes. The originality and specificity of the sexual sense lies in its capacity to respond to excitations of very various kinds, including some which can only be detected by a very close psychological examination. Odours, tastes, colours, and sounds are all independently capable of provoking sexual secretions—but only because they have already been associated with sexual excitation in the strict sense.Orgasm, which is of course intimately connected, both actively and passively, with the secretions, may also be brought about by reading or by looking at pictures. There is here a phenomenon analogous to the production of salivary secretion by means of smell alone, or by the mere picture of some favourite dish. The law which Pavlov has formulated on this subject is, in all essential respects, applicable to the sexual sense; and the individual is no more responsible for the production or the excess of his sexual secretions than he is for those of his salivary glands. Finally, there is no need to insist upon the fact that the emotions have as big an influence on the glandular secretions of sex as on the other secretions.

It must be admitted, therefore, that the sexual secretions can act both chemically and mechanically. Chemically, their presence in excess without periodical elimination would appear to lead eventually to a sort of auto-intoxication. Nothing surprises us less than to learn that the neuroses of sexual origin "show the greatest chemical resemblance to the phenomena of intoxication, and to those states of need which are brought about by the habitual taking of certain poisons (alkaloids)"[9] "These analogies", Freud has said elsewhere, "in my opinion necessitate the conclusion that the 'actual neuroses' result from disturbances in the metabolism of the sexual substances, either because toxins are produced in a quantity greater than the person is able to tolerate, or because certain internal, or even psychological, conditions disturb the adequate utilization of these substances."[10] The tendencies in modern physiology are so strongly in the direction of explaining all organic phenomena in terms of chemical reactions, that we cannot but be pleased with anything that brings us a little nearer to the final laws that have yet to be discovered in this realm.

Periods of Aura and Resolution. — In sexual excitation there is a period of aura which is probably more prolonged than that to be found in any other analogous manifestation. It is a sort of introduction to the sexual state itself. It may be confused with an incipient orgasm, or may long precede any indication of orgasm. It seems to affect the general tonicity of the body, exercising a more or less widespread influence on the specific organs. It is agreeable, especially if the subject foresees that he will eventually achieve satisfaction; indeed it is so pleasant that certain individuals prolong it by an effort of will, by postponing the period of satisfaction.

In many cases, owing to the distortions that modern morality has forced upon the sexual sense, the period of satisfaction does not occur at al, the period of aura is then characterized by well-marked accessory manifestations of the other senses (clenching of the hands, the smelling of a perfume, ecstasy, etc.), which all contribute to create a state of general emotion, in which only a relatively small part is played by the specific organs and their secretions.

The period of resolution — "post coitum animal triste" — is the third phase, following on the period of satisfaction. It is very variable from one individual to another. The depression of which the Latin poet speaks is not necessarily present in all subjects; in those of a highly sensual disposition, accustomed to frequent gratification, it is even replaced by the satisfaction of a *fait accompli*; and mere muscular fatigue, with the accompanying need of rest, must not be confused with depression. In all cases the process shows a certain resemblance to the onset of epilepsy. It is this, no doubt, which is responsible for the well-known saying, "amor epilepsia brevis". It is interesting to note, however, that a similar resemblance has also been discovered in the case of laughter.[11]

The Limitation of Sexual Responsibility. —If it is thus the internal secretions which influence individual sexual manifestations; if they act upon the nervous system; if, with the assistance of the sexual organs, it is they which determine sexual desire, together with what was formerly called the instinct of reprouduction; then the individual himself is not responsible for the quantitative aspects of his desire or instinct; the voluptuary can no more be blamed for his repeated needs than can the ascetic be justified in boasting of his continence both of them should refer us to their secretions as the determining factor of their conduct. We can see now how unjust and foolish it is to persecute those who are compelled to seek the necessary satisfaction for their strong sexual needs. It is ridiculous to imprison or to punish girls or boys just because they have manifested, without doing any harm to others, the sexual needs which are determined by their nature. Such an attitude is a sad reminder of those ancient punitive systems which, instead of looking upon the insane as persons who were ill and irresponsible, actually chained them up in prison. So long as we remain enslaved to unscientific conventions of this kind, we have no justification whatsoever for considering ourselves more civilized than were our fathers.

From the physiological role of the internal secretions in our general economy, we may infer that modifications of these glandular secretions may modify the responsibility of the individual. Anatomical modifications have the same effect. The extirpation of the pineal gland in young cocks develops the genitals glands and leads to sexual prococity; in young boys a tumour on this gland has similar effects.[12] The castrations of males and females has a general reaction on numerous systems such as the larynx, the uterus, the breasts, the skeleton and the hairs.[13] The hidden reasons of sexual inversion or, not to go as far as this, of those preferences which manifest themselves in "love at first sight", lie entirely in our physiological constitution and in the physio-chemical mechanism of our body. Our general common sense has long recognized this, in saying that we are all the slaves of our "temperament." But it has not yet been adequately realized how absurd it is, in most cases, to punish or to blame, as such, manifestations which are determined in the last resort by the laws of chemistry and physics.

Footnotes

1. These observations are of course strikingly corroborated by the experiments in artificial parthenogenesis (the experiments of Loeb, Delage, Bataillion) and the evidence concerning the phenomenon of spanandry (Marchal and Voudel).

2. Another corroborative statement: if one presents a monkey with some favourite morsel, he often experiences orgasm on taking it or eating it; here the sexual sense co-operates with the other senses in a way that is not even remotely connected with the reproductive process.

3. Compare what Freud has to say on the false theories of

procreation held by children (*Introductory Lectures on Psycho-analysis*). We must note, however, that Freud's remarks only apply to children in Western societies. In countries where nudity is much more frequent, and ethical conceptions have not created a custom of concealing the true nature of procreation (with the aid, incidentally, of stories which, looked at scientifically, are very undesirable), quite young children are very well informed on the subject; and this real knowledge has an influence on their mentality which is entirely beneficial. A Machard's book, *Printtemps Sexual*, would have no meaning for the inhabitants of such countries.

4. We would call the reader's attention also to the fact that even those physiologists who, through their love of the traditional and classical five senses, refuse to increase the number of the senses to six, are nevertheless unable to dispute the mutual independence of reproduction and of sexual pleasure, nor the very clear difference that exists between them. This is a definite triumph for our doctrine, one which is certainly destined to exert a profound influence on all future studies of sexuality.

5. *Physiologische Psychologie.*

6. Marcel Le Goff : *Anatole France a la Bechelleris*, p 190.

7. See G. Dumas : *Traite de Psychologie*, vol. II, p.107

8. See *Rejuvenation the Work of Stemach, Varonoff and Others*, by Norman Haire, London, 1924.

9. Freud's *Third Contribution to the Theory of Sex.*

10. Freud: *Introductory Lectures on Psycho-analysis.*

11. Raulin: *Le Rire et les Exhilarants.*

12. G. Dumas : *Traite de Psychologie*, vol. II, p.1093.

13. Ibid.

Chapter-4

The Morality of Sexual Acts

Chapter 4

The Psycho-physiological Teachings of Sexuality. — Our inquiry up to this point has led us to some very definite conclusions. We have not gone beyond the domain of physiology, or at least of a psychology which by the very nature of things is so intimately allied to physiology as to be at least as much physiological as psychological.

Now what does this science teach us?

1. There are organs connected with a special sense of pleasure; they are no more shameful in themselves than other organs connected with other senses, and no more or less worthy of consideration; they exist and that is all. There is no greater physiological reason to hide them or to excommunicate them than there is to hide the tongue or the ear; they are composed of the same tissues, the same cells, the same muscles, and vitalized by the same circulation of the blood, as are the others; they secrete, like the others, they have their appearance *sui generis*, about which there is nothing mysterious; they are a part of the human body, just as natural and familiar as any other part; there is nothing more shameful about them than there is about the hand or the nose; and every natural person — i.e. one who has not been infected by ideas that are contrary to the normal physiological ones-has clearly no more hesitation in letting them be seen or touched than he has with regard to any other part of his body (as is very evident in children and in primitive races).

2. There is a *specific pleasure*, very vivid, and at its height very intense, which comes from the physiological exercise of these organs; it is only natural that this pleasure should be regarded as desirable, should be appreciated and sought after, as equal to the best that the other senses have to offer, even including taste and smell, and it is, therefore, just as natural

that men or women should seek to procure this pleasure under the most agreeable conditions, as that they should seek to satisfy their sense of taste by food that is well cooked and daintily prepared. This much clearly belongs to our nature as human beings; all else must be regarded as an artificial or cultural addition to the normal exercise of the sense and the normal enjoyment of the specific pleasure.

3. There is a function of reproduction which is not necessarily connected with sexual pleasure: and it is natural that it should seek to realize its end in the same way that the digestive or respiratory functions seek to realize theirs.

This is all that scientific observation teaches us. In this it is, indeed, completely in harmony with everyday experience; for science does not always lead to greater complication. The fantasies of primitive mentality have often burdened our notions of the most elementary things with such a load of improbabilities that one of the first efforts of science frequently aims at brushing away all these irrelevancies and returning to the simple facts of nature.

The Sexual Conventions as Additions to Physiological Facts. — In truth, physiological and biological science teach us that the Lingam and the Yoni are neither god nor devil. Coitus is neither sacred nor diabolical; it is a pleasant, useful and necessary act. These are the essential facts; everything beyond this is a commentary, which has nothing to do with the sexual organs themselves, but which springs entirely from the human brain. It is this great organ of invention and fantasy which has felt a need to label everything, and to make classifications in which Nature herself takes not the slightest interest.

Thus the moral elements in sex are all creations of the human mind which have been superimposed upon the original physiological facts. They have no basis in these facts themselves. This morality is made up of *convention*, i.e. an understanding between certain human beings to interpret the physiological facts in a certain way. There was a time—at the period of the phallic religions—when convention took the form of exalting, copying and venerating the reproductive organ and placing it on the altars as a thing to worship. There is another and opposite contention, according to which this same organ is proscribed, dishonoured, and concealed; and in conformity with this second convention certain religions will even go so far as to prohibit their believers from looking at, or touching, their own sexual parts, even for purposes of cleanliness.

In the one case as in the other, the conventional moral valuation is something that goes beyond the mere physiological and anatomical facts; similar conventions could have been applied to the noste or the foot. In a certain novel the author has supposed the existence of a society where eating in public (i.e. the exercise of taste and of the nutritive function) meets with exactly the same reprobation and same punishment as would be encountered in our own society by the public exercise of the sexual sense. Samuel Butler, who had little respect for taboos, asked us in his *Erewhon* to imagine a society where to be ill or to talk about one's health was regarded as a moral indiscretion. To convention everything is possible; there is nothing that it cannot either decree or prohibit; except, incidentally, the establishment of an opposite convention.

Thus the conventions with which we supplement the simple physiological facts, such ideas, for example, as that the sexual organs ought to be concealed in a way that does not apply to the other organs of sense, that coitus and sexual pleasure must be treated with greater reserve and discretion than, say, eating and sleeping, that the organs of sex, alone among our organs, must not be talked about—these conventions, as the name indicates, are creations of the mind; they do not follow from the facts as revealed by physiology. This truth, once realized, must surely be of great importance for all rational minds: for such minds have generally a healthy suspicion of the fantastic products of the human imagination. It remains now to see on what foundation our present sexual convention rests, and how far it is justified.

The Origins of Sexual Conventions.— Speaking quite generally, we may truly say that nothing more clearly reveals the inanity of a convention than the fact that, at some time or other, there have existed other human societies with an exactly opposite convention. This is the case with the sexual convention, since, as we have already reminded the reader, certain social groups, recognizing the great pleasure which is derived from the sexual sense, found it more natural to express their gratitude by treating the phallus as an object of public worship, instead of paying their devotions in the privacy of the alcove, as we do to-day. The cult of the phallus was indeed a thanksgiving to the sexual organs, a very striking contrast to the modern practice of repression. Chateaubriand in his preface to *Paul et Virginis* very justly observes that the obstinate act which costs the latter her life (obsessed as she is by sexual thoughts and their repression) would appear merely ridiculous to a young Greek girl.This severe judgement, naïve as it seems from the pen of the Christian writer, is nevertheless very true. It makes us realize that the taboo of sexuality is the result of a special social and religious education and is very far from being a natural condition of affairs.

Contradictions of this kind are not enough to enable us to come to a definite decision on the matter. But they should at least put us on our guard and should enable the philosophically minded person to remain unmoved by the dogmatic tone of the sexual moralists, and to withhold his assent until the latter can produce some proof of their contentions.

But this proof, it we refuse to allow it to take the shape of mere assertion or personal conviction, is singularly unconvincing. Let us restate the problem; we desire to know whether, granted the existence of physiological organs adapted to the exercise of a function of undeniable utility and of a sense which affords us a pleasure of undeniable charm and intensity, it is legitimate and justifiable to impose a veto on these organs as such, and upon their natural manifestations.Put in this way, the question appears in all its true significance.Indeed a visitor from another planet would perhaps be astonished to see the question raised at all. His first impulse would be to demand, in virtue of what passion for denial and self-mutilation, such organs and their manifestations, far from becoming the objects of public gratitude, have been condemned to banishment and shame. Can we reply to him by pushing our analysis a little further?

Impossibility of a Physiological Justification of these Conventions. — We have already said, and there is no need to insist further on this point, that the organs of sexuality in themselves possess nothing–either in their constitutive elements or in their form – which should make them subject to a special taboo. On the contrary, they are undeniably the seat of an all-powerful attraction, as we have seen in the case of young children; and later on they exercise a no less compelling attraction upon lovers. It would be as absurd to attempt to prove the existence of this fascination as it would be to prove the existence of light. If, therefore, there were a prejudice of any kind, this would be in the nature of sympathy rather than repugnance. All the different practices which lend variety to amorous enjoyment, and which so often call in the other organs to aid those of the sexual sense, emphasize this strong predisposition. In a word, the hostility, the contempt, the disgust, that we find associated with the sexual organs have all been learnt; they are derived from the general character of the education in the first years of life, and form an integral part of the system of repression.

Added to this, there is, in those persons who are saturated with the Judeo-Christian doctrine of "sin", a certain distrust of these organs, which are the very instruments of sin. The organs thus become diabolic, after having been divine. But all this has nothing to do with the scientific and impartial interpretation of sexual physiology.

The same may be said of the special secretions of the sexual organs. Far from abolishing the attractions of sex, they afford, on the contrary, a well-proved means of stimulation, and this for both sexes. The *odor di femina,* and the dominion acquired by certain women-doubtless, we should add, by certain men also-over their sexual partners, in virtue of the odours connected with these secretions, are facts so well known that it is unnecessary to insist upon them. But the facts can be corroborated by observing the behaviour of other animals in this particular.

Neither is disgust inspired by the sexual act a deux, or by coitus (to consider the most usual form of this act). To believe the contrary would be to allow our prejudices to interpret the morality of repression as though it were a natural phenomenon. The truth is, as we know, that coitus is ardently desired, indefatigably sought, and practised with delight as one of the greatest sources of human pleasure. In the sentimental phraseology of love, it has been lauded as the "crowning joy" of passion. "To give herself," i.e. to allow coitus, is held to be by far the most valuable thing that a woman has to offer.

We have already made the necessary reservations concerning the celebrated adage "post coitus animal triste" (to which, however, the Latin poet makes an exception of the cock and the woman), which is a false physiological interpretation of the facts. The man is not rendered sad by coitus, he is generally tired by what has been a considerable neuro-muscular effort. Above all, he is deprived of the immediate prospect of a pleasure for which he is not in a position for the moment to supply the necessary means; but it is the very importance attached to this pleasure that makes him regret its dis-appearance (whilst the woman on her side is so physiologically constituted as to be able to recommence without delay). This feeling naturally vanishes with the fatigue itself and the return of potency.In those men who practise frequent and varied sexual relationships, and who have also cast aside the theories which invest these relationships with the ideas of sin and guilt, coitus brings only a normal and satisfying joy, without any element of sadness.

Impossibility of Justifying Conventions on Grounds of

Disgust.—Some authors have put forward an ingenious explanation of the sexual taboos in terms of a subsidiary physiological fact. They point out that the anatomy, both of men and women, is such that the sexual organs, which are the seat of sexual pleasure, are in close and confusing proximity to the outlets for certain toxic and malodorous excretions. Freud also considers disgust as a factor calculated to aid the mechanism of repression. We cannot deny the justice of this observation, nor the advantages which the enemies of sex have derived from the unfortunate proximity in question. But the psycho-physiology of love shows us, at the same time, that we must not exaggerate the significance of this fact.

In the first place we must note that scatological disgust does not apply to one's own person; psycho-analysis has clearly established this general fact, which was indeed already known. The individual feels but little repugnance for his own excretions, and the Romans had already expressed this fact in a proverb. I remember once making a railway journey with a man who continuously indulged mechanically, but none the less with obvious gratification, in scratching his scalp and eating everything which he could extract from his auricular and nasal cavities. The child feels no repugnance at all for its own excretions. As Freud says, in the beginning, "his own faces produce no disgust in him, he values them as part of his body and is unwilling to part with them; he uses them as the first 'present' by which he can mark out those people whom he values especially. Even after education has succeeded in alienating him from these tendencies, he continues to feel the same high regard for his 'presents' and his 'money'; while his achievements in the way of urination appear to be the subject of particulár pride: We may ourselves complete the great psychologist's analysis by a few corroborative observations. In certain countries, to step or excrement is regarded by the superstitious as "a sign of money"; words and expressions connected with excrement are often employed by the common people, and even by the educated, as exclamations and for the purpose of stressing a statement or opinion (*le mot de Camb-*

ronne); and lastly that pride which Freud tells us may attach in early years to micturition may later be applied to the process of seminal ejaculation in the adult. And indeed this process, if we look at it scientifically, is nothing but an elimination of a superiduous secretion the accumulation of which would be likely to cause discomfort. The cells concerned may be the carriers of human destiny, but this does not prevent them from being at the same time substances of an excretory nature.

Another interesting observation of the psycho-analysts is that the anal zone is capable of providing a sort of masturbatory excitation, the stimulus for which is provided by the retention of faecal matter. It is probable, therefore, that the pleasure from this source tends greatly to diminish the disgust that is associated with the excretory function.

Freud has also said, quite rightly, that though disgust may inhabit libido, it can also be overcome by it. We may unhesitatingly add that the cases where it is thus overcome are legion; as is proved by the widespread habit of *fellatio*. There are variations in the degree of this disgust, according to the individual, or, in the same individual, according to the object or the condition of desire or satiety. It is only in the hysterical — i.e. definitely pathological — cases that there is displayed a general and insuperable disgust for the masculine genital apparatus, on the ground that it serves also the purposes of micturition. But it would seem that, as a rule, the excretory processes are not a matter of grave consideration to lovers: the most that can possibly be said in favour of this theory of disgust is that the processes in question are simply overlooked and forgotten.

Where persons are in love with one another, the tolerance towards their own excretions seems to extend to those of the partner—in virtuc doubtloss of that strong identification which unites the lovers into a single being. Their bodily needs are then a matter of amusement rather than repugnance, and they become a definite and permissible part of the general intimacy.Lovers are often able to say, in the words of Sacha

Guitry: "How intimate we have grown; at the end of a fortnight we performed our little needs in front of one another....." Furthermore, by a regression that is natural consequence of the laws that govern love, the said needs suddently recover the repulsive elements with which education has endowed them, as soon as desire wanes as a result of habituation or separation. Lovers who felt no embarrassment at these excretions (neither at the menses nor at the odour of the sweat glands) during their first period of love, are not able to tolerate them when their honeymoon is over; then it is that the newely married pair begin to feel the need of separate bedrooms.

Disgust is thus a matter of education and environment rather than of innate endowment; the expressions and exclamations of adults are probably to a large extent responsible for its arousal in the child. In harmony with this does not exist in the child, but is shown by the adult; it may be aroused by the excreta of some persons but not by that of others; some individuals may experience it in relation to certain things (food), or persons (lover's embraces), while other individuals do not; certain races experience it for foods which are in no wise repugnant to other races: the peoples of Indo-China relish *nioc-man*, which is a residue of putrid fish, but are unable to understand our own love of cheese. All this shows that disgust results from a certain education of the senses and the mind; the true nature of this education is vividly revealed when one sees persons who were formerly "disgusted" by a particular dish partaking of it when they see others eating it, and soon becoming enthusiastic lovers of it.

We may reasonably ask how this comes about. The answer is no difficult : if disgust is the result of education (aided no doubt by certain atavistic traits), it is not a natural phenomenon. Indeed, how can it be an expression of nature?

Disgust has no place in nature. Nature, inorganic or organic, only knows substances, which are all of equal value in her eyes. One mineral is as good as another; one salt or gas is as good as another salt or gas; there is no hierarchy among them.

Hierarchies are established by our needs or our subjective preferences. It is we who decide whether a thing shall be pure or impure, good or bad, sweet-smelling or malodorous; exactly in the same way as we declare, often according to very varying formulae, that this is beautiful and that is ugly. Nature is as indifferent to an excrement as it is to a rose; for her, both are momentary chemical combinations of substances which could just as well have undergone some other combination, and which perhaps tomorrow will recombine so as to produce a totally different result. We have therefore no need to be astonished that so purely human and subjective a notion as disgust should be swayed this way and that, as our capricious senses may dictate.

Furthermore, how can the manifestations of disgust conceivably be other than subjective? Man reasons in terms of his own nature, and tends always to take his own structure as the general rule. But this structure is, in reality, only one type among many. There are some animal types in which "the genital apparatus is intimately related to the mouth," and others in which "it is inseparable from the excretory apparatus" (Freud). Our subjective preferences have created a word which is constantly at variance with reality.

Finally, we have the phenomena of rapid habituation, which, as has been said, shows our organism to be "remarkably plastic" (B.Bourdou). If we can learn to eat and relish Munster or Livarot cheese, we may conclude a *priori* that there is no limit to the extent to which our senses are willing to oblige. The power of imagination is such that it comes to the aid of this process of habit formation, and there are few more favourable fields for its development than that of the sexual relationships. On the other hand it may exercise an inhibitory function without any material justification for so doing; there are few persons who could eat jam from a chamber-pot without nausea, even though the pot were quite new and had just that moment come from the factory. These examples of opposite kinds show how fragile is the element of reason which we must expect to meet when it is question of the objective appreciation of sexual values or of anything that is connected with them. Observations of this kind should make us very wary, showing, as they do, what an enormous part is played hereby subjective impressions, by the state of excitation or desire; and should lead us to attach but little importance to the standards of appreciation or disgust which are current in other cases.

Let us add that, if we are to believe the specialists, there are many men who prefer rectal to normal coitus, men with a women; and that these men find willing partners. If, in normal cases, lovers are moved by each other's sexual organs to feelings which border on the fanatical and idolatrous; if, in a jargon which is tolerated even by sexual morality itself, they speak of these organs as "treasures" and as "charms", and do not hesitate to bestow upon them kisses and caresses; it is difficult to see in all this the influence of repulsion about which some physiologists are wont to write. And finally, the choicest present which a woman can make to a man, when she is desperately desirous of showing him her love, adoration, admiration, and devotion—is it not her body, her flesh, her sexuality? This in itself suffices a priori to give the lie to all those statements about the supposed disgust of human beings for sexuality and "the flesh". In truth, this explanation, considered in itself alone, is unable to justify the taboo of the sexual organs.

Impossibility of Justifying Conventions on Grounds of Modesty. — According to another system, the convention which taboos the organs of the sexual sense and the pleasure which they give is justified by a special sentiment, i.e. that of modesty. Modesty consists in experiencing a feeling of shame in the exposure to other people(or even in extreme cases to oneself) of the sexual organs, or in the manifestation of sexual pleasure. The feeling is so well known that it is unnecessary to define it further; modern society, in distinction to many ancient societies, has been at such pains to develop this feeling, that it is perfectly understood even by those who experience it very little; and it has even been considered a feeling sufficiently imperious in character to justify, for its protection, the creation of a new and special crime, which was unknown to the ancients, that of outrage on public decency.

The view that modesty is a natural and necessary feeling among human beings (for there is no question of its existence among other animals) rests, however, upon a gratuitous assumption which has no foundation in experience. What is natural to human beings, as to all other animals, is a state of a-modesty, that is to say, the absence of all shame until it has been instilled by education. Even atavism itself, influential as it is in bringing about varieties in the species, counts for little here.

In the child, modesty is non-existent; he has to be constantly told (and indeed the injunction is repeated *ad nauseam*) that he must not exhibit or touch his sexual organs. "The young child," says, Freud, "is utterly lacking in modesty, and in the years of infancy takes an unconcealed pleasure in exhibiting his body and in drawing attention to the genital regions." When he begins to abstain from these satisfactions, it is not because he personally subscribes to this prohibition, against which his whole sexual sense rebels; it is for fear of being punished. This is clearly shown by the numerous cases where children come together without the knowledge of their parents in order to talk about the sexual organs or to indulge in sexual practices; their pleasure in the exercise of the sexual sense being supplemented here (as the result of a gross pedagogical error) by the pleasure of doing something that is forbidden. In other words, it requires a whole process of training and repression before "official" modesty becomes easy enough to pass muster as a normal and innate characteristic of the human mind.In certain individuals, moreover, this repression only achieves a superficial adhesion and a hypocritical acceptance of the social conventions, which are not really understood, and against which the sexual sense continually rebels. In primitive races, which have remained closer to nature modesty, as we have seen, is no more apparent than it is in children; the reader can be left to himself to imagine what must have been the state of modesty in pre-historic times.

The number of women who are definitely a-modesty is just as large as that of men.This fact is shown, in the first place, by the ease with which many of them become prostitutes—either openly or secretly. The prostitute affords a striking instance of a-modesty, inasmuch as she represents an individual in whom neither the manifestations nor the organs of sex are able to inspire a feeling of disgust or embarrassment.But many women who are not professional prostitutes are a-modest with a succession of lovers; i.e. once they have made up their mind to pass the threshold of each new love, they experience no embarrassment whatsoever when they first undress or first indulge in intimacy.Thus the temperament of the courtesan is not an exceptional one; and indeed, since the members of her profession can be numbered by the million, we are not justified in speaking of an exception, but rather of a well-marked type.

The artificial arousal of the sentiment of modesty takes place in obedience to social conventions; it is not a spontaneous manifestation.The triumph of modesty is a relatively recent phenomenon, for, although shame was known to the ancients, it was very far from enjoying the importance which was given to it by Judeo-Christian ethics and by the social systems founded thereon; it is a triumph which, in the immense majority of cases, is very superficial.

It is very instructive to see how, in the majority of mortals, this sentiment of modesty, the result of a laborious process of education, is easily broken down as soon as it is no longer imposed by convention.All young girls, however obedient they may be to the behest s of modesty, look forward to the moment when, under cover of marriage, which frees them from the convention, they may officially throw aside their modesty; for the married state is the opposite of that which their education has ordained, i.e. it implies liberty to exhibit and to use the sexual organs.If modesty were a natural sentiment, not only would this intense desire be absent, but shame would make us revel against love and marriage also.In reality, however, these latter socially permissible expressions of sexual pleasure are so highly valued,just because they afford a means of overcoming the constraint of modesty, that heavy mortgage on nature and the happiness of life. The most modest of brides is delighted to trample on her modesty as soon as she knows that she can do so and still remain within the bounds of social convention. Between lovers, and even between married couples, there is continuous immodesty; it is the daily bread of such people, our sexual moralists, powerless to prevent it; call it intimacy; it implies a mutual liberty, freed from the influence of society prudery, in the use of all the organs and the sexual secretions.

Thus nothing is easier to break down than this convention of modesty; in prostitutes it is broken down with reference to all men, in the married girl (for the time being) with reference to one only; but this is merely a matter of degree. Even the most legitimate of sexual unions is based on the abdication of modesty. All male, and female alike, in the human race no less than among other species, are equally at the mercy of the demands and expressions of the sexual sense; the most ardent apologies of modesty must, in their own marital relations, resign themselves, like others, to the highest possible degree of obscenity, if obscenity exists.

The fact that men so often praise the modesty of women and regard it as one of the great feminine virtues, does not in any way invalidate our contention. In the first place the apologies of sexual morality and social convention have made a stock argument of this line of defence. In the second place those men who attach great importance to the exclusive possession of a particular woman have special interest in extolling modesty, which seems to constitute a guarantee of what they desire, and puts their minds to rest as regards the danger of having to share their possession with others. Lastly, it would seem as though men often attach a high value to female modesty in order to enjoy greater thrill whenever they are allowed, in all privacy and intimacy, to crush and trample on this modesty and to transform it into immodesty. It was in this spirit that Richelieu considered that a woman was all the more attractive for possessing "un petit air d'honnectete." It is a specific of sadism; the man delights in venging himself on modesty and repression, in teaching the woman of his choice a lesson which is diametrically opposed to, and destructive of, those lessons of modesty which had previously been taught to both. That this interpretation is correct is shown by the fact that just those men who have remained in touch with nature, and have been but little influenced by the teachings of modesty (which they look on as a very artificial thing), are not specially attracted to women who parade their prudery. On the contrary they are pleased when they can find women who will respond to the imperious call of sexual desire in a straightforward way, with a frank and free immodesty, and who will look on this response as a legitimate indulgence of which there is no cause to be ashamed. In terms of our current sexual morality, these men are more "perverse" than those who prefer modest women; but a psychological analysis shows that in reality it is the "modest" who at bottom offend most against the code of modesty itself, and who are skilful in using it, only in the end to flout it all the more effectually.

Modesty is the very ensign of repression. It is the tangible symbol planted on the fortress of sexuality which indicates that it has been conquered and annexed by repression. And this explains everything. This flag was not hoisted during the first years of childhood, for at that time sexuality was still free, and not subject to censorship. If modesty is not a natural phenomenon, this is just because repression itself, of which it is the emblem, is a declaration of war against nature. The role played by modesty in the Judeo-Christian system is the apotheosis of repression. Thus everything falls into its place; if we apply this criterion to the facts of sex, they are all explained by it. Here is one example out of a hundred that we could give. People who are perfectly a-modest, who are hostile to repression, and who exhibit no shame in their sexual relationships, experience this sentiment of modesty solely in connection with their parents; they would not undress before them; they are embarrassed if obscene words are spoken in their presence: for the parents are intimately connected with the first attempts at repression, and therefore with the birth of modesty. The impression thus created is so strong and durable that it persists even when an ardent temperament, or a deliberate decision, has banished the convention of modesty from all sexual relations with the habitual partners.

In view of this, there is no need to be astonished by the fact that modesty, like sexual morality as a whole, varies enormously both in space and time. The philosopher will remain sceptical about a virtue which is so much at the mercy of temperature or fashion. Thus it comes about that in civilizations of long standing, which have passed through every phase of thought, modesty loses much of its respectability as a simple taboo. Except in unsophisticated circles, where thought is still governed by convention, it is scarcely spoken of, except perhaps in tones of irony. In the year of grace 1927 Abel Harmont summed it up as follows:"...The sentiment of modesty, which is apparently the same everywhere, finds it expression in certain conventions, which in one place signify modesty, though in another place they may signify the opposite. The manifestations of modesty are, if we may be permitted to say so, essentially geographic. Even in the same place, this virtue is subject to strange variations, like those of which we are the bewildered witnesses at the present day. Let us not be deceived. Some moral rule is indispensable; but its particular formula is a matter of indifference; modesty is indispensable, but its demands on one side of the Pyrenees have no necessary relation to those on the other."

If modesty is not a natural sentiment, if it is nothing but the symbol of a social convention, as artificial and arbitrary as the convention which it represents, it is utterly incapable of explaining the taboo which lies upon the sexual organs and the sexual sense. Unknown as it is, alike in the infancy of the individual and in that of the race, it represents the end of a process of development rather than its beginning. It is clear that we must look elsewhere for the cause of the taboo in question.

Necessity of Justifying Conventions by Metaphysical Conceptions.— We must indeed, in this case as in every other instance of convention, examine its origin and study its sources and its history, if we are to understand its nature.

The ascetic religions have a system which is very logical, once we grant its premises, and which can be summed up in a few words; they promise to their believers a future life, which is both better and more permanent than this life on earth. But, as a condition of obtaining this future life, they insist upon a renunciation of the pleasures and enjoyments of earth. This is, in particular, one of the express injunctions of Judeo-Christian dogma, which regards this world as "a vale of tears." Such a view automatically produces a tendency to avoid everything which could make our present existence appear desirable. It is a general theory and does not apply to sexual pleasure only; it logically implies a condemnation of everything which is capable of giving pleasure: the pleasure of the table (sin of gluttony), of drink (prohibitionism), of the theatre, of music, of dancing. It would seem as though such a doctrine aimed less at the attainment of heaven by the renunciation of earthly pleasure, than at the proof of the reality of the "vale of tears"; for it does its best to make life agree with this description, in spite of all the pleasures which could otherwise be found in existence here on earth. "The joy of nature makes us forget the gods," said Octave Mirabeau. This explains the origin of all modern prohibitonistic movements, eager as they are to destroy everything which has a semblance of pleasure; it explains even such minor details as the campaign against tobacco in certain parts of America, and the obsolete decrees of certain official busybodies, who are anxious to prevent women from smoking in public. For those who are eager to destroy human pleasures often have an exaggerated notion of the importance of these pleasures, and distort the most trivial acts without ever seeking to understand them.

When we contemplate the fury with which the prohibitionistic systems are wont to pursue the unfortunate pleasures of man, even the least important of them, it is easy to realize how tremendous, even in the earliest times, must have been the taboo against the most intense, the most powerful, and the most desired of all pleasures, i.e. that of sex. In this general proscription sex has naturally headed the list. Its free development would indeed, more than anything else, have endangered the reputation of this world as an abode of sadness. It triumph would have turned our thoughts and desires from vague and distant compensations to more certain and immediate advantages. It has, therefore, been denounced above all others: proscribed in common with other sources of enjoyment, it has also been accorded the honour of special denunciation in view of its position as the supreme enjoyment. It has been qualified as shameful and impure; though, by a further convention, which is contradictory and does not bear examination, it is *not* considered to possess these characters when it is obtained under special authorized circumstances, and in connection with the process of reproduction (civil or religious marriage). But can the purity or impurity of a physiological act vary according to the term which we use to describe it?If we regard coitus as impure, does it not remain so even when carried out by a couple whose marriage has been duly soleminized?

It will be noticed that the prohibitionistic tendency is directed only against such things as are capable of *giving pleasure.* Thus it is only the enjoyment of sex which meets with disapproval and not the process of reproduction, which has of necessity to be permitted, and which indeed is given an official blessing.In truth, every prohibitionistic doctrine has, from the beginning, shown a complete understanding of the important principle with which we dealt in the preceding chapter: the distinction between the sense of sexual enjoyment and the function of reproduction.Prohibitionistic systems have tabooed the former and tolerated, organized, and blessed the latter; the important thing was to reproduce, but, since enjoyment was inevitable, we ought, according to this view, to carry out the work of procreation with as little pleasure as is possible, hurriedly and regretfully. Celibacy was enjoined on certain Atheninan and Mithraic priests. St. Paul declared that, though marriage might be good, complete abstinence was better.

The Judeo-Christian system, which finally came to control the whole of Western morals, has always shown the strongest antagonism to sexual pleasure as such. This attitude is revealed in a simple but instructive manner by a fact which can be easily verified by those who are familiar with simple country priests or bishops of humble origin. Such ecclesiastics, though duly hostile to "sin" are as indulgent as Rabelais himself to coprophilic jokes: for to sin is to enjoy, whereas dirtiness signifies but little. In family life, too, many parents who would never give their children sexual explanations, even of a strictly scientific kind, are in no wise disturbed by humour of this type. This also explains the fact that the unashamed exhibition of the sexual organs of young boys arouses no indignation, and that the Mannekenpiss reigns officially over a Brussels square; it is only where there is a possibility of orgasm, i.e. of pleasure, that the puritans begin to protest.

The prohibitionistic doctrine based on these metaphysical presuppositions must surely appear untenable to all rational beings who are anxious to organize life on earth for the increase of human profit and satisfaction–for all those who, far from abolishing pleasure, wish to increase it by making life itself a better and more desirable thing. But it is a doctrine which, through the strength of its history and traditions, has exercised an enormous influence on the illogical structure of our sexual ethics, and which in itself is sufficient to explain why, without any adequate reason either in physiology or logic, certain normal organs and a quite legitimate source of pleasure have been proscribed, condemned, ostracized and regarded as unclean.This proscription cannot be understood unless we trace back its origin to the mighty metaphysical systems which have so greatly influenced the destinies of men. So difficult is it to escape the influence in question that even those members of our modern societies who have deliberately abandoned Judeo Christian metaphysics, have not yet recognized that the anti-sexual morality, which they still profess with such docility, is only an application of these metaphysics□that it is a fundamentally illogical and irrational morality, incapable of justification by science or reason, if once its essential metaphysical support be withdrawn.

The Fundamental Error of Sexual Morality. — Thus, both from the physiological and the philosophical points of view, it would seem that for centuries human beings have laboured under the weight of a scientific error which has crushed their lives, i.e. the devaluation of sexual pleasure, the procuring of which has, in defiance of all logic, been treated as a shameful and immoral act.

The few centuries of past human history are as nothing in the evolution of the race; and however permanent our moral conventions may seem to superficial minds, they have nothing behind them but a tradition which is insignificant enough when confronted with the millennia to come.Difficult as it is to imagine, the most powerful doctrines of the present day will appear to our remote descendants only as so many vestiges and ruins, the creations of children and savages as yet scarcely alive to the impartial light of science and of reason. That contemporary sexual ethics will one day have to join the geocentric theory or the doctrine of special creation, would seem to be an inevitable consequence of the progress of the human mind.

It is, indeed, a very dangerous step for an ethical system to link its fate with that of metaphysics or religion of whatsoever kind. An ethical system can only be permanent in so far as it is based upon scientific and logical (that is to say, natural and independent) conclusions. But if it is the slave of metaphysics system, it will share the fate of that system; will be opposed or rejected in the same way as the system itself. This is what is actually happening to modern sexual ethics. Incapable of invoking rational and scientific principles in its support, its strength is derived solely from the metaphysics of renunciation: instead of existing in its own right, it is merely an item in the programmes of this metaphysics. Its increasing discredit among all rational minds is therefore no matter for surprise, "There is a phase in every love affair." H.G.Wells has written, "when death and ruin are agreeable additions to the prospect. It gives the business a gravity, a solemnity". These alarming words give expression to psychological fact which undoubtedly has to reckoned with.And what can be the ultimate reason of this apparent contradiction, of this resignation of despair, unless it be some deep-founded conviction on the part of the lovers who accept it? The conviction that it is they themselves who are in the right; that their conduct, confirming as it does to natural laws, is of greater worth than any servile adherence to variable and temporary social conventions; and this dishonour with which they are menaced is only a dishonour in name, a false and hollow sham, while they themselves, in their own hearts, believe it honourable to live according to the eternal truths, which our sexual prohibitions and repressions, with their lack of comprehension and cowardly adherence to tradition, do their best to stifle. Our so-called sexual morality stands condemned by the fact that, whenever there is a conflict between truth and pretence, it reserves all its severity \for the former and bestows all its praise upon the latter.

Necessity for an Advance of Thought in this Matter. — There can be no doubt that progress in human thought consists in replacing *false* associations of ideas by *true* ones. False associations abound primitive peoples; they gradually disappear in so far as a precise and scientific observation, and a more logical method of thought, bring to light the true relations between things. Certain minds, through their love of the *status quo* (often called tradition),or through false sentiment, fight hard to retain the old false associations, and to oppose the advent of new and truer ones; either by directly refusing to accept the new, by accepting it in word only and not in thought or deed, or else by evading it with the help if a thousand ingenious but futile subtleties of one kind or another. In the end, however, they are as powerless as were the inquisitors who tried to make Galileo withdraw his statements about the rotation of the earth.

False associations of ideas, without any basis in experience, are common enough among primitive people. Here is one example among ten thousand; "There was a rule of the Spartan constitution that every eighth year the Ephors should choose a clear and moonless night, and, sitting down, observe the sky in silence. If during their vigil they saw *meteor or shooting star*, they inferred that the king had *sinned against the deity*, and they suspended him from a his functions until the Delphic or Olympic oracles should reinstate him." The italicized word represent the two terms of the false association. Superstitious practices of this kind are very widespread, and it is not astonishing to find that they play a part also in the attitude adopted towards the sexual organs and the sexual life.

The false association in these cases consists in the creation of a mental relation between two facts which in reality are unrelated: a bad harvest and an incestuous coitus, for example. What error of judgement may have led to this association is of little importance here; we need only remind the reader that the savage has plenty of opportunities to make faulty observations, since he has no notions of scientific method or of experimental technique, and is perpetually worried and harassed by anxiety. But false relation brought about in this way engenders the further idea that the abolition of the supposed cause will abolish the supposed consequence; in what follows we shall see the important part played by this idea in the creation of taboos especially taboos of deprivation taboos which, in their further development, are translated, though in a still more or less recognizable form, into the fields of sociology, ethics and religion.

We cannot for the moment imagine our own modern societies encumbered with all the superstitions, constraints and prohibitions which are so prevalent in the folklore of primitive peoples. A reference to the pages of Frazer's *Golden Bough* is sufficient to make us realize the vast difference there exists in this respect. We have enormously reduced the numbers of demons, gods, ghosts. lemures and devils, which dogged the steps of our remote ancestors through the terrors of the dark. Too many of these whimsies are still with us, but their power has waned. Yet there remains a host of illogical conventions which have proved more difficult to overcome, and still continue to affect our actions.Some of them it is true, have succumbed to impartial observation, and in the eyes of many people already stand condemned. But others have offered a more formidable resistance, and this is often because we do not take the trouble to examine them closely and without bias. Our so-called sexual morality teems with superstitions of this kind.

Progress in this sphere must consist in a ruthless examination of all facts. We must see to it that we are guided, not by any traditional sentimentality, but by reason only. When we do this, we are surprised to find that many views we usually accept without question are merely so many inaccurate and unprovable assumptions, a heritage from the remote superstitions of our primitive forefathers.

There is nothing new in this. Tyrannical as our sexual morality has been, there have at all times existed certain free and critical spirits who realized how false and empty were these reasonings. If they possessed enough strength of character to reject them and to refuse to look upon them as indispensable rules of life, they were taxed with immorality. This "immorality,"which is nothing more than a spirit of criticism And free inquiry, has greatly increased in recent times. The enthusiastic supporters of conventional sexual morality, in common with all those who have an interest in maintaining it, have to admit this tendency, much as they are alarmed at it. They call it "the collapse of morality", but that is to beg the question.

The problem is much wider than this. It is not our business to uphold the claims that sexual morality makes on our respect, as though it enjoyed a feudal privilege; we must, rather, ask whether it is worthy of this respect; that is, whether it is the scientific, rational, and logical expression of the teachings of physiology. We must no longer ask it to lay down rules for us, but rather to justify itself. We must examine the accuracy of its implications and verify the truth of its postulates. Let it emerge successfully from the test, if it can. Since none of the ancient dogmas has survived such a test, neither in religion, nor in politics, nor in sociology—it would be very surprising indeed if sexual morality alone were able to escape.

Criticism of Sexual Conventions.—If we submit sexual morality to a critical examination of this kind, we find that it is based:-

(a) On false associations of ideas; for to attribute *moral* value to *physiological* organs is a false association. It is equally false to attribute purity or impurity to the exercise of a sense or a function, even though it be sexual. Such things as the testicles, the neck of the womb, or the act of coitus can be neither good nor bad; valuations of this kind rest entirely on convention, and in no wise on reason and necessity.

(b) On false reasonings, derived from false associations which have become converted into postulates. Thus it is false reasoning to condemn people who freely exercise their sexual sense as morally inferior, even when this exercise involves no violence or deceit, and is carried out with the full consent of their partners: for such exercise is only in accordance with the demands of physiology and hygiene; nor is abstinence in any way a sign of superior morality. To place "the honour" of a woman in her sexual organs is, as de Brosses has already hinted, childish conception originated by our primitive ancestors, who possessed a lively gift for metaphysics, but who were ignorant of biology, of evolution, and of the true nature of living beings.

(c) On conventional classifications which are impossible to justify scientifically or even logically. For example, the representation of a naked body is permitted in our picture galleries, though it is always understood that the public hairs must not be indicated; and yet these latter are in no way more than the hairs of the head or of the armpit. Similarly, it needed a great effort before the chorus girls in French theatres were allowed to appear with naked breasts, although women nursing their children are to be seen everywhere in public places.

(d) In the last resort, on a complete confusion between physiology, which is one thing, and morality, which is another. It is strange indeed that morality should have been able to take possession of certain physiological manifestations and erect them into a criterion of good behaviour. The sexual act is in reality as a-moral as are eating, breathing, or sleeping; and it is self-sufficient. There can therefore be neither honour nor dishonour when two beings agree to give each other sexual pleasure: there is merely the deliberate exercise of a perfectly admissible physiological need.

Positive Rules.—If, now, we try to extract certain positive teachings from this critical examination, we may summarize such teachings in the following rules:

(i) *The convention which regards the sexual organs as shameful is without any foundation in reason, logic or physiology; it would be just as possible and just as foolish to regard the nose, the tongue or the act of swallowing, as shameful.*

(ii) *The acts accompanying sexual pleasure find their only and sufficient justification in the pleasure that they bring; sexual pleasure is therefore just as admissible as any other natural satisfaction, and its exercise, in whatsoever form may be preferred, has nothing to do with the morality, the virtue or the dignity of either sex.*

(iii) *There should therefore be no disgrace, either for the man or for the woman,in procuring or giving sexual pleasure it is the lawful and natural exercise of a physiological act.*

(iv) *Sexual pleasure is always lawful, whether it is obtained with a view to reproduction or as an end in itself, i.e., for the mere purpose of obtaining a specific satisfaction.*

(v) *Everybody has the right to exercise quite freely his own preferences in matters of sex, so long as he is guilty of no violence or deceit to others; the right to sexual satisfaction is just as inalienable as the right to eat.*

(vi) *The hygiene of the sexual sense and sexual organs is a matter of science and of personal responsibility, just as is the hygiene of the nutritive function.*

Thus we are led to realize what inestimable advantages would be gained by a substitution of the term "*neural pleasure*" for that of "*sexual pleasure*". Not only should we, in so doing, re-establish a physiological truth, but with one stroke we should abolish all those conventional and ethical prejudices which so distort the observations of psycho-analysts and independent moralists within this field. So-called sexual morality would retire in favour of the natural laws of biology, physiology and hygiene; and the confusion between neural pleasure and the function of reproduction would automatically cease.

Conclusions as Regards the Morality of Sexual Acts. — This return to a logical conception of the sexual sense and its exercise is the only means of making us realize what heights of absurdity are reached by those doctrines which have turned sex into a sort of artificial monster. As R.de Gourmant says, "the Greeks seem to have been always very vague as regards sexual morals, though this has not prevented them from playing a certain role in history"; or as E. Faguet has naively remarked. "The Roman mimes, however obscene or licentious they may have been, were yet full of highly moral maxims, which the Latin grammarians have preserved for us. We may explain this curious contrast and admixture as we think best...."

How easy it is now to explain these supposed contradictions! The fact is that, among the ancients, morals had remained morals, i.e. a code of virtue teaching people not to harm their neighbours. It had not become completely sexualized. Sexuality and its pleasures had remained questions of physiology and not of morals. It was therefore still permissible to speak about sex, which could be treated with the same frankness with which to-day we can discuss our meals (i.e. the nutritive functions) and the condiments that we consider right to add thereto. The ancients were still in touch with truth; whereas we moderns, for certain special reasons, have lost sight of it. A certain prelate once thought that he ought to defend France against the charge of not observing the ninth commandment of the Christian Church. By this very fact he showed how close for him was that relationship, to which we have already referred, between sexual repression and metaphysics. But we on our part have to recognize that, in addition to the doctrine, the prelate was defending, there exists another doctrine, that of rationalism, which in turn considers that these "commandments" are themselves primitive, unjustifiable and inadmissible; and which calls our attention to the fact that there are many people of fine intellect who refuse to observe them, not so much for reasons of taste as of principle: in other words, the reproach from which the prelate sought to defend his country, whether it be supported by the evidence or not, has no meaning or interest for the modern rationalist.

A critical examination of the facts, therefore, fails utterly to give any support to the theory (itself based on a faulty physiology) which maintains that men and women who adjure sex enjoy more dignified lives than those who freely lend themselves to sexual pleasure. Dignity is no more concerned here than it would be in the question as to whether we should travel by foot or in a car. This imaginary *dignity* is only the counterpart of the imaginary *defilement*: the latter was a punishment, the former a reward; the aim of both being to ensure the triumph of false conceptions. It is just as ridiculous for a person to consider himself worthy or respectable because he abstains from neural pleasure as it would be to consider himself morally superior for going without one of his daily meals. These supposed moral values are, every one of them, distorted: they only exist as so many arbitrary and artificial categories for those who are incapable of understanding physiological truth.

It will no doubt in future be considered a triumph of modern rationalism, especially in France, that it was able to draw the distinctions that were so urgently needed in this field, and that it has brought order into a problem which had hitherto suffered from such an obstinate, passionate, not to say perverse, confusion of ideas.

Chapter-5

The Sexual Taboo and its Origin

Chapter 5

The Origin of the Prohibitionistic Sanctions. — An important problem arises at this point of our research. We have seen how absurd, unreasonable and unscientific it is to look upon the sexual organs as though they were, in their very nature, shameful and in need of covering, and to regard the natural desire for sexual pleasure as though it were intrinsically wicked. We have seen too that physiology can give us no sound reason why we should be more secretive about these organs and their pleasures than we are, for instance, about the organs and pleasures of nutrition. Finally, experience and observation have revealed the fact that modesty is nothing but an unnecessary and variable convention. How and why then has it come about that our official morality is so bitterly hostile to sex?Under what circumstances did this morality arise, how did it become so firmly established, so generally accepted? How was it able to arouse such passion and cause such persecution?How comes it that even to-day exercises a veritiable dictatorship over humanity, and turns our legal and punitive systems to its own uses?

Indeed, we should naturally imagine that it would have been an extremely difficult matter to make humanity accept such a regime.If men had been psychologically normal (as they are physiologically normal), they would have strongly opposed these prohibitions, directed as they are against a pleasure which they esteem above all others. They would have found the greatest difficulty in understanding why one particular part of the body should be regarded as shameful, while the others are not.They would have smiled in derision at a theory that was so illogical as to prohibit the very things that under other names (love and procreation) it approves and enjoins. Nor would they have easily been led to suppose that a pleasure which gives the most lively satisfaction could have engendered anything but a desire for its renew and a sense of gratitude (such as the phallic worship) with undeniable logic, were wont to express in their rites).

This paradox is so evident that sexual morality has often pointed to it as a proof that there exists an innate sense of modesty. This argument forgets to take into account the existence of the phallic religions, and loses sight of the fact that, in certain well-established cults, the manifestations of the sexual life have been considered as being themselves a homage to the gods; a system which is the exact contrary of that which prohibits these manifestations in order to please God. Contradictions such as these are very significant, since they show us that the prohibitions of sex are the result of a temporary and local system and do not correspond to any universal law of human nature.

Nevertheless, the servile readiness with which an important part of the human race has accepted this prohibition, with all its inconveniences, restrictions and tyrannies (though many of these have been secretly flouted and set at nought by the great majority), has remained a sociological mystery which pedants have found it easy to exploit. The study of the origin and development of religion among primitive races has at last thrown some light upon these obscure facts. This work has now shown that sexual morality, unable to find any rational justification for its teachings, has bound itself in close alliance to certain sanctions, which themselves have been established for purely metaphysical ends. It is from these sanctions that sexual morality derives its apparent strength.

We must now proceed to give a careful and detailed proof of this statement.

Role and Importance of Taboo.—We must begin by a definition of taboo, in the form in which it has been observed by European travellers, especially in Polynesia, where they discovered hitherto isolated peoples fortunate enough to have escaped the distorting and crippling influences which have so much affected the Occidental world. Salomon Reinach gives the following definition; "Taboo, in Polynesia, signified, strictly speaking, that which is removed from current usage; a tree which cannot be touched or cut down is a tabooed tree, and people will speak of the taboo of a tree to designate the scruples felt by a man who is tempted to touch or cut down that tree. These scruples are never founded on any practical reason, such as, in the case of the tree, might be caused by the fear of hurting or pricking oneself. What gives the distinctive character to taboo is that the prohibition is not adequately motivated, and that the punishment that is expected in the event of a taboo being violated is not a penalty inflicted by civil law, but a calamity, such as death or blindness, which descends upon the guilty person.

The word is Polynesian, but the idea which it expresses is very familiar to us; especially in those countries where people have not yet forgotten their Bible. At the very beginning of that book, Adam is warned by the Almighty not to eat the fruit of a certain tree-on pain of death; this is a characteristic taboo, for the Almighty does not say *why* Adam should not eat the fruit of that tree.

Later on, in the religious legislation of the Hebrews, it is forbidden under pain of death to pronounce the sacred name of the Almighty. Here we have a case of a tabooed name. Another example of taboo appears in the Second Book of Samuel. The Ark of the Covenant was not allowed to be touched except by the members of a certain privileged family. When David wanted to carry it to Jerusalem, he had it placed upon a chariot drawn by oxen; in the course of the journey these oxen stumbled, and a certain Uzzah rushed towards the Ark and held it up. He was struck dead on the instant. The Ark was taboo, and death was the punishment of the violation of the taboo. In the form in which it appears in our text of the Bible, the story is not a little shocking, for it is said that the wrath of the Lord was kindled against Uzzah and that He "smote him there for his error"; though, according to our present sense of justice, it was no error. But take away the notion of the Lord; consider the Ark as a vessel full to overflowing with an invisible but terrible force; Uzzah, touching it, pays the penalty of his imprudence, like a man who dies from an electric shock on having touched the terminals of some powerful battery. The proof of the antiquity of this story is that the editor of the Book of Sameul, in the form in which we possess it, did not understand it, and somewhat distorted it in the course of his account.

The concept of taboo is one of the most fruitful which nineteenth-century ethnography has given us. In the transition from taboo to a reasoned, logical and adequately motivated prohibition we see reflected almost the whole history of the progress of the human mind.'

Freud for his part has written: "For us the meaning of taboo branches off into two opposite directions. On the one hand it means to us acred, consecrated, but on the other hand it means uncanny, dangerous, forbidden and unclean. The opposite of taboo is designated in Polynesian by the word *noa*, and signifies something ordinary and generally accessible. Thus something like the concept of 'reserved' is present in taboo; taboo expresses essentially a prohibition and restriction. Our combination of 'holy dread' would often express the meaning of taboo... The taboo prohibitions lack all justification and are of unknown origin. Though incomprehensible to us, they are taken as a matter of course by those who are under their dominion."

If we bear in mind particularly this last sentence, we can see to what a great extent it applies to the ritual injunctions which still characterize many religions of the present day. But we must note one further point: the notion that it is *impossible to do* a given thing, though of the essence of taboo, is, needless to say, completely relative, completely a matter of convention. The act in question is, in fact, possible for everybody, but it is put in a special category which makes it impossible for those who are unwilling to transgress the law.Just as the eating of pork, is as a matter of fact, possible for every Jew, but has become impossible and tabooed for those Jews who desire to conform to their religious laws. In opposition to the view held by N.W. Thomas, we believe that there is here more than a mere analogy; and that in reality, although it may be possible to distinguish, as he wants us to do, between the prohibitions of taboo on the one side and the prohibitions of religion on the other, we should never allow ourselves to forget that the latter are at any rate derived from the former, and are closely related to them.

In the notes made by R.L. Stevenson in the course of his travels in Oceania there are to be found many very interesting details regarding Polynesian taboos. These latter are modern equivalents of long since vanished practices of our ancestors and reveal to us the far-distant origins of many rites found in present day religions. Stevenson tells us that taboos of this kind "forbade the use of certain words of the language, particularly those words which related to women". Women indeed had to obey innumerable taboos. The sanction was the same as that mentioned by Salomon Reinach: "Every infraction is immediately punished by consumption or some other mortal malady. Those who have eaten tabooed fish are attacked by a slow wasting disease". The impression made on the mind of the individual concerned is so terrible that even more striking cases have been reported. In "Dr. Campbells" *Paenamo* we may read," says Stevenson, "a story of a young New Zealand girl; she had eaten a tabooed yam; they had been so stupid as to tell her; she immediately fell ill, and died two days afterwards of sheer terror". The same deadly power of auto-suggestion, though in an opposite aspect, appears in the cures made at Lourdes, Analogous cases cited by Freud will be found in his book, *Totem* and *Taboo*.

All primitive rites abound in taboos of this kind; prohibitions affecting gestures, garments, articles of food, bodily attitudes, industries and trades; a strange procession of picturesque, childish, bewildering, disconcerting and unexpected associations, which indicate at once the wealth and the torment of our forefathers' imaginations, and which will be found in that precious monument of folk lore, Sir *J.G. Frazer's Golden Bough*, to which we must here refer the reader.

The Birth of Taboo.— The origin of taboos appears to be a simple matter, and is connected in many ways with the origin of religious rites themselves. Taboo is a function of the physiological sensibility possessed by all organic beings, a sensibility which has gradually developed in the course of age-long evolution, and has reached its highest point, up to the present, in human intelligence and thought. The price of this sensibility is pain, a much dreaded experience, as can be seen in the case of the animals, who pass their time in trying to avoid it; much dreaded also by man, in whom it is complicated by the idea of death, which (except perhaps in certain pathological cases) is looked upon the supreme pain – since; as the wisdom of peoples very rightly insists, life is the most precious of good things. These notions underlie the whole of modern psycho-physiology; we mention them only in order that we may draw the necessary conclusions from them; there is no need to enter into further details here.

Pain, a specific psychological response of the living organism, has in turn given rise to the fear of pain. The reasoned control of fear through the agency of the will is a relatively late development. In primitive man fear is instinctive and all-powerful; it holds the animals completely in its grip; and, in the case of most of them, determines their migrations, habits and desires. It has doubtless been the fertile source of many now atavistic tendencies, and has given rise to certain special habits and abilities (such as those involved in flight, climbing trees or burrowing under the earth); to deny the dominating influence of ear in animals would be to admit that we had never observed the terror of a horse when approached by some brutal carter, of an illtreated dog, of hunted game. Moreover, in considering the matter scientifically, we must beware of reading into the word "fear" that element of disapproval which we so often attach to it; "fear" must be distinguished from cowardice. We must look upon it as a simple and useful reaction that protects the organism against everything which (because of the organism's specific sensibility) would give rise to the specific sensation of pain. Sometimes great fear will suddenly produce great courage, the courage of despair; this is because the organism is driven in these cases to the only possible means of escaping pain, i.e. by a counteroffensive.

In man, the animal which has specialized in cerebral development, fear has not remained solely on the physiological level. The knowledge of death (that event which organic sensibility fears more than anything else) has created the fear of death. And from this point onwards it is easy to engender other associated fears; the fear of what may happen after death, the fear of strange phenomena which might have some connexion with death, the fear of unknown or invisible beings who might cause such phenomena or who might otherwise exercise an alarming influence on human affairs. As soon as man developed his brain, he developed fresh fears unknown to the animals; his imaginations and his associations created in his mind a whole world of fresh terrors, those which had to do with death and the life beyond- a species of metaphysical fear.

To deny the influence of this fear among primitives, or even among people of to-day, would be to forget the impressions made on them (and on us) by death and darkness, and generally by things of which we do not understand the cause. The terror of these things often takes possession of even the least credulous of modern persons; cemeteries, corposes, haunted houses, panics and collective hallucinations still remain for most men (if they are frank enough to avow it) as impressive reminders of the terrors of yore. But among primitives, these fears-unclassified, unanalysed, uncomprehended-were veritably legion, and in their combined influence altogether overpowering. Even to-day the negro is much more subject to so-called superstitious terrors than is the white man. Similarly, as regards the Polynesian, Stevenson says: "It is scarce possible to exaggerate the extent and empire of his superstitions; they mould his life, they colour his thinking; and when he does not speak to me of ghosts and gods, and devils, he is playing the dissembler, and talking only with his lips."

We have every reason to believe that our own childlike and trembling ancestors were in the same condition. They imagined themselves, especially at night-time, surrounded by ghosts and devils, by evil and dangerous beings. Such imaginations left them in a constant state of terror, especially when the kindly sun, the destroyer of nightmares, was no longer in the sky. More than one of them must have died of fright, in the same way as the young New Zealand girl already mentioned. Fear of the dead dominated one of the strongest, but at the same time one of the most superstitious races of the world, the Romans; who, so far as concerns their metaphysical notions of the Beyond, were indeed but little above the level of the Polynesians. "Hecate and the evilwilling dead who composed her train," says Jobbe-Duval, "were terrible and mysterious forces; in general always ready to do an ill turn to the living, they could be induced by means of the *sacra nocturna* to turn particularly against any of them." The same author mentions that in the heroic period of Greece, "the victor mutilated the corpose of the vanquished; he cut off the hands, the feet, the ears and nose, threaded them on a string and hung them round his neck". These acts (which show us once again how closely these direct ancestors of our civilization resemble the inhabitants of Africa or Oceania whom we choose to call "savages," because, from a certain conventional stand point, they have not developed so rapidly as we have) find their explanation "in the idea of self-defence against the ghosts of the vanquished."

Such was the origin, both in the East and in the West, of those many religions which attempted to give a timid explanation of all this fearsome mystery, to allay these innumerable anxieties; the rites of religion, destined to placate all these unknown and hostile beings (and perhaps sometimes to make them actually favourable), have all been born of this fear; the spirit of religion is essentially a spirit of terror.

This much, however, must be added; the invisible beings are, as a matter of course, looked upon as evil, as engaged in activities harmful to men. "The great fear of the living," H. Gaidoz has said, has always been lest the sad and jealous dead should return to torment them." E. Jobbe Duval, who quotes this author in his book *Les Morts Malfaisants*, very justly adds: "In many primitive societies, it is those who have recently dies who are feared most of all; even when they have been harmless during their lives, they become evil after death, because they are supposed to suffer while their bodies are decaying" (p17). As regards Polynesian societies the same idea is well illustrated by Stevenson, who shows that the ghost of a dead man is always evil, even if, during life, he lowed the person whom he subsequently haunts. The gods themselves are scarcely any better; the Jewish Jehovah with his dogma of original sin, with his unjust punishments, inflicted without rhyme or reason as by a spoilt child, is a late but clear-cut example of such a peevish and ill-tempered deity.

On the Restrictions Caused by Taboo. — The origins of taboo are now becoming clear to us. It is true there have been taboos of all kinds; and it is evident that the institution of taboo once created must have proved very useful to the chiefs of primitive tribes, who were often hard put to it to enforce obedience even to the wisest of their orders, and who had not at their disposition the *mise en scene* of Moses on Mount Sinai to help promulgate their laws, nor the assistance of the angel Gabriel to dictate the Koran. Indeed, we must agree with Freud and N.W. Thomas that taboo is by no means merely a matter of phantasy; it has also a practical and useful side. Drawing a general conclusion from the authors we have quoted, we may say that, in all its divers forms, the ultimate aim to taboo is to *protect* oneself or other people against the evils, general or particular, which so cruelly, so unjustly, and often too so unexpectedly, oppress humanity; though sometimes the purpose may be to ward off certain ill chances, such as may affect, for instance, a hunting or a fishing expedition. But in every case it is sought to avoid some eventual hindrance, danger or misfortune.

We are now in a position to take a further step. We have already emphasized the importance for human psychology in general, and especially for the psychology of primitive peoples, of that emotional state which we call fear. At the same time we have seen how the savage is inclined to believe everywhere in spirits–good or (more usually) evil-in ghosts and supernatural beings; and it is clear that, far from considering the need of protection against them as a special and separate field, he sees in these beings the authors of all the disasters and catastrophes that befall him, such as illness, accident, lightning, famine, flood, etc. To his mind, protection against these disasters must include protection against those who so cruelly inflict them. The methods of protection were therefore no mere empty formulae; it was fear that inspired the need for defence against supernatural enemies. From this point onwards, the further develop is clear. The hostile beings must be conciliated, mollified, cajoled; and here, I think, we are in agreement with the profound significance which is attributed to taboo by the theory of Wundt. By a still further extension of the original notion, this idea of protection will sometimes be employed with reference to human beings or to material objects, if these latter should happen to posses, either permanently or temporarily, some harmful quality or are able to communicate this quality.

Primitive societies would seem to have discovered two methods of dealing with the fearsome problems that confronted them. The first and most obvious was the offering up of some valuable thing, i.e. the rite of sacrifice, which is found in all primitive human societies. This often includes the "sacrifice" of loved or cherished persons; a kind of sacrifice which could be either individual (as in the case of Abraham, Iphigenia, etc.), or collective (as in Crete, among the ancient Jews, the

Aztecs, etc). The underlying idea is that the loss of some good thing (i.e. the process of deprivation) will conciliate these ferocious powers which control (with but little show of tenderness) the destinies of human life- a life which at its best is short and difficult.The second method, which is closely related to the first, consisted in procuring the favour of the gods or of Fate by abstaining from certain acts. Such abstentions were not left to the choice of the individual: they soon took on the definitely social character of taboo, of which we may find endless examples in Frazer's *Golden Bough.*

To illustrate this, we may begin by quoting some typical instances of these prohibitions, chosen preferably from the sphere of sex.

(a) When a chief priest of the Congo travels for the purpose of meting out justice, married persons must refrain from sexual relations; otherwise the priest would meet with disaster.

(b) In Assam, a chief must abstain from sexual relations with his wife on the day before a public observance of taboo; otherwise the religious ceremony would fail in attaining its end.

(c) The Creek Indians must undergo a similar deprivation for three days and three nights preceding their departure on a campaign; otherwise the campaign would end disastrously.

(d) The Ba-Pedis and the Ba-Tongas of South Africa extend this prohibition to those who remain behind in the village.

(e) There are numerous examples to show that hunters and fishermen must avoid sexual relations before setting out on their expeditions; otherwise they would catch no game or fish.

(f) Among the Kochins (Burma) a woman who prepares yeast for making beer must abstain from sexual relations during this time; if not, the beer would be bitter.

(g) Quite generally, incestuous relations must be avoided because they impair the fertility of the soil and spoil the harvest.

(h) The gathering of the sacred cactus by the Huichol Indians (Mexico) is sure to be successful if men and women practise chastity while those who have to go and fetch it are away.

(i) In Sarawak, if a wife is unfaithful, it will interfere with her absent husband's search for camphor.

(j) In Rome at the time of kings, incest was forbidden because it caused famine.

(k) In the Congo, if a high priest was away from home, he would die if his flock failed to observe chastity.

(l) Certain Indians can assure themselves success in hunting the whale... if they abstain from coitus with their wives. Curiously enough, the hunters of Madagascar do the same.

We often find that the main idea of deprivation has become complicated by certain secondary notions; but this only adds to the force of the original conception. The mere proximity of a woman in an unclean (tabooed) condition may be sufficient to ruin many a fine project; for, as is well known, owing to the influence of homoeopathic (imitative) magic, the mere contact or proximity of a being in an unclean (tabooed) condition is considered sufficient to transmit the defects of this being to another (as in the case of certain taboos where the warriors abstain from eating hare lest they should become cowards). To the primitive mind the ideas of sexual pleasure and of the uncleanness of women are almost inseparable. The feminine sex, with its peculiar periodic phenomena, constitutes an awe-inspiring mystery, in which the useful and the pleasant are associated with the terrible. The restrictions on pleasure thus become linked up with other taboos, in which the mere presence of a women becomes a menace.

We may note that in every case there exists a relation between an act of abstinence or privation and a certain object, this object differing however from one instance to another.

The variation in the object depends, not upon the significance of the deprivation itself, which remains constant, but upon the circumstances in which it occurs. The deprivation applies not, as in the case of sacrifice, to some material good, but to the mental act of enjoyment. The constant element which is found behind all the apparent diversity consists in the *forgoing of something precious or agreeable in order to avoid some disaster*. These restrictions are closely related, therefore, to taboo itself; and the resemblance becomes all the more striking when we remember that, like taboos, they are devoid of all logical foundation.

There is here a close relation also with ritual sacrifice. Now what is the nature of sacrifice in primitive societies? It is a present made to supernatural beings or powers; the present of something valuable which the suppliant possessed: fruit, sheep, bulls, weapons (hung in temples), etc. The greater the value of the object sacrificed, the greater the merit of the sacrifice, the supreme sacrifice would be that of a loved child, or, in the case of the group, of its young men or maidens. But what is a taboo if it is not the deprivation of some valued object? Instead of sacrificing this object when it is already possessed, it is sacrificed in advance; i.e. it is renounced before it is possessed. This extension of the idea has the advantage that it makes sacrifice more elastic, and widens its range. The opportunities for sacrificing a real object are necessarily limited; the sheep or bull must be obtained before it can be offered up. In sacrifice by abstinence it is possible to forgo a very great variety of things; above all, it is possible to refrain from acts which, though they do not aim at the possession of any material object, are none the less precious on that account. When the savage, desirous of success in war or fishing, abstains from the sexual relations that are so infinitely attractive to him, he is making a true sacrifice to the gods or spirits, who, he imagines, will duly appreciate the price that he is paying. An advantage of this form of sacrifice, which has no doubt played a great part in bringing about its widespread use, is that an offering can be made even by those who have no material possessions.

Their abstinence is itself the offering, and is a very useful method for associating all the members of the clan, even the least fortunate, in the general supplication made to the supernatural beings in the hope of obtaining their good graces. The great difference between the loss involved in ritual sacrifice and that involved in taboo lies indeed, not so much in the intrinsic nature of this loss, as in the fact that in the former case it is voluntary and spontaneous (in so far as the sacrifice is not decreed by law or custom), whereas in the second case it is compulsory and is sanctioned by punishments which are immediately inflicted on the transgressor of the taboo.

A childish notion indeed, it will be said; it is difficult for us today to conceive of a deity (i.e. a being who is by definition endowed with intelligence) who is capable of being pleased with men just because they deprive themselves of a pleasure. But the more childish an idea was, the more easily could it find a place In the primitive brain. The unknown beings, who were supposed to be hostile to men and to all human joys and satisfactions, and to exercise their ingenuity in preventing human happiness, must indeed have been pleased to see men depriving themselves, of their own free will, of such joys as were within their reach. To prohibit or diminish human joys was a natural form of homage to such beings, a natural method of conciliating them. Human joys, therefore, became subject to prohibition or restraint; but the process of taboo they were, without any reason other than primitive ancestral fear, prevented from playing their natural and healthy part in life. Thus, as a ransom from terror, the taboos of deprivation settled down upon the human race, a heavy mortgage on its happiness; and needless to say, as usual with taboos, no discussion of their merits was allowed, and every protest was treated as a heresy.

Application of Taboo to Sexuality.—Since, of the various sources of pleasure, the sexual one is the most highly prized of all, it is easy to foresee that its deprivation will play a part in those renunciations which must be made to the gods as the price of their protection; and that it will even become the object of a particularly strong taboo of its own. This indeed is what has actually happened, and Stevenson is right when he says that the majority of Polynesian taboos aim at erecting a barrier between the sexes. Our Western taboos on sex have the same intention and the same results.

In truth everything conspired here to produce taboos of exceptional severity. The taboos found themselves opposed to an instinct of quite exceptional urgency and strength; it became necessary therefore to extend the taboo not only to the organs themselves, their use and function, but also to their very names – in brief, to interfere by all possible means with the passionate desires which these organs and their functions naturally inspire.

In primitive societies, no doubt, certain sociological considerations also play a part. Brute force was master among savages. It manifested itself in the procuring of sexual pleasures at the expense of weaker beings (whereas we ourselves have recognized this pleasure as legitimate only when it is obtained without violence). The taboo was no doubt complicated by the necessity of preventing the quarrels and bloodshed which so often followed a conflict of desires for the same female, perhaps also for the same male: quarrels which were a natural consequence of the egoistic desire for sole possession (jealousy, individualized love, etc.). All these deep desires must have caused innumerable conflicts in primitive societies; sexual desire is certainly use of the most disturbing elements in the primitive clan. The religious taboos also added its force to the social taboo, and the chiefs were glad enough to make use of it in order to ensure a blind obedience and to impose an absolute prohibition of certain socially disruptive acts with a view to diminishing the number of such acts.

Here is another accessory cause of a sociological kind: the desire which men have in primitive societies to assert their proprietary right over a woman and her children – a desire which corresponds to real material advantages. The desire for possession, i.e. the translation into legal terms of the egoistic sentiment, is largely developed in man. The same is true of animals, as is shown by the anger of the dog or the monkey when we true to deprive it of some object, even though the object itself be of a relatively useless kind; it is shown also by the fury of bees when we rob them of their honey, etc. In our own time this assertion of the rights of possession is coming to apply less and less to persons; slavery now seems to us an indefensible institution; *patria potestas* is no longer absolute; the right of a husband to kill his wife, if he has surprised her in the act of adultery, has been abolished in all modern systems of law. In the beginning, however, the idea of property extended to everything; material objects, animals, or human beings. It was simply the expression of the complete appropriation by an individual (ancestor) of all that he had been able to obtain by force, or skill; of everything, in fact, within his power. The idea of property everywhere implied complete control of what was owned.

Woman, valued as a means of satisfaction of the sexual sense, as a means of reproduction, and as a sort of slave to whom all inferior kinds of work could be delegated, was naturally a precious object, just as was a stone axe. Children were the property of their progenitor, as much at his mercy as the game that he had captured in the hunt; they also had a value, a value which was constantly increasing as they grew older. It is probable also that, at this period, the father made no distinction between a mother and her daughters from the point of view of sexual satisfaction. In due course the spirit of taboo came to the assistance of the sentiment of property, by laying down rules for the sexual act, by treating it as something out of the ordinary, and by making laws in virtue of which the possession of a woman was looked upon the same way as the possession of a weapon; if adultery is punished by death, just as is theft, it is because it is looked upon as the theft of a woman considered as a piece of property.

An interesting line of thought is opened here. "It would be easy," Frazer has said, "to prove by a long *array* of facts that the sexual relation is associated in the primitive mind with many serious perils' but the exact nature of the danger apprehended is still obscure." It is clear that we must consider this terror in relation to all that we have learnt about the primitive functions of taboo. One further factor must be added, however: beyond a doubt the fear of disease also plays a part – a fear which is very strong among savages, ill-protected as they are against physical pain and the various mischances that cause inflammation or destruction of the organs and the living tissues. Where hygiene is unknown, the sexual organs are delicate in both sexes; the pathological conditions, organic or microbic, to which they are subject, are both startling and alarming. Those who realize how closely–even in our own days – disease and superstition are allied, will understand how these considerations reinforce and confirm what we already know about taboo.

I believe that too little emphasis has been laid upon the profoundly disquieting impression – closely connected with fear – that is made upon the primitive mind by the sight of blood. This is shown in very characteristic fashion in a number of taboos. Blood is intimately associated with the ideas of death (either by violence or by ultimate decomposition of the corpse), or wounds (through accident or war), or disease (vomiting of blood, ulcers, bleeding abscesses, etc.)of sexual relations (menses, childbirth). It plays an important role, and when it appears it is always under circumstances that compel attention. In those times when terror was for ever abroad, there could be no neglecting the presence of blood; which suggested alarming consequences, against which it was necessary to protect oneself. One of the best methods of defence was to regard all individuals who had had any special relations – direct or indirect - with blood as though they were unclean (i.e. to isolate them, and avoid contact with them, at least until they have been purified). This would seem to be the conclusion to be drawn from the following observation reported by Freud (from Frazer); "Among the Monumbos in New Guinea a man who has killed an enemy in combat becomes 'unclean', the same word being employed which is applied to women during menstruation or confirnement. For a considerable period he is not allowed to leave the men's club-house, while the inhabitants of his village gather about him and celebrate his victory with songs and dances. He must not touch anyone, not even his wife and children; if he did so they would be afflicted with boils". We see here how third persons are adroitly protected by the fear aroused in the "unclean" person himself, who will carefully abstain from touching them lest he should be visited by the punishment that is inflicted for a broken taboo.

Examples could easily be multiplied. In particular, we find almost everywhere cases analogous to the one we have just quoted, where a warrior who, as we might at first imagine would be greatly honoured because he has killed an enemy, is, as a matter of fact, rewarded, at any rate in the first instance, by having to submit to isolation (as though he were infected) and to long and trying purificatory rituals. The case is similar with women who are considered "unclean", i.e. those who are menstruating, in childbirth, etc. We must refer to Frazer's book for particular examples. But we must remember that the fear of blood or of the complications that it suggests has led quite naturally to the erection of a number of severe taboos affecting all the circumstances in which it appears – including those of sex. Thus we are told: "Among the Tinnehs and many other American tribes, there is scarcely any creature who inspires so much fear as does a menstruating woman." And the blood of childbirth "seems in the eyes of the natives of South Africa to be even more dangerously polluted than that of the menses."

The Theory of Sexual Taboo.— If reason fails to provide any grounds for the shame which (at a superficial level at any rate) attaches to the organs and physiological manifestations of sex, we must obviously look elsewhere for the origin of this association.

Now we have seen that sexual pleasure, which is quite distinct from the function of reproduction, is connected with some of the strongest desires of living beings. We have seen also that certain metaphysical doctrines are compelled by their very nature to condemn pleasure, since this upsets the system according to which they contrast the present world with that of a more blissful future; since, indeed, it contradicts their axiom that this terrestrial world is "a vale of tears". For these doctrines all joys are unwelcome; the happy man has no need of them, is not interested in them, or may actively deny them. Sexual pleasure, which is greater than all other pleasures, is therefore quite naturally regarded as the most detestable of them all. And this inevitably leads to the further step on which this philosophy lays so much stress; to be happy; to have pleasure, to give the lie to the description of life as a state of misery, to be content with this life, still more to regard it as agreeable and to be uninterested in the next life; all this is shameful, since it is opposed to the intentions of a divinity who is very much more concerned with putting people to the test than at making their lives easy. Here we meet the supreme triumph of a false association of ideas; what we might justifiably regard as an ingenious move from the point of view of a particular metaphysical assumption is treated as though it possessed a universal application and validity. A specific moral attitude towards pleasure and sexual satisfaction is mistaken for a general rule; and it is forgotten that, if we deny the premises, we must reject their consequences.

If now, to this generally hostile attitude towards all pleasure, we add the influence of the ancient taboos relating to the organs of the sexual sense and their manifestations, taboos which are admirably calculated to reinforce the above-mentioned metaphysical system, everything becomes clear. The prohibitions which relate to sex are in fact nothing but taboos. The taboo prohibits all *contact*, and extends, not only to the touching and manipulation of the sexual organs, but also to such indirect forms of contact as are constituted by the sight of these organs or the mention of their names.Coitus, which is the extreme form of contact, naturally becomes itself taboo. And these taboos can only be removed by special acts of grace (such as marriage, or certain ritual festivals, in which sexual relations are specifically permitted.)

Lastly (and this is of the very essence of taboo), there is no adequate motive for the sexual prohibitions: and indeed this could not be otherwise, since neither physiology, psychology, nor logic can provide the philosopher with satisfactory reasons for excommunicating a few particular muscles and sensory organs. From the standpoint of to-day, we have to admit that prohibitions of this sort deliberately flout all scientific knowledge and all common sense. We rightly demand that all judicial pronouncements should be based on reason, should be unimpeachable examples of logic and of legal science. But a rule that is enforced just because we *wish* to enforce it, and which is regarded beyond all criticism—such a rule is not capable of explanation; it must of necessity take refuge in taboo. The typical instance of taboo is that of the "grown-up" who replies to the child's question "Why mustn't I do this?" with the simple and peremptory retort: "Because you mustn't." It is true that, as Salomon Reinach would say, an arbitrary imposition of this sort is profoundly shocking to the more rational part of our nature, when we have reached a stage at which we are no longer content with prohibitions but demand reasons. To this indeed is due the weakening of mystic beliefs, so rich in riddles and taboos; it is this part of our nature which, beyond all doubt, has led so many people of to-day to raise disrespectful hands against one of the most formidable of still existing taboos, that of sex; because, without reason and in open contradiction of logic and common sense, it has decreed that certain organs shall be shameful, that it is wicked to touch them or use them — just as was formely the case with tho Ark of the Covenant.

We may recall in this connexion that the compulsive prohibitions, which neurotic patients impose upon themselves, are, as Freud has said, "as inadequately motivated and as mysterious in their origin as taboo itself." We may add that, from the point of view of the logician, they depend upon false associations of ideas, which have no counterpart in reality; and this too, as we have seen, is one of the characteristics of the moral prohibitions with regard to sex.

The peculiar terror which is associated with taboos is the only possible explanation of that unhealthy tyranny which is manifested by certain minds with regard to everything connected with sex, a tyranny which is sometimes carried to almost incredible extremes. A single word, look, or gesture, may be enough to constitute incriminating evidence, a sign of all that is vile or filthy. In some schools and families the lives of young people are made almost intolerable in this way; subject to a system of perpetual spying and suspicion, sooner or later they are inevitably found guilty of some crime or other; they are often accused in the most unreasonable way and punished with the utmost harshness. Taboo alone can explain the ferocity with which many people will persecute sexual pleasure, which with them becomes an object of the fiercest hatred, the most violent abuse, the most bitter and relentless opposition. The taboo attitude is incapable of realizing that a pleasure loses much of its obsessiveness as soon as it is freely permitted; it has no understanding of the joy that is the recompense of healthy and normal behaviour. Every taboo is, by definition, dictatorial, intolerant, meddlesome and spiteful; the sexiual life of man has learnt this to its cost.

To those who are completely under the dominion of a taboo, death seems preferable to any infraction of the rules. Miss Helyett, in a well-known operetta of that name, looks upon her accident in the mountains as an irreperable calamity, just because an unlucky fall reveals her nakedness to a rescuer, who providentially but indiscreetly appears upon the scene. Our present-day society would consider the feelings of this young lady by no means so very extraordinary; and yet she possesses a thoroughly Polynesian mentality, and, civlized though she believes herself to be, she is as much under the sway of her taboos as a New Guinea Papuan could desire. The same applies to Virginie, who preferred to die rather than to show herself naked; it applies indeed to the majority of the "sins" which encumber the ethical systems derived from metaphysics: gluttony, the use of alcohol, dancing, music, the theatre, etc. Rationalism, on the other hand, seeks to determine the true value of things, and, where necessary, to bring us back to a proper sense of this value; there can be no doubt that the much lesser admiration which it is inclined to bestow on useless sacrifices and primitive taboos qualifies it much better for the task of constructing a humane, tolerant and scientific system of ethics.

We should note, in conclusion, what a close relation exists between the origins of taboo, which we have just been studying, and the metaphysical conceptions which, as we saw in the last chapter, constitute the foundations of the taboo on sex. In their growth and development taboos are undoubtedly associated with very definite conceptions of the life beyond, of the beings who exist there, of the reincarnations which await us after death. These eternal problems have been solved in different ways by the various religions; but everywhere men have tried to establish a relation between their acts and their metaphysical beliefs, in the hope that, through the former, which they could to some extent control, they might allay the terror which the latter so easily aroused within their timid minds.

Chapter-6

The Triumph of Sexual Taboo

Chapter 6

The Morality of Sexual Acts in Ancient Societies.— Turning now from the very primitive societies where the system of taboo had its origin to those much more highly organized societies, often of high cultural standing, which developed in ancient times on the shores of the Mediterranean, in the middle East, and in Asia, we find that in those latter taboo had lost much of its original power, and that, as a consequence, the right to carry out sexual acts was rarely called in question. The decay of taboo had been a natural process, partly because of the mere antiquity of the institution itself, the origins of which were already lost to view, and partly because the facts of sex had come to be looked upon with less bias and greater physiological insight.Indeed there remained only a few societies which, like the Jews, remained firmly attached to a very primitive system of metaphysics and taboo, and which regard abstinence as a virtue in itself and all sexual behaviour as a moral blemish.

But we must take care to be clear as to the sense in which we use these terms. By "the right to carry out sexual acts," we mean that the sexual organs and the sexual acts are looked upon as fundamentally natural, that there is no cause to be offended when they are seen or sought, and that they are in no sense derogatory to human dignity. This very rational view of sex had been achieved by most of the societies of the ancient world; though with the triumph of Judeo-Christianity, it was entirely forgotten, and was replaced by the view that the sexual act was a sin deserving of the strongest censure and the sternest measures of suppression. We mean that the mere fact of men and women manifesting their sexual desires and putting them into execution did not itself. Offend against any principal or convention: reference to sex in behaviour or in speech was looked upon as an integral and normal feature of life, comparable to eating or drinking; furthermore, the various modes of sexual conduct (those which were subsequently called *perversions*) were looked upon as merely matters of taste and were left to the discretion of the individual. This is confirmed by the esteem which was accorded to courtesans, some of whom were looked upon as sacred, and by the open relations which philosophers, statesmen and others in the public eye enjoyed with them, without damage to their own reputation.

These are facts of great importance. As we shall see when we come to speak of the so-called "perversions," they reveal very clearly the error of the arbitrary theory of "degeneration," a theory which is contradicted by the whole nature of human civilization *before* the triumph of sexual prohibitionism. They show also how easy it would be to bring back that truer appreciation of sexual things which was once so general. They are in harmony too with all our foregoing observations, which showed us that, in primitive societies, men and women would freely seek each other and look upon a sexual offer or proposal as a welcome sign of homage rather than as an insult or offence.

But, to avoid any possibility of confusion, we must realize that right does not mean liberty. It is true that sexual liberty was not unknown in the ancient world, and this condition, which is certainly an advanced as compared with the sort of muddled slavery which we enjoy to-day, has found its prototypes in certain societies of the past. But it has always been an exception. Even though the manifestations of sex were considered legitimate and unobjectionable in themselves, nevertheless many circumstances frequently conspired to curtail sexual liberty. In the first place, there could be no true sexual liberty so long as the more general conception of individual liberty was still almost entirely lacking; above all, where women were not free, but were on the contrary, in a condition of tutelage or semi-servitude throughout their lives (for this was the case in the majority of ancient societies). Almost everywhere, civilization began in the totemic group or in the patriarchal family, where any talk of liberty was a mockery. A little study of this subject reveals the fact that the heads of families very soon began to understand the interest that they had in retaining the girls of their households as valuable assets for a variety of purposes; for, when suitably married, these girls would be the means, not only of maintaining the purity of their race or class, but also of securing useful alliances and of adding to the wealth or territory of the family; they could even be used for insinuating themselves skillfully into the private lives of neighbouring and hostile chiefs. Under these conditions, the sexual liberty of women could be nothing but a dream, and when the girls eventually became wives, the terrible sanctions of adultery (which was generally punished by death) soon taught them that they had only changed one master for another. These restrictions were particularly severe in the case of the ruling classes; in ancient times, as at the present day, a free development of the sexual life was easier for the peasant than for the princess. Furthermore, so far as the sexual act itself was concerned, there inevitably remained certain relics of taboo, which kept alive the traditional restrictions of earlier days, and which were supposed to be endowed with a magical efficacy against calamities of every possible kind.

There is no need in the present volume to pursue further these questions of sexual liberty. We must reserve their treatment for another work. But it was important to prevent a possible confusion between right, which was a rare exception in ancient societies. We must note, too, that there is no contradiction involved here, for whereas the admission of right represented the reasonable adoption of a position founded upon undeniable facts, the refusal of liberty was based entirely upon instinct—instinct, moreover, of a supremely egoistic and imperious kind.

Social Taboo in Primitive India. — As is well known, the Hindus have, from the earliest times, been thoroughly at home in the realm of metaphysics, and have fully explored even its most bewildering subtleties; and this long before Greek thought had approached the problems of being and non-being. The taboos on sex, together with those on a multitude of other things, had not failed to prosper among the original clans of India, as among so many primitive communities. We find them sanctioned in many local religions by the menace of infernal torment: Hell has always been the *post mortem* Penal Code of taboo.

But, contrasting strongly with the more or less gross conceptions of its contemporary religions, Buddhism approached this delicate question with remarkable subtlety and success. Following a very human tendency, but one which was here pushed to its utmost limits, Hindu philosophy had from its very beginning expounded a doctrine of unmitigated pessimism. We have elsewhere tried to show that this doctrine has its origin in the fact that life is good, too good; and in the regrets inevitably engendered by the necessity of abandoning these too great joys beyond all possibility of recall; we have summarized this view in the formula: "since we are beaten from the start, it is better not to live at all." The primitive inhabitants of India, whether aborigines or invaders, had a very vivid realization of these inevitable evils. Disease, old age, death — these three facts, together with the impossibility of overcoming them, were perpetually recurring in their speculations. It was from these ills, from this gnawing obsession, that they sought to be delivered; and it was only after several analogous but unsuccessful attempts in this direction that Buddha finally appeared.

We know that the *raison d'etre* of Buddhism is to bring that deliverance which the Hindu mind so passionately desired. It would be outside the sphere of our present subject to examine here the doctrine of Cakiamouni. We need only indicate its relations to our present study of sexual ethics. Now, the foundation of Buddhist discipline, the means of obtaining deliverance, is the suppression of desire. The wise man, he who will soonest obtain the higher reincarnations and who will finally achieve deliverance on attaining Nirvana, cannot enter on this path except on the condition of suppressing desire, the origin of all our ills; and inevitably the sensual desires, and therefore also the sexual desires, must be included in this general sacrifice.

It is true that Buddhism did not fail to recognize the difficulty of the aim which it had set itself. To abolish the torment of desire is no doubt the most radical cure for all human ills; unfortunately it is beyond ordinary human strength. Buddhist morality, therefore devised a certain technique, if we can call it such, to help in the work of eliminating desire. As L. de la Vallee-Poussin says, we must combat *nimitta* by another *nimitta* of an opposite kind; the qualities of pleasantness, purity and permanence by the qualities of hatefulness, impurity and transitoriness. Desire will die when the appearance of desirability, already broken and weakened by a study of the defects inherent in every desirable object, has become finally eliminated." Furthermore, ":that disease of the mind which we call desire compels us to create inaccurate ideas, ideas which are not in harmony with reality, which do not correspond to things as they are, but as we should like them to be, ideas which are the result of an effort of imagination. In this way the element of sex can be driven out by the element of the impure or the horrible, when we think of the living body as a decomposing mass, blue, putrid, eaten by worms; considered as such it is no longer the living body".

We may add: it is no longer the real body. But the important fact in this system is that everything is based upon general ideas which are logical, acceptable and relatively practical. Buddhism suggests a remedy for the everlasting misery of man, a remedy which is applicable to this present life. "The great effort of the Saints", says the same author, is directed to seeing pleasant things in their unpleasant aspects". Above all, and herein Buddhism shows its superiority over other contemporary theories, sexuality is-not made an object of special odium of an unreasonable and almost pathological kind, as was the case with primitive taboo. Buddhism is not hypnotized by sex; it does not distinguish sex from other sources of desire, and if sex is regarded with suspicion, it is because it falls in the same category as these other sources, and is deliberately condemned as a consequence of a general principle, which has its foundation in reason and its use in practice. Chastity is recommended in the same way as fasting and the distaste for pleasure in general, because it involves a renunciation which in turn constitutes a step towards deliverance. Compared with this ingenious, original and subtle conception, how crude and inefficient appears that fanatical system of taboo which found such blind and irrational expression in the development of the Jewish religion.

The Triumph of Sexual Taboo in the Hebrew Theory of Sin. —Sexual taboo achieved its complete triumph in the religion of the Jews. Christianity, which was derived from this source, in turn inherited all that doctrinaire suspicion of the sexual organs which was characteristic of Hebrew culture; and analysis shows that we have to deal here with irrational prohibitions in one of their most primitive forms. As Dr. Norman Haire has justly remarked in his book *Hymen*, the striking contract between the sexual attitude of the Greeks and of the Jews respectively exhibits an exact correspondence with the political needs of the two societies; the Jews were "a small race with great ambitions,: for whom a large army was a necessity and who felt themselves called upon to obey the order of Jehovah to "increase and multiply"; their whole social organization was therefore directed to this end. The Greeks, on the other hand, distributed as they were in small states with limited food supply, found themselves in circumstances which demanded a voluntary restriction of population. They were thus able to approve and to tolerate sexual pleasure as an end in itself, without reference to procreation.

We know that the idea of original sin is not exclusively Christian in its origin. It was accorded a place in the Orphic mysteries. As Salomon Reinach says in dealing with this cult, "the soul was thought to be confined in the body, as in a tomb or prison, and this as the punishment for a sin committed long ago by the Titans, the ancestors of man, who had treacherously killed the young go Zagreus." St. Paul seems to have been particularly concerned to revive this notion of sin and death, which served excellently to explain the coming and the sacrifice of Christ, and to redeem men from the sin committed by their ancestor Adam. This doctrine has been much discussed ever since the time of the monk Pelagius, who contended that it was unjust; but in truth it was no more primitive than was the Orphic doctrine, which had met with great success. The point which interests us here is that, owing to the virulence of sexual taboo in the Judeo-Christian story, the crime is no longer a murder, as in the case of Zagreus, the first of men, who was cut to pieces, but is the sexual act itself.

The theory of sin was a valiant attempt to give an appearance of logic to what in reality was merely a taboo. For, as humanity advances, taboo is apt to find itself in danger if it maintains too obstinate a silence as to the reason of its existence. The theory of original sin is an explanation of taboo with the help of a fairy tale such as would be given by a child or a savage. If we consider the important part which original sin, the crime of Eve and the subsequent necessity for the intervention of the Messiah play in the Judeo-Christian system, we are driven to a conclusion which is very unflattering to humanity, namely that one of its greatest intellectual efforts — Christianity itself, which has taken possession of so many minds-arose from a mistaken conception of a physiological act.

In truth, the Judeo-Christian notion reflects very accurately the uncompromising dogmatism of primitive taboo; according to its merciless reasoning, sexual enjoyment is equivalent to eternal damnation, even though the equation may be stated in somewhat ribald terms by the incorrigible Abbe of Voisenon:

Fe Vous avertis, pecheurs infortunds:
Et zague, et zague, et zague et vous volid' damnds.

Unbelievers, for whom this enjoyment is a legitimate physiological recreation, must needs to make a great effort before they can understand the state of mind which may result from such a conviction among the faithful. If they succeed, they cannot but be astonished at the ease with

"I warn you of it, miserable sinners;
F—and f—and f—,and there you are, damned."

wich so many Christian women, either in free love or in adultery, consent to run such risks, even with confession as an eventual means of reparation. And this only serves to exhibit once again the colossal influence of the sexual sense, which celebrates its supreme triumph in those who, according to the terms of their own belief, are risking everything in order to assure this triumph.

Having achieved this great success with the theory of sin, sexual taboo hence forward imposed its rigid prohibitions on all further attempts at explanation. Even at the present day we still have an admirable illustration of the close alliance between taboo and the doctrine of sin in those naïve statements of our priests who, reformulating an ancient doctrine in modern language, solemnly declare (in the true spirit of primitive taboo) that coitus (except in marriage) is an offence against God; and that sexual enjoyment "causes sorrow to *le Bon Dieu* or to the Holy Virgin". A striking illustration of the slow development of the human brain, and a witness to the difficulty which human beings have in outgrowing their ancestral fears!

According to the theory of sin, sex is taboo, the sexual organs are taboo, their names and functions are taboo. All our actual social prohibitions are derived from this: they have tended to separate the sexes in order to avoid transgression; disgrace to him who does not respect the taboo (formerly it would have been death!) Since the formulation of this doctrine, the whole of human evolution has had to bear the burden of this heavy mortgage, which still makes itself felt to-day in our laws and prohibitions, in the fanatical activities of the various societies for opposing sex, in numberless arbitrary interferences with private life.

Taboo and Fudeo-Christian Doctrine. — The Christian Churches have therefore, in logical conformity with their principles, adopted a very severe attitude towards the pleasure of sex. "For the Fathers of the Church," says Remy de Gourmont, "there is no middle course between virginity and debauchery; marriage is nothing but a *remedium amoris* which God in His goodness has granted as a concession to human weakness." Let us add that these Fathers of the Church are perfectly logical upholders of taboo: if coitus is not just a physiological act, neither moral nor immoral, then, as we have already said, it must, according to their system, be looked upon as degrading, even for those who enjoy the official sanction of marriage. Remy de Gourmont reminds us of the system of prohibitions drawn up by the monk Campanella for the ordering of human love – "a terrible organization."

Sexual taboo maintained its triumph for long centuries, as did also the related metaphysical taboos. Its power varied however to some extent from one epoch to another. In general, Catholicism showed itself more indulgent than Protestantism. Friedrich Schlegel, whose erotic poem *Lucinda* (1799) contained a final apologia in which Shamelessness triumphs over Decency and Modesty, discovered a few years later (1808) private reasons for changing from Protestantism to Catholicism; the Court of Rome, which raised him to the rank of nobleman after 1815, willingly shut its eyes to the existence of his earlier writings.

It is remarkable too that at the present day it is still the Protestants who for the most part are the organizers of the modern crusades in favour of chastity, whether among themselves or in non-Christian countries. This is in no sense due to chance, but is a matter of definite policy. The Protestantism of men like Luther and Calvin was in the nature of a violent ascetic reaction against the *laisser-aller* of Rome. It is difficult to conceive of religion in Italy or Spain without an echo of Paganism. The sumptuously apparelled Madonnas, the incense of solmen ceremony, the hypnotic rhythm of ritual chants, and, above all, the colour and the *mise en scene* in which the mitred actors move pompously to and fro in golden vestments, as though they were almost supernatural beings whose world was the world of miracles, all these are necessary to the religious spirit of the countries of the South. There is sensuality in all this, if by sensuality we mean the charm of the senses. There is moreover a certain emotional preversity in confessing the evil one has committed – an element that is well appreciated by sensitive individuals whose feelings and imaginations are already stirred by their environment. The Catholicism of the Popes, at the time of the Reformation, had become an artistic and sensual religion, possessing all the charm, the vice and the inconsequences that are to be found in art and sensuality. Public opinion was scarcely ever shocked; there was little astonishment at the wrath of Julian II or the perversities of a Borgia, occupying as they did a throne which by very definition was possessed of all the virtues. In truth, none of these could really appear shocking in the brilliant sunshine of the Roman Campagna, so different from the twilight of the North, that Goethe, when he crossed the Alps, no longer recognized it as coming from the same luminary.

The Reformation was the revenge of the hungry, gloomy parts of the world, those lands which are hard to cultivate and hostile to idleness, beaten by the wintry winds which shake the snow-clad pine forests or ruffle the melancholy lakes of Eastern Germany. It was the response of the imagination to the austerity of nature, and it began by throwing overboard as superfluous all the sensuality of the useless, garish, flashy ornaments. The bitter tongue of the Wartburg monk delighted in disturbing the harmony of the papal chants, and the icy winds of the Alps, which carried it to Rome, gave it a voice of thunder. But this bare, austere and simple faith, which so affrighted Rome, was one in which the peoples of the North felt themselves at home. For them it was the true religious edifice, built on rigid and uncompromising lines, one which suited the background of their misty Northern homes. The Reformation heralded itself as an attempt to strangle sensuality.

It is this which explains the moderate degree of success which it enjoyed in France. Flouted in Italy and Spain, where it did not even obtain a footing, triumphant on the shores of the North Sea and the Baltic, in France alone did it have its ups and downs, its fanatical upholders and no less fanatical opponents; here it was not a question of all or nothing, but a thing of fleeting fortune, one day on the point of disappearing, another day on the point of seizing the very throne; a thing that had to be reckoned with. France indeed, as always, had the singular destiny of representing a mean between two opposite extremes; it belongs to the Southern races in virtue of the warm plains of Provence and Gascony, while the heavy monotony of Flanders and the simple melancholy of Lorraine proclaim it as belonging no less to the North. It is continental like Germany and maritime like England; it speaks a language as far removed from the clusters of sparkling vowels which are to be heard south of the Pyrenees or the Alps, as from the harsh and turgid consonantal agglomerations of the North – causes and effects which are difficult to disentangle to-day, but which nevertheless explain the influence exercised by this nation; for the mean is in many cases not far from the truth.

French minds are thus perhaps in a better position than others to resist the fascination of big words, and to appreciate at their true value the relations between sexuality and morals. For them there is not a single field which is allowed, to evade critical investigation; there are no dogmas, but only scientific laws. Since the supreme dogma, that of the existence of God, has had to submit to the test of reason, how could there by any question of other dogmas escaping this primary necessity? It is because they work under the assumption that science cannot profane but only investigate, that the French are better qualified than all other Western peoples critically to examine and to define the bearing of science and logic on the phenomena of sex. Whether we like it or not, the conclusion to be drawn from all this is that the Judeo-Christian doctrine has been the true fortress of the prohibitionistic attitude towards sex. We need not insist on the fact that Christianity itself does not seek to deny this. Changing circumstances, and the necessity of taking account of the rapid development of ideas in the field of sex, have only modified the methods of attach; a theory which has now grown somewhat out of date has been abandoned in favour of a more direct form of criticism. The Congress of the Y.M.C.A., at Helsingfors in July 1926, where the Americans predominated, stressed the importance of sexual problems, and, true to the political tradition of sin which is the buttress of this doctrine, pronounced a sweeping denunciation of certain modern tendencies of an opposite kind, such as :the dancing mania", "the passion for liberty"(*sic*), postponement of marriage, and Freudian psychology. No better illustration could be given of the fact that we are here faced with a conflict between two systems which are as old as the world itself and which are everywhere in opposition to one another; liberty of thought and the spirit of criticism on the one hand, arrayed against traditional authoritarian doctrine (with its metaphysical foundations) on the other.

It will be admitted, therefore, that agnostic and rationalistic minds are in a much better position to consider with the necessary detachment the problems raised by the morality of sexual acts than those which, whether directly or indirectly, are still under the influence of Judaism. Indeed, this is only a particular instance of a general rule; a rule which applies to every question that demands an unprejudiced examination carried out in a logical and scientific spirit.

Platonic Love as a Means of Escaping Taboo. — The pretence of "pure" or Platonic love must certainly be looked upon as an attempt at reconciliation between the severe precepts of Christianity, permitting sexual relations for purposes of reproduction only, and the natural human desire for unrestricted satisfaction. As sexuality gradually emerged triumphant from all the moralist crusades, three main elements became distinguishable amid the general confusion: the act of reproduction, the pleasures of sense (supposedly intended to make this act more agreeable), and the feelings of sympathy and tenderness between the two partners. The Church accepted the first, proscribed the second, and was more or less indifferent to the third. Men naturally sought therefore to make the most of this last element.

Love, which under the pagan skies of the Mediterranean had once been so triumphant, thus came back into fashion, though by a roundabout and discreet road. The new method consisted in permitting, and even in exalting, the feelings of affection, devotion and self-sacrifice which were inspired in men by the magical influence of women. But how did men become capable of harbouring such feelings? Merely as a preliminary step to the act of carnal pleasure? We cannot doubt it. If Platonic love itself chooses one woman rather than another, it is because the possession of such-and-such a woman permits more readily of a certain definite form of satisfaction, one in which Venus does not lose her rights. If the Platonic lover trembled with emotion at the mere thought of touching the hand or the cheek of his mistress, it was because her flesh filled him with a strange excitement; how much more strongly would he have been moved if he had gained possession of other and more secret parts, parts more specifically destined for sexual pleasure! Rest assured that his subconscious mind is in no uncertainty upon this point. But Platonic love, doubtless in all good faith, protested to the contrary. To seek a culmination of the process of sexual pleasure was against the laws of metaphysics. Very well! Love pretended to be pure, it sought to keep the tender sentiment free from contamination by the flesh, the sexual organs, and the processes of reproduction. It thus developed into a sort of morbid excitation, which speculated on a sensual pleasure, without ever making use of it.

A long artificial, moralizing process was necessary before this simple fact could be lost sight of. Language itself, however, has been a partner in the conspiracy; it pretends that a man asks for the "hand" of a girl, while all the time the essential element in view is a physiological organ of quite a different kind. The defenders of Platonic love have "friendship" and "love" as their only refuge, but as soon as they pronounce this latter word, they inevitably call to mind the relations of the sexes and the specific sensations connected with them; and though they refuse to seek these pleasures, they have implicitly to admit that in these only can be found the crowning joy, the complete fulfillment of their desires. The mistress of such a lover who did not feel that she was the object of a discreetly veiled passion of a more ardent kind would look upon her adorer as a frigid enunch. Moreover, the little intimacies of Platonic love, even the most "innocent" of them – contemplation of the loved being, enjoyment of the perfume which surrounds her, admiration of her movements, pleasure in her voice, the emotions stirred by her look – all these, as we know, create a special aura which reverberates throughout the organism, timidly, but no less certainly, affecting even the specific sexual organs themselves. This fact reveals Platonic love as belonging, beyond doubt, to the general category of love; albeit the sexual sense is here kept in check by inhibitions from the intelligence or will.

From the physiological point of view, therefore, this "pure" love is more or less comparable to the act of gazing with an empty stomach on a well-served table. Nevertheless it was enough to fill the chivalric romances of the Middle Ages. We see Tristan and Yseult lying side by side with the sword between them, for the greater edification of King Mark: a symbol of the most ardent love, here destined to *prevent* the tabooed act. The voice of Wolfram von Eschenbach has glorified the chastity of those elect ones who were guardians of the Holy Grail. Hrotsuith sings the praises of virginity. Lichtenstein chooses "the most chaste" as the lady of his thoughts. At a later date, Jahn demanded, in the name of German virtue, that statues of the nude should be suppressed (proposing at the same time that bachelors should be deprived of their civic rights, a remarkable illustration of a campaign directed solely against sexual pleasure). The perfect knight eventually came to be looked upon as one who, though guided by the love of his lady, did not dream of demanding any satisfaction from her in return; neither had Don Quixote any knowledge of the (entirely superfluous) body of his Dulcinea. Salomon Reinach, in dealing with the - relatively late (fifth or sixth century) cult of Mary the Virgin Mother, justly remarks that this cult, rich as it is in the most astonishing developments in points of detail, corresponds to "the necessity for a feminine ideal in the Christian Pantheon," and that its function was to minister to "the unsatisfied love of the religious orders."

How far can all these manceuvres be regarded as sincere? Some minds no doubt were really in earnest in the matter: those, for instance, who were strongly imbued with the Christian faith and were genuinely hostile to sexuality. Such men thought as did the author of the Gospel of Philip, a gnostic work of the second century, in which both marriage and reproduction are condemned as evil in themselves; and as did the Encratites of the first few centuries of Christianity, who regarded marriage itself as a form of vice. But for many, consciously or unconsciously, the movement represented a reaction against the brutal monotony of the mere act of reproduction, the only sexual act that was permitted; it corresponded to a need for - something more – and what else in truth, if not sexual pleasure? The purely psychic joys to be found in a state of passionate exaltation seemed to promise a way back to the physiological satisfaction of the flesh, now less proscribed, because more decorously hidden. Platonic love, to which the Church shut its eyes (in so far as this method of adoring a created being did not interfere with due worship of the Creator) was thus nothing but an attempted compromise between the process of reproduction, which was tolerated, and the pleasures of sex, which were prohibited but still desired.

Finally, by a new concession to the exigencies of the time, the prohibitonistic doctrine took a further step, and became sentimental even in relation to non-Platonic love, especially, when this represented a step on the road to a legitimate and conventional union. Love-with a capital L, official Love, tenderly symbolized by Cupid and his arrows, regularized by a betrothal, by legal bonds, by civil and religious ceremonies–has been a safety valve, highly necessary and wonderfully efficacious. With its help taboo has been circumvented. The sexual act, formerly so much in disgrace, has thus once again been recognized in all its power, exalted in all its joy. Thanks to love, we now speak of little else.Our books, our plays, our newspapers, our arts, our sermons, our everyday talk, are full of it. There it is, in spite of all; and stronger than all – imperious, omnipotent, omnipresent. But it is decently concealed, either by a page on the municipal register, which plays the role of fig-leaf, or by one of those healthy adventures, the irregularity of which is lost sight of in the flood of sentimentality which it arouses. In this way the pleasures and preoccupations of sex once more make an appearance, and reassert themselves (though in an idealized form) in the speeches of the Mayor and of the priest, in the sentimentalizings of parents and elderly cousins, in the fond dallyings, intimate but tolerated, of engaged couples. It is true that, by a piece of conventional hypocrisy, they are now called by another name. As before, however, these sexual manifestations still culminate in mutual contact and in a fusion of secretions.

The Extending Range of Taboo.— When we strike a balance of the moral and social prohibitions which are the inevitable consequence of sexual taboo, and which have been adopted by the nations without discussion as official dogmas, we can see them extending with a tireless ingenuity to everything that has to do, either closely or remotely, with the sexual organs, or with sexual pleasure.

The most direct consequence of taboo consists in prohibiting the sight or even the name of these organs – a prohibition which a *fortiori* extends to copulation also. Aretino, reproaching Michael Angelo with the indecency of his "Last Judgement," exhorted him to "imitate the modesty of the Florentines, who placed golden leaves over the shameful parts of their beautiful Colossus"; and we know that a pope followed this advice to the letter by insisting that certain angels, who offended him by their nudity, should be duly clothed in drawers. A similar attitude is shown at the present day in the emotions of those men or women who think it a catastrophe, or at any rate an event of the first magnitude, if their private parts are seen by another, and who will take childish pains to prevent such an occurrence: the amusing story of Miss Helyett, who considers herself bound to marry the only mortal who (in saving her from a perilous fall on a mountain) has seen her nakedness, is an example of a modern taboo worthy for any seaside resort. Here is another example of a self-imposed taboo; in his preface to *Orgie Latine*, Felicien Champsaur says, "In my childhood I knew at Digne an elderly magistrate of the old style, Pecou by name, a very pious churchwarden, who, before unbuttoning his trousers to 'pass water', always carefully took out a piece of paper so as not to soil his hand by contact with 'the vile member'. Taboo can scarcely go further. Consider also, in this connexion, the notices found in men's urinals, asking the users to "adjust their dress before leaving," so as not to affront decency. In this last case it is the mere touching of a garment which is affected by the taboo, doubtless because, to the taboo-ridden souls of those who drew up the notice, the slightest gesture in the direction of the sexual organs suffices to call them vividly to mind. In the United States a "special assistant district attorney – general" a few years ago drew up some rules on the length of women's chemises, which required that these should fall below the knee; at Coney Island there were disputes as to whether women should be compelled to wear stockings while bathing; at Newport, an elegant watering-place, close-fitting bathing dresses were forbidden, and a large notice warned bathers not to loiter on the platform in wet bathing costumes, lest their too clearly outlined forms should inspire tabooed thoughts. For the same reason, the Director of a Congregational Educational Colony near Boulogne-sur-Mer in France took the children under his charge to a little-frequented beach, where thirteen of them were drowned. When accused of manslaughter through neglect of reasonable precautions, he said that his action had been dictated by a desire "to avoid arousing the children's curiosity." "A well-meaning minister," Judge Lindsey tells us, "recently came to me with a bill which he wanted to see introduced into the legislature. Among the things the bill prohibited was the display of women's lingerie in show windows.... Lingerie in shop windows! Now just what short of a cesspool do you suppose that man's mind contained?"

Passing now to the prohibitions relating to copulation or physical contact between the sexes, we find that in the Middle Ages they were positively legion. The disfavour with which country priests (down to Paul-Louis Courier) looked upon dancing was due to the fear of these physical contacts; for the same reason the chorus of disapproval still continues, and in America policewomen have been known formally to prohibit certain dances which they considered "dangerous"

In Italy in 1926 ten dancing halls were closed at Milan, twenty at Naples, twenty-four at Mantua, twenty at Bologna; in this last town, at a single large establishment where the police made an unexpected raid, they arrested 150 girls of between fifteen and eighteen years, and 250 boys of the same age. At Mantua they similarly arrested in a single hall twenty-four young girls still under age: they were promenaded in the town, four in a row, and ten of them were immediately dispatched to a reformatory. In France in 1926, the Mayor of Rocroi prohibited boys under fifteen or girls under eighteen from attending public dances unless they were accompanied by their parents. A decree of the Chief of the Police of Long Beach near New York "forbids couples walking on the beach or bathing to approach each other closer than 6 inches or 15 centimetres; inspectors will be provided with foot rules in order make sure that bathers shall preserve this distance."

All this could be looked upon as an amusing exhibition of childishness, were it not for the facts: (1) that in the opinion of all rational minds it is based upon false and illogical associations; (2) that it endeavours to give the force of a general law to the doctrine of taboo, which is really only the peculiarity of a particular sect; and (3) that, without any logical or scientific justification, it adds to the restrictions upon individual liberty. For, in truth, it is liberty itself which is threatened by the taboos on sex: in Spain and in Italy in the eighteenth century (according to the Memoirs of Casanova), the Inquisition forbade unmarried people to sleep together, and (to the great profit of thieves) ordered hotel proprietors not to close the doors of their rooms, so that inspection might be easy. In the reign of Maria Theresa, Austria was under the power of a police which was tirelessly engaged in putting down the pleasures of sex. The prison or the cloister were the punishments provided by law. In these places the unfortunate neurotics who were constitutionally incapable of submitting to the taboo ended their days in presume to pass judgement on their wives' dresses. About the same time the Greek Dictator Pangalos succumbed to the prevailing temptation and issued an ukase prohibiting the wearing of short skirts. He himself did not long survive these skirts. Who can say whether some subtle feminine hostility may not have had something to do with his rapid fall? The same taboo led the Hungarian Government in 1928 to rig up their schoolgirls in trousers, so terrified were they by the short skirts then worn. In Catholic countries, the pronouncements of Archbishops on this subject are legion; they provide a more or less happy linguistic expression of the dress taboo, by means of which it is hoped to ensure the triumph of the sex taboo. Promulgation's of this sort are in the true Judeo-Christian tradition, as an Archbishop of Catania reminded us when he quioted the apostle (I Timothy, ii, 9): "Let women adorn themselves in modest apparel, with shamefacedness and sobriety....." It has been reported recently that, on the representation of the clergy, the Japanese authorities, formerly so free from the spirit of taboo, have decreed that dresses shall not be lifted too high in rainy weather, lest the enemies of the flesh be scandalized. . . . A worthy municipal councillor of Glasgow has extended the taboo to the wax figures in shops, which reveal to the eyes of passers-by the "alluring mysteries" of feminine underclothes, and which he accused of corrupting the morals of youth much as Socrates was supposed to have done of old. Other manifestations of the working of taboo are to be found in the petitions which the women members of the Italian "National Council" sent to their Queen, complaining of feminine fashions as a cause of moral and social degeneration (1928); in the attacks of the reformed Dutch Church of South Africa against the light dress materials which the heat encourages the young girls of that country to wear (1928) in the objection to nudity on the part of certain bathers at Juan-les-Pins, which resulted in the prosecution and acquittal of the painter D—before the tribunal of the Alpes-Maritimes in 1926......It would need a whole volume merely to enumerate all the cases of this kind, which are sometimes based on sincere conviction, but which too often represent merely a servile acquiescence in the activities of a few busybodies, and which, in spite of their appearance of modernity, are at bottom always associated with the ancient fears and superstitions of an ignorant and bygone age.

The Sociological Effects of Sexual Restrictions.— Modern extensions of taboo, in countries where laws have been passed for the nominal purpose of protecting women, have had some curious and unexpected results, the chief of which is that man in his turn has found himself in need of protection. A women's word is always believed when she complains of a want of respect; and in a court of law such complaints are translated into hard cash in very liberal measure. In some Anglo-Saxon countries, if a man has occasion to see a woman in an office, he will, if he is prudent, provide himself with a secretary to act as chaperon! Speaking of Bernard Shaw's *Man* *and Superman*, a witty critic in *The Times* recounts that "as soon as the hero of the piece notices that his ward has matrimonial intentions with regard to him, he straightway leaves England in headlong flight for the furthermost point of Spain, with all the speed at which forty horse-power can carry him. A futile effort at escape! The girl pursues him, finds him in a remote corner of the Sierra Nevada, and plays the well-known trick of fainting in his arms before witnesses. On coming to, she murmurs that he has just asked her to marry him, an abominable lie, but one which nevertheless forces him to propose marriage in real earnest!" In similar strain Paul Souday writes that "there can be no doubt that under the pretext of protecting women, who are supposed to be defenceless, the English have passed laws which have led to a striking increase of blackmail. In the United Kingdom, a man who is alone in a railway compartment, and who sees an unattended woman about to enter, jumps out instantly on to the platform at the risk of losing his train or breaking his neck, for, if he has a proper sense of proportion, these dangers will seem small as compared with that which he would run if he remained alone with her." Things have reached such a pass that a Cabinet Minister, after an adventure which had been given much publicity, declared in Parliament that if these crimes on the part of women went on increasing, he would be compelled to have recourse to flogging as a punishment to adventuresses of this sort, who enjoyed too much protection in our modern civilization.

In the United States there is an enormous wealth of laws, which have been passed in the service of taboo. Listen to what Ferri Pisani writes in his recollections of Los Angeles (*Au pays du film*): "Through the efforts of feminism, a movement born of neo-paganism, there has arisen a legislation with regard to sex, which is unique in human history. In the United States every gesture on the part of a man is translated into terms of damages payable to the woman. It is not only a question of the "Law of Alienation of Affection"; there is also the 'Law of Breach of Promise', much feared by the disturbers of marital bliss. There is the 'Right of the Spouse in Common Law,' which may insist that an imprudent night of adventure be regularized by marriage. There is the Law of Respect, which pitilessly condemns a man who, through lack of courtesy or perhaps merely through excess of enterprise, speaks to a woman against her wish. There is the 'Law of Alimony', which throws into prison the divorced husband who delays by even an hour in making the appointed payments to his former wife. There is the 'Law of White Slave Traffic', which punishes by penal servitude the mere taking of a woman from one state to another, for the sole purpose of putting some proposition before her in more comfortable and congenial circumstances. There are a thousand other feminist laws in wait for the Yankee male, who is compelled to live in an Orphic atmosphere, pursued everywhere by the ghost of the great misogynist, the victim of the Bacchantes."

We have here a most interesting and curious social experiment that could only have been made in a country, the people □ or at any rate the ruling majority – of which had unreservedly accepted the Judeo-Christian metaphysics, i.e. the doctrine of a soul destined for eternal life, provided it maintains a strict observance of the conventional rites and taboos. Indeed, it may be said that, in North America at the present day, this metaphysical system is accepted with as little discussion as in Europe during the Middle Ages. The observance of the sexual taboo, pushed to its extreme, limits, leads us straight to the historic doctrine of Sin. In a system of this kind, women herself may be said to be taboo, except in cases where the prohibition is officially removed by "a duly solemnized marriage." This is indeed the simplest and most certain manner of assuring the triumph of the taboo. For it has a double effect; in the first place with reference to the man, who has to obey it for fear of social consequences; in the second place with reference to the woman, whose sexual desires (even if she belongs to the clitorid type) are inevitably thwarted and mutilated by the (quite reasonable) suspicions of the man, who is systematically discouraged, and always on the look-out for some trap. The tabooed woman comes to resemble the Ark of the Covenant among the Jews; an object which must not be touched, on pain of punishment by a thunderbolt from heaven.

It is not surprising, therefore, that certain English legislators should have proposed the institution of severe punishments for women who exploit the benefits of the law which "protects" them; for it is now man, who, in his turn, has need of protection, though his wily companions have known quite well how to protect themselves from the very beginning...... Thus the perfection of taboo, as exemplified in its modern legal form, has provided a strong and quite unexpected encouragement to the blackmailer. We may note, in passing, how these very abuses provide yet another proof of that special power of fascination possessed by the sexual organs and the sexual sense. a fascination that we were at pains to emphasize in the earlier part of this book. For the Puritans, who, in the name of their fanatical metaphysics, are never tired of opposing and condemning sex in any of its manifestations, through this very ardour reveal their own complete domination by sexual thoughts their perpetual preoccupation with the subject; the only difference is that they are engaged in fighting their desires instead of satisfying them.

The Anti-scientific Influence of Prohibitions. – One of the most serious consequences of taboo lies in the fact that it has prevented us from realizing the necessity for a logical and scientific study of sexual pleasure. According to Sarcey "improper words" – and by these he means the terms which relate to the sexual organs or to sexual pleasure, and which from our present point of view appear just as legitimate as the things they denote—"are inevitably associated with certain revolting ideas which lead us to turn from them in disgust". We could hardly find a more naïve and childish acceptance of taboo than in this sentence of the amiable and good-natured bourgeois critic; for if these "revolting ideas" and this "disgust" are characteristic of certain minds which unhesitatingly subscribe to the taboo, it is none the less true that they undergo a complete transformation whenever the possessors of such minds are themselves behaving sexually. If the sexual act and the sexual organs were really disgusting, they should logically still have continued to be so, even when the good Sarcey was himself indulging in the sexual act, proud as a rooster and very satisfied with what he was doing; but no sooner had he put on again his taboo-coloured spectacles than he lost all sense of proportion, and the very same act, when carried out by others, now appeared to him as loathsome.

For many centuries taboo prevented any reasoned or scientific examination of the sexual organs or the pleasure which they give; just as certain other taboos of a religious character long prevented the anatomical study of the human cadever. In fact, these same prohibitions, sadly bound up as they are with all the traditions of ignorance, are to be found everywhere impeding the advance of science. In our own days, the sexual and the metaphysical taboos have joined forces in opposing the methods introduced by Voronoff, thus re-enacting the campaign of squeamishness and childish vanity which in earlier years had been waged against Darwin. In this way a highly interesting and fruitful experiment has been denounced as "an offence against morality, hygiene, and decency"; and this moral indignation takes the place of all scientific consideration of the matter. Our education is still hampered by formal restrictions relating to such subjects as copulation and the organs of reproduction. Some dictionaries still exclude all reference to sexual terms. A publisher recently brought out a collection of ironical eulogies on our vices and defects (*In Praise of Gluttony, Untidiness, Egoism, etc.*) The list was a very full one, but he did not dare, even in the paradoxical tone that was adopted, to include a eulogy of sexual wantonness.

So great is the prejudice against sexual questions that science has often been prevented from making even a purely theoretical attack on the most urgent problems. Freud's books are forbidden in some countries. In certain works of pure science, such as G. Dumas's *Traite de Pshychologie*, in the course of an otherwise very important discussion of psychoanalysis, we find expressions like the following: "Freud makes certain observations which we cannot repeat here...." (p 1034); "Freud quotes certain sexual impressions of infancy which it is impossible to reproduce..... (p 1038). These "impossibilities," which cannot meet with the approval of the rationalistic thinker, betray the great influence which taboo still exercises on science. Surely it is absurd that the spirit of inquiry should still allow itself to be put off by such "impossibilities" – impossibilities which have insidiously led us, step by step, away from the realities which our forefathers could openly face, and have eventually produced in us a sort of general castration of the power of thought. Sexual truth has become something that we cannot bear to contemplate. "Decency" is like a cosmetic which has been mistaken for a natural complexion. Balzac, who is so in love with the conventions that he scarcely dares to consider the possibility of their being called in question, is appalled when his own very lively power of observation reveals to him the "effrontery" of the Ego, which he considers "scarcely decent"; resolutely turning his back on nature, and remaining faithful in his admiration of all the virtues of convention, he does not hesitate to say that the writer should "soften", "prune" and "emasculate" reality; these three expressions are his own. And yet, in this twentieth century, Leon Blum in his book on marriage, a book in which he treats sexual questions with a quite unusual breadth of mind, has conceded so much to the generally prohibitionistic attitude of his environment, as to say, in referring to Balzac's *Physiologie du Marriage* "with a wealth of detail which I cannot repeat, he shows that the use of separate beds by husband and wife. . . etc."; and these details given by the prudish novelist are at least a century old. . .

The relations between the sexes, the various manifestations of which are so important for humanity, are thus exposed to all the ignorant phantasies that anyone chooses to create; hence our many unhappy marriages and the innumerable tragedies of our private lives. Health itself is endangered by our absurd prohibitions and our ridiculous customs. And, worse still, sexual cleanliness has been impaired by the taboo; indeed the Middles Ages saw the triumph of a saintly filthiness. Felicien Chamsaur anxiously inquires what can have been the state of cleanliness of the "vile member" of the chief of the arch-prohibitionists. He comes to the said conclusion that intellectual individuals of either sex were walking cesspools-an inevitable result of the intrusion of taboo into a field that should be sacred to hygiene. The classic precautions taken in bourgeois societies to send the young girl out of the room when a sexual subject is introduced; the whispered tones in which such a subject is discussed in her presence; the roundabout phrases which are used to speak of it in front of her; the stories about storks or cabbages which serve to veil the actual processes of human reproduction; the books which are "fit to put into any hands" — all these things, to which habit has inured us, but which are grotesque enough if considered in themselves, are, at bottom, manifestations of taboo, instances of the survival of privative magic. They are the expression of a social condition which is still ruled by irrational prejudice and has not reached the stage of science.

The Limitation of Taboo to Sexual Pleasure. — In this way the sexual taboo spread throughout the human race; a taboo which, we may repeat, is directed exclusively against sexual pleasure, and, as we have shown above, makes no secret of this, since it does not claim in any way to extend to scatology.

It has, however, been very greatly aided by external circumstances.Remy de Gourmont has suggested that sexual taboo in Europe had the good fortune to encounter a strong ally in the spread of syphilis, which placed a barrier in the way of relations between the more turbulent individuals of both sexes, and which furnished the prohibitionists with an alarming weapon which they brandished most effectively. The fact that syphilis was, in all probability, non-existent in ancient societies must certainly have helped to make sexual intercourse an easier and less dangerous proposition; the almost certain disappearance of this disease in the future will, however, again favour a more rationalistic attitude towards sexual relations. The enemies of sex have no delusions on this matter; they have groaned in horror every time that some new progress towards the final extinction of venereal disease has been announced. Confirmed prohibitionists have been known to acclaim with joy these same diseases-an abuse of human intelligence that is not a little disconcerting. The purity societies and certain Anglican bishops have contended that it is not right to teach the means of avoiding venereal disease, and that the pro-phylactic methods now available should be regarded as so many invitations to debauchery.

One of these fanatics has said that "if medical science should succeed in doing away with the punishment (*sic*) which nature inflicts on those who have abandoned themselves to vice, this discovery would have anti-social and demoralizing effects, for it would bring about a syphilis of the mind, which would be even worse than syphilis of the body". Such "extravagances" (to use the very mild expression of the author we have quoted) are in truth a crime against humanity; the least that we can say is that such statements reveal an arrogance and self-complacency on the part of those who make them that is only equalled by their complete lack of understanding of the relative nature of all moral judgements.

The moral rule of taboo, which dominated the Middle-Ages, has been carried over wholesale into modern legislature; it is responsible for the framework of our penal laws, which were only codified at a relatively late date, chiefly from the beginning of the nineteenth century onwards. The sexual taboo enters into these laws without a question ever being raised as to its logical or scientific value — in much the same way as the crimes against religion which figured in our primitive penal code. Regarded as an indisputable principle, the taboo became sanctioned by legal penalties: and, worse still, these penalties, supported as they are by the never-ceasing purity campaign, have (little the restrictions of taboo itself) shown a tendency to steady increase; they tend in fact to deny the right to sexual pleasure. There has even arisen a theory, which would have astounded the civilizations of old, that the mere fact of the indulgence in sexual relations by unmarried persons in itself constitutes an infraction of the law.

If this theory were put into practice, it could fitly be regarded as the crowing achievement, the supreme triumph, of the tendencies expressed in modern taboo.

Chapter-7

Chastity as the Complement of Sexual Taboo

Chapter 7

Chastity as Complementary to the Sexual Taboo. — In primitive religious doctrine, and especially in the Judeo-Christian variety, the natural and inevitable complement of taboo has been the theory of Chastity, i.e. the exaltation of sexual abstinence into a virtue. Indeed, according to this special terminology, chastity is regarded as the virtue *par excellence*; for a "virtuous" girl in this sense is one who abstains from sexual pleasures, or at least from those that are forbidden by the moral rules. In the same way this system of ethics is fond of assimilating the idea of chastity to that of "purity" (by which is meant—to put the point bluntly—that a person has not yet been exposed to the "defilement" associated with the sexual secretions). It is clear, however, that this conception of "defilement," and therefore also that of "purity", have a merely conventional value, one moreover which is incompatible with scientific, and in particular with physiological, reality.

The exaltation of chastity has thus been a necessary complement to the taboo on sex. One of the chief figures of the Christian Olympus is the Virgin Mary, who (just as is the case also in certain ancient Asiatic myths) is supposed to have performed the remarkable feat of conceiving, carrying, and giving birth to a child while remaining all the time *virgon intact*a – a conception which corresponds to one of the most frequently recurring products of the religious imagination.

In this way there arose the very special and peculiar theory that "purity" was agreeable to God, and in consequence worthy of admiration by man. Doubtless it is necessary to have the true metaphysical spirit in order to appreciate at its full value the principle that ignorance is admirable.

Purity or Cleanliness. — Accepting this view of chastity, certain religious systems of morality then proceeded tc base their whole appreciation of sex on one central idea, viz. That the exercise of the sexual sense was unjustifiable, except for purposes of reproduction; while even here it was regarded merely as an unfortunate necessity, better avoided if possible (as shown in the celibacy of priests).Woman was *impure*; doubtless because her organs and her periods constituted an ever-present reminder of the function of reproduction, and because her body exercised an attraction on the male, which incited him to the act of copulation (among Jews, women occupy one part of the Synagogue and men the other). The sexual act, except under prescribed conditions, was a crime which might eventually be punished by death (as in the case of adultery). This view represents the triumph of a system based upon a confusion between moral qualities on the one hand, and physiological organs and sensations on the other.

The idea of purity is not a natural one; what is natural is the idea of material cleanliness of the organs, which is by no means the same thing. The idea of purity is, indeed, contrary to nature, since it leads to the suppression and neglect of the essential mechanism of a sense or function; while at the same time it tends to reduce the facilities for the proper exercise of certain organs to which nature has allotted a very definite role. To propose chastity as a substitute for the normal functioning of the sexual organs is at bottom the same thing as to bandage our eyes or block our ears. Organs should be used as nature intends them to be used; there is nothing to be proud of in subjecting our organs or senses to an inactivity which at its worst may lead to atrophy, and at its best involves needless restraint. The mechanism of a sense or of an organ, in so far as it causes no harm to others, is neither moral nor immoral; it just exists and that is all.

In reality all love between the sexes has at bottom a physiological foundation. The possibility of the final act is seldom absent from the mind, and all preliminary caresses lead in this direction. Otherwise, there would be no special point in sex attraction, and we might just as well satisfy our longings with a work of art or a cream bun. Our novels are very fond of telling us about lovers who "exchange chaste embraces" or "pure kisses". Such literature does not deign to take account of the state of aura that is inevitably present in such cases, nor of the physiological secretions and mild orgasms that such behaviour inevitably provokes.

Criticism of the Idea of Chastity. — It is true that this whole mechanism of sex is accompanied by a pleasure of specific kind. But is there anything to complain of in this? In itself, and allowing for differences of individual preference, sexual pleasure is neither more nor less valuable than any other kind of pleasure; thus certain individuals might even consider it inferior to the pleasures of taste. It is no more meritorious to abstain from coitus for a long period than it is to live for a week without eating; both cases represent a *tour de force*, and in neither of them can we hope to find a foundation for a rational system of morality.

The reasoning that applies to the functions in question naturally applies also to the organs. The mere fact that certain organs are related to certain functions surely affords no ground for indignation or disgust.The sense of vision is rendered possible by the existence of the eye and of the optic nerves; we ought to be able to admit, just as impartially and objectively, that the sexual sense, together with the pleasure that accompanies its use, is rendered possible by the existence of certain organs, which happen to be different in the case of men and women. But, just as the eye is a neutral organ, in the sense that it is neither pure nor impure, in the same way, every other portion of the human body, whether composed of cells, muscles, or mucous membrane, is nothing but a neutral organ, in itself containing neither purity nor impurity.

It is for this reason, incidentally, that nakedness, especially of the sexual organs, has as a rule a much slighter effect on those who are unaffected by taboo than on those who are perpetually obsessed by it.It is only through the sexual prohibitions themselves that a special value comes to be placed upon the exposure of the sexual organs. It has been decreed that they shall remain hidden; the mere fact of their appearance thereupon becomes a cause of emotion and embarrassment. If human beings were in the habit of walking about naked in the streets, all this emotion would disappear, together with the sense of mystery that surrounds the whole subject; our domestic animals continually expose their sexual organs, but we seldom trouble to look at them. If our children were given a true and full account of the processes of reproduction, if they had frequent opportunity of themselves observing these processes, or even of using anatomical models, they would, other things equal, be less sensually excitable than children who are brought up in the idea that sex is a mystery (a mystery which they desire to solve as soon as possible and to which their thoughts and actions will often be directed).

Philosophical analysis thus brings no support to the defence of chastity; as is indeed to be expected after what has been already said concerning the legitimacy of sexual pleasure. But it is necessary to stress this point in order that the reader may appreciate the full logical weakness of the argument for chastity.

Stendhal has described chastity as a comic virtue. This is a view which enjoyed a certain vogue for many centuries, especially among the Latin races, but which is now meeting with official disapproval. The French Minister for War even went so far as to draw up a circular letter explaining to his subordinates that it was possible to be chaste without being ridiculous; an effort which seems to have been inspired chiefly by the praiseworthy desire to reduce the incidence of venereal disease in the Army (since taboo still prohibits instruction as to how such disease can best be prevented). Under the further influence of the taboo, a women's congress at Milan in 1923 improved upon the above statement by saying that chastity was a necessity and a duty–thus making light of all the teachings of physiology. Finally, the medical profession, prostituting science to the service of taboo (and taking the latter for granted), has endeavoured to show that it is possible to forgo the sexual act *without* injury to health, and that in consequence the individual had no right to plead the imperious desires of nature as an excuse for not remaining chaste.

It goes without saying that all declarations of this kind imply an *a priori* acceptance of taboo; they take over the sexual taboo in its traditional form and make no effort to inquire whether it is justifiable.In striking contrast to this attitude was the feminist propaganda that accompanied the revolution of 1830 and demanded the abolition of compulsory chastity for women (which, according to a manifesto published at the time, was considered to be a "virtue that springs for the most part from weakness and timidity"). As for those medical men who have succumbed to the taboo, they forget altogether to take into account the existence of the neuroses or of individual differences in constitution; they fail to realize that in some persons the liberation of the sexual secretions and the accompanying release of nervous tension are almost in the nature of a compulsive necessity. Rationalists have no alternative but to refuse to take part in the discussion of a problem which has been so falsely stated.

Indeed, the question is not whether it is *possible* to be chaste, with help of a certain amount of special training. The real problem is as follows. Is it not, even on purely *a priori* grounds, contrary to logic and common sense for us to deprive ourselves on principle of the most intense natural pleasure which Nature gives us? Is it not, rather, perfectly legitimate and reasonable for us to seek this pleasure, and to make every effort to procure it, so long as we do no harm to others?

With this much understood, the attitude of every clear thinking person should be plain enough. For such persons chastity is *a matter of no interest*; it is merely an unfortunate result of a primitive and irrational view of things. Indeed, can ignorance ever be of interest? The most charitable thing that we can say about it is that it is useless: and that, if we look at the matter closely, those who lead chaste lives appear to be the victims of an illusion. In other words, chastity is a state of being, a condition, or, as the doctors say, a constitution. It merits neither admiration, praise nor criticism. There are people who have a large appetite, others who have a moderate one, still others who have no appetite at all; it is a matter of constitution, a strictly personal affair. To turn this into a question of right or wrong, and to use it as a pretext for meddling with other people's private lives, in order to discover whether more or less use is made of a certain physiological function, is surely a most lamentable outcome of false reasoning.

Philosophical consideration thus finds nothing to admire in chastity.How indeed can chastity lay claim even to our sympathy, since it is contrary to nature, and is nothing but an erroneous translation of moral values? Far from creating happy human societies living according to the laws of nature, chastity imposes on the world that state of gloomy ennui which is so dear to the hear of the Puritan. This joyless organization of society is hardly a seductive argument, especially when we bear in mind the fact that it would be possible to make human life radiantly happy by the intelligent organization and aesthetic exercise of this great sexual joy, the influence of which no society can, in any case, hope altogether to escape.

The Psycho-physiology of Chastity.—It would seem, furthermore, that individuals who lead a chaste life often get too much credit, and that their chastity is often nothing more than a sort of gastritis of the sexual organs. Or else that they get too little;and this applies to those fierce and combative persons who are dominated by a veritable antisexual paranoia, who regard sexual pleasure as diabolic, and who make martyrs of themselves-in mind, in spirit, and in flesh—in order to avoid it.

But even these latter are illogical and inconsistent. The ardent purity campaigns which have been carried on in Anglo-Saxon countries—by clergymen or unmarried women, usually with little understanding of the matter-are only feeble echoes of true chastity. They only preach a relative chastity, which is almost a contradiction in terms. A woman who has a husband can no longer be pure; a wife at the moment of copulation is no purer than a prostitute. It is easy for everyone to follow up this comparison in detail. In reality, this purity which is so much extolled is a purely relative affair. It is merely an arbitrary expression of the desire of certain fanatics to see the sexual act practised *only in those conventional forms in which they practise it themselves.* But it is sheer tyranny to demand that sexual pleasure shall be realized always under the same social and legal conditions; and it is hypocrisy or idiocy to call these pleasures impure, just because they do not happen to accord with one's own personal preferences in the matter. At bottom of all the fervour we invariably find the same old motive, i.e. the compulsion of taboo, in one or other of its forms.

We must admit, however, that the persistence of an atavistic taboo is not the only reason why many men demand chastity in women. If they value female chastity so highly (while attaching relatively little importance to chastity in men), it is through the persistence of an idea which has dominated our matrimonial conceptions for several centuries; women (and children also) were the *property* of the male, and every breach of this law was considered as theft and was punishable by death. This idea of property was the only conceivable justification for the use of those abominable "girdles of chastity" which, regardless of their possible effects on health, were padlocked on a woman by her lord when he departed for the wars. In our own day, chastity is still extolled by the male, because he sees in it a means of assuaging the pangs of his own jealousy. Often also, to refer once again to a fact which we have already encountered, he experiences a sort of sadistic pleasure at the – real or imagined – rape of a chaste women. His attitude is sadistic, because the deliberate acceptance of sexual pleasure by a woman who has freed herself from conventions is not sufficient for him. Our own view, on the contrary, is that normal individuals of either sex are those who can take their pleasures without unnecessary complication, and who can appreciate the full joy of complete mutual harmony. Such persons can dispense with the preliminaries dictated by convention; their attitude is based on the free mutual acceptance of acts which are regarded by both partners as being perfectly moral and legitimate.

The moral Value of Chastity.— It may be that chastity is a virtue from certain special points of view; nobody will deny the right of a religious or philosophical system to expound its views and preferences and to impose these views upon its own followers. But we have no right to say that chastity is a virtue in itself. A mode of being cannot be a virtue. To the rationalist chastity can never be a virtue, for to him sexual relations are strictly physiological processes, comparable to those of nutrition and respiration, which can only be looked at from the point of view of hygiene, and to which such notions as honour or honesty can only be attached through a false association of ideas.

Chronic chastity, however, is not merely a mode of being; it only too easily develops into a disease. Physiological organs are adapted to play certain roles in the vital economy; if, owing either to some external reason or to the intervention of a morbid will, they are prevented from playing these roles, the organism is no longer healthy but diseased. Sexual organs that are not allowed to function are no better than a stomach that cannot digest, or a lung that cannot breathe. Listen to Anatole France, as reported by his friend and confidant J.J. Brousson.The great writer considers that "virtue" (in the sense implied by conventional ethics) is an infirmity. Chastity "demands treatment, just as does anaemia or tuberculosis". He called chastity "the most cruel of the gods," and though that modesty was "hideous". He also said "there are no really chaste people; there are only hypocrites, invalids, maniacs and madmen..." Anatole France was too much of a pagan to be chaste. Rejecting taboo in virtue of his rationalistic principles, he was able to see chastity in its true light, without any sentiment or prejudice; he saw that it was always one of three things; (a) a consequence of mere deficiency; (b) the result of the prolonged influence of a fear-inspiring taboo; or (c) merely a manifestation of hypocrisy (on the part of those who publicly approved of the rules of this taboo in order to escape from them in their own private lives).

If we were to push this analysis further, we should come to the conclusion that chastity is a prejudice–one that is found neither among very primitive peoples, nor among those who are truly civilized. The former still enjoy a state of nature unperverted by arbitrary conventions. With the latter a full and rational analysis of causes and of values must inevitably lead to the suppression of chastity as a moral virtue, when its conventional and childish nature has once been realized.

It is the *half-civilized* races which believe in the superiority of chastity; such races as our own at the present time. The civilization of which we are so proud will doubtless seem a semi-barbarism to those who study it four or five thousand years hence. Between those distant descendants of ours and ourselves there will be as great a gulf as that between us and our ancestors of the Middle Ages; our descendants in their turn will look upon us as semi-barbarous, because of our wars, our intrusions upon privacy, our childish explanations of the Beyond, our misguided sense of values (which leads us to mistake foolery and fanaticism for divine inspiration), the illogicality of our repressive system....But it is just in these half-civilizations that the want of adequate reflection, the continuance of ancestral prejudice, the inability to think reasonably about fundamental human needs, the ignorance as to the true importance of physio-logical functions, the confusion between ethics and hygiene, or between ethics and law, the incapacity to see social values in their true perspective, a childish and absurdly conventional organization of the sexual life, a puerile disapproval of sensual satisfactions – all these combine to give a spurious value to chastity, and to make it appear (ridiculously enough) as though it were a virtue in itself. A truly rational civilization will, without a doubt, reject chastity, together with all other forms of asceticism; it will look upon them all as puerile or paranoiac. But this will only happen when, with the help of reason, we have so far succeeded in distinguishing truth from error, that we are able to reduce our confused moral values into some kind of logical or scientific order.

The "*Strength of the Chaste*". — It has sometimes been maintained that chastity confers on those who practise it certain advantages in the struggle for existence. We have been asked to admire the "strength of the chaste" a paradoxical slogan of the kind beloved by certain types of unscientific mind, who extol the artificial and despite the teachings of nature and who use striking statements of this sort to bolster up out-of-date taboos.

But what is this supposed strength? The man who takes no alcohol and no narcotics is stronger, physiologically and psychologically, than he who resorts to drugs and stimulants; for these drugs and stimulants are unnatural. Thirst and water, on the other hand, are natural; there is nothing extraordinary in the fact that the sober man is the stronger; it is just because he eschews artificial stimulants.Sexual pleasure, on the other hand, is certainly not artificial.On the contrary, to abstain from it is to declare war on nature.Do we speak of the superiority of the blind or the deaf? It is always foolish to oppose the laws of nature; and we shall see presently that nature does not fail to take her revenge; her answer to taboo is neurosis.Is it a question of the physical fatigue which may follow sexual satisfaction? It is ridiculous to speak of this in young persons, who indeed experience a feeling of additional poise and well-being after the normal exercise of the senses and the muscles; if it is pathogenetic excess which is condemned, we must of course agree, but then excess is everywhere an error.

"Professor Metchnikoff, who as is well known, is engaged in the endeavour to prolong human life"– so writes Leon Blum— "considers that the state of virginity is eminently harmful to the species. He sees in it the cause of a sort of permanent toxic condition, and he regards the hymen as belonging, like the appendix, to the class of useless organs which no longer do us anything but harm". I would like to corroborate this by the following statement, which I have taken purposely from a work which adopts the orthodox and traditional view of the sexual act: "Those who live strictly continent lives are more than usually liable to certain neuroses, to certain disorders of the circulation (arterio-sclerosis) and to certain affections of the sexual organs."

Continence is praised by certain doctors; but they take good care not to practise it themselves.They prefer the feeling of poise and satisfaction which is produced by the normal exercise of the sexual sense to a state of anxiety and neurosis. Who indeed would not be suspicious of continence? Old maids, who are perfect living examples of this virtue, afford a glaring illustration of its disastrous effects. Conversely, who has not noticed the occurrence of a profound and beneficial physiological transformation in many girls who have just married (to confine ourselves to unions of an official kind)?So long as they are condemned to virginity, they vegetate-pale, languishing, morose, envious of those who have escaped from compulsory continence; when they get engaged, they wake up and begin to take a fresh interest in life; on returning from their honeymoon, they are often so transformed, so improved in appearance, that their parents can scarecely believe their own eyes. And in truth continence is a terrible form of excess.Like all excess, it has a depressing, fatiguing and debilitating effect, which to some extent makes itself felt throughout the nervous system.

In reality, the chaste individual is not (as the orthodox view might lead us to suppose) a valuable or desirable member of society.He is unstable, restless, nervous. He is often peevish, because he demands of others that they shall undergo the same privations that he imposes on himself. If they do not consent, he hates them because they have freed themselves from the restrictions which he himself finds so burdensome. Sexuality obsesses him, and robs him of all peace of mind; and for that very reason, he objects to peace of mind in anyone. This is why so many old maids are always busy destroying the happiness of others, prying out the details of their private lives, condemning pleasures which they do not understand. The chaste person is an anomaly of nature. He is more or less vaguely aware of this, suffers in consequence, and seeks his revenge in making others suffer. Those who make ostentatious profession of their own chastity are nearly always most unpleasant people.

As Judge Lindsey has very rightly observed, our present society lays much more stress on the physical aspects of this much-vaunted virtue than on its mental aspects. A person is considered chaste if he is too frightened or timid to attempt anything in the nature of open sexual behaviour. His mind may be a mass of erotic visions, but nobody worries about this. We may safely go further and say that, when he declares war on the "impure" he is quite as much obsessed by sex as others are; his fanatical zeal is fed by images which are a torture to the flesh–a condition with which we are already well acquainted. Many of the chaste are merely cowards, afraid of what will be said about them; they then fall ready victims to hypocrisy and make-believe, qualities which often go with cowardice. "What many other persons would call the 'moral law', says the above mentioned American sociologist with his characteristic frankness, "I regard as not moral at all. In fact, I consider it often cruel, unjust, savage and ignoble.Take, for example, the value we place on chastity in women. It is part of our 'moral law'. It masquerades under all sorts of aesthetic names. It is identified by poets with the 'purity' of the lily. This implies that sexual relations sully that purity. It even insists on an "immaculate conception' in order to make sure that its particular chief deity, a man-god, should be free from this taint. And then, by a special magic, it excepts married women from the general rule. They have had sex relations, but they are chaste and pure – even in a loveless marriage –

all by virtue of a bit of magic called a wedding ceremony.On the other hand, some sinning sister, unmarried, who has committed the same act in an ecstasy of love, is impure, polluted, tainted and what not. What all this means is simply that women are property; and that society swats any woman who yields up her virginity irregularly by branding her with a mark of shame, and making her taboo. The 'moral law' – where under heaven is there a name to fit this thing?"

What remains of this supposed "strength" of the chaste, if physiology gives not support to the idea? Is it meant that the chaste, owing to their egoistic withdrawal from the passions of love and their careful avoidance of all possibility of contamination, remain ignorant alike of jealousy and of the torments of desire, of the fear of abandonment and the tragedy of separation? Doubtless! But neither do they know the thrill of sex, the joys of passion and possession. They are the misers of life, and pass their whole existence without any realization of the profounder human emotions. Their days are spent in niggardly and timid fashion. Is such an existence enviable? Everyone will reply according to his temperament, but of those who have enjoyed a full and satisfying love life, there are few who, if asked at the end of their lives whether they would like to begin all over again, would not choose to do so if it were only possible.

In reality, the supposed strength of the chaste in our anti-sexual society is an illusion; due to the terrible strength of our taboos. Taboos make love so complicated, so hard to obtain without falling into the snares of conventional morals, of social rules, or prohibitions, that to abstain from it clearly relieves us of many difficulties. The warm-blooded individual who desires to follow the natural law of love is likely to find himself in constant conflict with a prohibitionistic social organization, which is everywhere in opposition to this law. Man or woman, such a person will inevitably lead a "stormy life", the exciting episodes of which, in their constant repetition, may sometimes easily develop into tragedies. Chaste, he remains protected from these disasters. But that this should be so is purely a consequence of the taboo itself.

If a society were to defy taboo and deliberately adopt a system of complete sexual freedom, we may be sure that both the individual and the social danger connected with amorous adventure would be very much reduced.We should see the disappearance of the sexual neuroses; since desire would be more freely satisfied, people would enjoy greater equanimity and greater *joie de vivre*, which in turn would have widespread and beneficial effects on our whole social condition, on the relations between individuals, on work and productivity.The "strength of the chaste" is merely the inevitable complement of the persecution of sensuality in prohibitionistic countries. It is a phrase which any natural being would think ridiculous. True strength, true repose of mind and senses, true satisfy, and the perfect balance, physiological and mental, which this implies – these are to be found, not by defiance of nature, but by a healthy and sensible decision to obey her invitations.

The Psycho-physiology of Virginity. — For long ages past, men would seem to have attached great importance to feminine virginity; for it is not worth speaking of masculine virginity, since there exists no means of proving its existence. The anatomical constitution of woman, however, has allowed this problem to arise in her case; the history,the history of virginity is in fact the history of the hymen. The desire of men seems to have been peculiarly stimulated by the idea that they were the first to possess a woman, the first to break this membrane. A curious sentiment, and one that is not universal; the process of defloration has a charm only for brutal minds, and at the present day it is no rare thing to meet men for whom it has no attraction whatever, and who are careful to avoid it. But among our crude ancestors brutality seems to have played an integral part in the sexual embrace, so that it is not very astonishing that they should have found pleasure in this sport.

On the other hand, we have seen that repression, in spite of its apparent triumph, weighs so heavily on human beings that it is a great relief for them to escape from it for a time – as in the intimacies of love. With this act of deliverance there are associated certain powerful feelings and sensations, which have left a permanent impress on the mind; it is as though by a single mighty stroke the powers of repression had been overcome; nature regained, Prometheus freed from his bonds. The more certain, sure and decisive is this return, the greater is its value, and the more widespread are its effects. To enjoy such a return with a woman who succumbs to a man's solicitations is good; but if this woman is not a virgin, she has already experienced this return to nature at the hands of other men; it still charms and transports her, but it is no longer a novelty. The girl who is a virgin, on the other hand, enjoys it in all its fullness and originality. The pleasure of both partners is increased by the fact that they have defied all restrictions on their natural liberty, and have regained this liberty in their intimate embraces. The man's joy is all the greater in that he brings this revelation, this deliverance and relief to a virgin who has up to now been a prisoner in the unyielding shackles of repression. The overcoming of virginity assures this maximum of pleasure. This is why some women attach so much importance to the first act of coitus, often indeed to the first sexual advances of whatever kind; and why this first moment in which they were able to deliver themselves from repression becomes, as it were, a nucleus around which all their other sexual feelings are grouped, so that they sometimes speak of it as a "revelation", and always retain a vivid impression of the man to whom they owe their first initiation. Some men, for whom all this is not altogether lost, find, therefore, a certain real satisfaction, both physical and mental, in virginity—at first in hope of destroying it, and eventually in the act of destruction itself.

Virginity seems therefore to have had, at first, the effect of increasing the value of the girl who still possessed it. Modern marriage and the "capital" (i.e. the economic value of virginity), on which so much store is placed by the mothers of the *danseuses* of the Paris opera, show that this tendency still exists. But virginity has also been looked upon, not so much as a means of increasing the sexual value of a girl, but rather as a sign of physical and moral superiority which was pleasing to the gods (e.g. as in the case of The Vestal Virgins), and therefore worthy of all respect. It should be clear, however, that virginity in this sense is only a particular aspect of the general problem of chastity; all that we have already said about this latter applies therefore to virginity as thus conceived. To those who have once adopted a moral and metaphysical system which implies the desirability of chastity, feminine virginity is the most convenient means of assuring the cultivation of this virtue, and indeed it is the only method which admits of objective control. In this way there has come about the most complete and perfect example of such a system, the Christian virgin, the final and most perfect product of sexual taboo, either veritably ignorant of the physiological phenomena which control her own species, or vertiably hypnotized by the horror of nakedness and of the flesh, a martyr to herself and a torment to others, ready to die when necessary, if she can thus escape from the natural law of coitus and reproduction. Herewith its attained the highest measure of artificiality, the apotheosis of repression.

As we have already said, virginity has not the same attraction for all men; those who marry widows or divorcees must of necessity dispense with it. In the East, where sexual initiation takes place at an early age, comparatively little importance is attached to virginity, and even in the case of a young girl, no exaggerated or exclusive emphasis is laid upon it as a condition of love; the girl is taken as she is found, without indiscreet questions as to her past. As is well known, in Japan the daughters of the lower classes used to be quite willing to pass a few years of their youth in the Yoshiwaras, in order to collect a little sum of money, after which they had no difficulty in finding a husband. The Chinese of the corresponding class often take a wife from a brother, and a girl would be astonished if objection were raised on the score of her no longer being a virgin.Even in Europe it would seem that the value attached to virginity has diminished with the advance of rational thought; in some twentieth-century novels we find that the heroine, far from being proud of her innocence, deliberately conceals or denies it, thinking that in this way she will be more certain of the man whom she desires.

We have to recognize, finally, that women may show an attitude towards virginity that is analogous to that of men. The "South Russian," whose very valuable confessions we have already had occasion to quote, tells us that from the age of thirteen to twenty he has in the habit of pretending to be completely naïve when the "lady" of his choice was older than himself. "It is astonishing," he remarks, "how they love to play the instructor in this matter! Every woman in turn would like to be the first to initiate her young partner... My own experience makes me believe that the attraction to children who have not yet reached the age of puberty or of adolescence, or have only just reached that age, is no rarer among women than among men. We are all acquainted with cases like that of Cherubino, where initiation took place at the hands of an elderly mistress, often a family friend, who is able to bring with her love both a wide erotic experience and a tenderness that is almost maternal in its quality.

The (Sexual) Moral Sense as a Breviary of Repression.—These considerations help us in understanding the value of a term which has been much used and abused, the *moral sense*. We are here of course only concerned with it in so far as it bears upon our subject, i.e. the manifestations of sex.

The moral sense is in no way a physiological concept, and is not comparable with the real senses described by physiology. The word "sense" is indeed wrongly used in place of the word "sentiment".We should really speak of the *moral sentiment*, if (as is usually the case) we mean to designate a state of mind which has reference to a collection of sexual rules and conventions the truth of which is accepted without question, and which are therefore unhesitatingly applied to individual cases.

Now it is just this collection of conventions which repression has substituted for the true sexual sense – that sense which is really based on physiology, which is so imperious in its demands, which rules without opposition in earliest infancy, and would have continued so to do if it had not been opposed by its rival, education. To have "moral sense" is to practise the fundamental rules of repression; not to have it is to return to the primitive demands of the sexual sense. This is so true that, if anything brings about a relaxation of repression, the sexual sense reappears in all its force, and people say that the individual has *lost* his moral sense; in certain diseases he can unblushingly admit to acts which our code considers as offences against morals, because, owing to a weakness of memory, fatigue, or an oversight of his enfeebled will, he has forgotten the rules of the game and returned to the spontaneous behaviour of nature.

The state of mind due to repression is so strong, so much resembles "second nature" (the first having been entirely lost to view), that it completely substitutes its own rules for those of the "sexual sense", which alone has its foundations in natural physiology. Indeed, the substitution is so complete, the expulsion of the sexual sense in favour of repression is carried out according to laws of such Draconian severity, that the disappearance of the sexual sense necessarily leaves the individual with a gap, a void, with something lacking in his mental equilibrium. To fill this gap, in such a way as not to reveal a gross discrepancy, it has been decreed that the moral sense shall take the place of the sexual sense. It is true that the latter corresponds to the former much as night corresponds to day; nevertheless, it is capable of providing an answer (of more or less exactly the opposite kind) to all the problems raised by sexuality.

In other words, the moral sense is the breviary of repression, the outcome of the determined opposition with which education has confronted the sexual sense. It does therefore represent a genuine system, but it does not, for all that, constitute a universal law. It participates in all the variations which sexual morality itself has undergone, both in space and time; the moral sense in a polygamous society is not the same as in a monogamous one. Indeed, it is not astonishing that it should vary, when we remember that the sexual acts themselves are judged according to a number of vastly different criteria, such as those of the spiritualist at one end of the scale, and those of the rationalist at the other.

Rationalism and Chastity.— The conclusions, as manifested in the various systems of education, have been such as we might have expected from the given premises. Education has so completely turned its back on nature, and has been so profoundly influenced by the idea of chastity, that it demands, as though it were an obviously pedagogical maxim, that the eyes of the new generation should be closed to certain natural acts, acts which are essential to the maintenance of life. The Western world, with its stories of children born from cabbages or brought by storks, affords a striking revelation of the ever-increasing strength of the taboo mentality; whereas, in other countries, there is not a single child, if he is capable of reasoning at all, who does not realize in main outline (greatly to the benefit of himself and of his understanding of life) the part played by the female in the acts of conception and of birth. In excluding the subject of animal propagation from our educational programmes, we are opening the way to indirect and misleading sources of information, to ignorance of the nature of venereal disease, and of the methods available for its prevention.

What should be the attitude of rationalists towards this problem of chastity? Surely one that displays a greater humanity and toleration. They will admit that it is possible to regard chastity as an ideal; they have no quarrel with other people's preferences. But they will deny that this ideal is the only possible one, that it is the only moral system that has any value; they will, in short, refuse to believe that chastity is moral in itself, nor will they admit that the partisans of taboo have the right to impose chastity on other people; they will reserve to themselves and to others the right of refusing to submit to chastity. They will, rather, stoutly maintain their own right to dispose freely of their own bodies, and their own sexual sense, though they will abstain from interfering with the freedom of others. It would seem such a simple thing not to meddle in the private lives of our neighbours; it would indeed appear to be one of the most obvious services we can render them. Yet in fact it is quite otherwise; man has evinced a singular desire to impose his own preferences on others, to make those preferences a law for others; herein lies the great danger of all taboos, and hence of all systems of metaphysics and morality.They cannot maintain a neutral attitude; they endeavour to make converts, by violent methods if they can. The strongest passion of those who hold such systems is to interfere in the affairs of others. The rationalist philosopher has exactly opposite ideals; in virtue of his very principles, he demands liberty for himself and accords liberty to others – exactly the contrary of the famous phrase of Veuillot. Some day, no doubt, this will become the general view, but only when we have grown out of the endless meddlesome prohibitions with which primitive taboos have plagued unfortunate humanity.

Thus the false prestige of chastity, a prestige which finds no echo among rational minds, is nothing but a relic of our ancestral fears, crystallized into abnormal and unnatural conventions. The arguments on which our anti-sexual morality is based appear strong only so long as we refuse to analyse chastity. As soon as we submit this idea to the light of reason, it is seen to be a consequence of the theories of taboo and sin, with no more scientific value than is possessed by these theories themselves.

The Relation between Metaphysical and Sexual Taboos. — We are now in a position to elucidate a point of some importance.The anti-sexual moralists are wont to conduct their campaign with the most intense ardour and pugnacity; they bring *an almost religious passion* to their fight against sexual pleasure, a degree of emotion which indeed causes considerable misgiving to more balanced minds.Unpopularity has no terrors for them; if necessary, they will abandon a peaceful private life in order to interfere with other people who have never asked for their advice; to carry on their work of propaganda, they will unhesitatingly intrude into the private lives of others, and do their best to imbue everyone with their own views of sexual life. To what end, we may ask, not without surprise? For we may justly be astonished that matters of an essentially physiological order should arouse ardour and fury of a kind that are generally to be found only in conflicts of a religious or political nature.

The answer to the problem is now easy enough. The explanation lies in the close association between the original taboos, metaphysical and sexual. There is, as we know, a most important metaphysical element in the sexual taboo.Cut out the supposed interest of the higher powers in the human sexual act, and the whole edifice of the sexual taboo falls to the ground. In the various Western faiths, the prohibitions on sex are put forward in closest association with religious dogmas (e.g. the ninth Christian commandment), and the anti-sexual moralists are usually recruited from the religious sects, or at any rate from the more religious sections of society. This is a fact that surely deserves our attention.It shows us how illogical it is for those who have once called into question the old metaphysical system not to apply the same scientific criteria to the sexual systems which have been built up on these very metaphysical foundations, and which cannot be otherwise than closely associated with their dogmas.

Finally, this should serve to remind us that current sexual morality, far from being of universal validity, is only *one particular kind of morality,* which we are at liberty to accept or reject, and which, therefore, should not be allowed to determine rules of behaviour for every member of the community. All these reasons probably play some part in the fact that anti-sexual campaigns have always enjoyed a greater success in Anglo-Saxon countries, where there is less inclination to discuss the value and justification of religious ideas. The Latin people have generally shown themselves more cautious, since they have felt that the sexual taboo ought doubtless to come in for its share of all the reservations and objections which, in their own countries, have been so freely brought to bear against metaphysics. This too is the reason why rationalists have always shown a tendency to assert their right to sexual enjoyment; because their reason, with the support both of their principles and of their inclinations, rebelled against the irrationalism of *all* taboos without exception.

This analysis should therefore serve as a definite assurance to a large category- probably indeed an imposing majority – of very worthy people who are good, law-abiding and public-spirited citizens, and are anxious to be of assistance to their fellow-men, but who, to their own surprise and pain, find themselves in revolt against the anti-sexual modes of life which convention would impose upon them. In spite of their good will, in spite of their evident and thorough honesty, it has happened only too often that their lives have been ruined and their careers wrecked because they have committed the so-called crime of indulging in sexual pleasure, without the slightest violence or deceit, but still in a manner that infringed the anti-sexual prohibitions. They realize vaguely that they have reason on their side, that it is wrong to proscribe and punish the act for which they are held guilty; and that, although they are regarded as immoral, it is they who are really following the path of nature. Such people should now be easier in mind. A sexual taboo is just as open to challenge as is a metaphysical dogma. *It is part of a system; it is not a part of morals.* We have every right to question or reject it. We are perfectly justified in preferring a rationalistic conception of existence in which sexual pleasure is regarded as avowable and legitimate, as a matter which has nothing to do with individual honesty or honour.

Chapter-8

The Neuroses Due to Sexual Repression

Chapter 8

The Neuroses Due to Sexual Repression.— It is perfectly clear - even before we bring the light of medical science to bear upon the matter - what must inevitably be the outcome of the conditions that we have described. On the one hand there is the sexual sense, as permanent as it is imperious; on the other hand the taboo, which is in everlasting combat with this sense. We can foresee that such a conflict cannot take place without giving rise to serious physiological troubles among the unfortunate beings who are its victims, continually tossed to and fro between their moral ideals and their physiological needs.

It is easy to show that this is what really happens. The depression, the boredom, the irritability the taedium vitae often manifested by people who appear to have everything to make them happy, are due almost always to the fact that their sexual desires are unsatisfied or inadequately satisfied; indeed our sexual prohibitions see to it that these desires shall be frustrated, even in their most legitimate and reasonable expressions. Freud, comparing the child and the adult, very justly remarked that we demand of the latter that he should abominate that which he formerly adored: "The individual when he grows up is expected to feel aversion and repugnance for the very things which, as a child, he had enjoyed." If we add that the former condition was a natural one, whereas the latter is entirely artificial and conventional, we can scarcely be astonished that neurosis and moral discomfort should result.

Further, when, on turning to the medical point of view, we find that sexual satisfaction favours sleep, whereas "most cases of nervous insomnia are due to a lack in the sexual life", we can easily understand that repression which is responsible not only for this lack, but for the conflict necessary to enforce it, is the gateway of all neurosis. In certain adults the nervous tension brought about by sexual abstinence causes much discomfort and reacts upon all the other functions. How indeed could it be otherwise, when we find that in animals the periodical rut is liable, especially if it is opposed, to cause a veritable state of madness (as in elephants)? We have therefore no justification whatsoever for treating these conditions lightly; above all, it is absurd to imagine that they are *necessarily and in every case* preferable to a state of satisfaction, as our general theories and conventions would seem to imply. All that we can admit is that the need for satisfaction varies from one individual to another; whence the error of the prohibitionistic school of medicine, which says that it is possible to forgo sexual satisfaction. "An old Italian abbot, seventy years of age, told Courier that he had been faithful to his vow of chastity, but he added that he would not like to return to the age of twenty and have to pass through the same trials again...." We know the story of the priest of Cours, near La Reole, who, as a result of his attempts at continence, became a victim to satyriasis, and died of it at the age of thirty-two. Such can be the terrible results of the obstinate conflict between physiology and morals!

It seems not unlikely that the exercise of the sexual function and the sexual sense (which controls the secretions) follows certain periodic laws, which are just as regular in a given subject as are those governing nutrition. But, as has been justly remarked, "this natural rhythm has, in man, been so completely upset by intellectual and social influences," that the laws in question are now very difficult to ascertain. They can therefore be misunderstood or even denited *in toto* by those who profess chastity and continence; though these latter conditions are assuredly not natural, but are on the contrary highly artificial states due solely to the influence of the moral systems which preach renunciation. Nevertheless, this flouting of "normal rhythms" in our artificial societies seems to be very prejudicial to human health, and may even endanger the continuance of the race.

The neuroses produced in otherwise healthy subjects by the prohibitions connected with the sexual taboo are legion, and have been clearly brought to light by the Freudian method of psycho-analysis and the various other methods of treating neuropathic victims of anti-sexual repression.Being called upon to treat neurotic patients, Freud naturally asked himself what was the origin of their neurosis.It is this question, indeed, which would seem to have led him to his whole system of psycho-analysis. As regards the question of etiology, he found that in all, or at any rate in the vast majority, of cases the responsible factors were the censorship and the sexual repression of which we have already spoken.

Here we must content ourselves by referring the reader to the studies which have been made on this subject by the Viennese savant and by the Zurich school, and their classification of nervous disorders into actual neuroses, psycho-neuroses, and narcissistic neuroses-a classification which covers all cases, including such well-marked affections as neurasthenia, hypochondria, hysteria, obsessional neurosis, melancholia, etc., etc. The clinical observations in this field are very numerous, and there is no need to repeat them here. It will be more interesting to add certain general observations of our own, and to see what conclusions of importance for sexual ethics can be drawn from pathological studies of this kind.

Various Types of Collective Sexual Neuroses. — All we can do here, by way of supporting and emphasizing the Freudian theory of sexual neurosis, is to describe certain types of neurosis which are particularly significant because they are in a certain sense collective, that is to say, common to groups of individuals living under certain similar physiological or social conditions.

(a) *Infantile Neurosis.*— This neurosis affects young persons of both sexes from childhood until the age when they are "grown up" and able to enjoy a relative degree of liberty, which, with the help of a little effort and intelligence on their own part, may enable them to remedy the trouble – if it is not too late. This first type of neurosis manifests itself in the state of enervation or anaemia (the precise symptoms varying according to the individual) to be found in young persons whom nature has endowed with an intense desire for the (prohibited) sexual act.In some cases, family or institutional life may become a veritable torment as a result of sexual prohibition; not to speak of the conflicts–latent or overt—thus occasioned between these young persons and their parents or teachers.

To this class belong all those languid, melancholy, sullen, strangely silent, timid, and introverted individuals who lead cramped lives, bounded by the family circle or the walls of their school. Auto-erotic practices are their only refuge, and may be resorted to even in excess. We cannot too much insist upon the paradox that it is just at the age when sexual desire appears in its most intense and ardent, and also – we may add – most charming and lovable form, that it receives least recognition and gratification. Not to speak of the possibilities of enriching and beautifying life that are thus lost, this attitude inevitably predisposes to neurosis, puberty manifests itself as a sort of exasperation, which may sometimes lead to insanity and which always exerts a profound influence on the character and emotions. It is not in the reformatory, a place which only teaches the child to hate our repressive society, that such neurotics can be cured; their only ray of hope lies in a freer attitude towards sex and better opportunity for sexual exercise. Those who have the intelligence to apply this remedy are astonished at the rapidity of the cure; it transforms these abnormal, excitable, melancholic or listless creatures into lively, healthy, active specimens of youth. While, on the other hand, every educational system which definitely bans all sexual activity until a comparatively late age is a veritable hot-bed for the development of sexual neurosis.

(b) *Conjugal Neurosis.*—The state of marriage (not to speak of free union), permitting, as it does, a regular satisfaction of the sexual needs, might seem at first sight to afford a condition unfavourable to the creation or continuance of sexual neurosis, but this is not necessarily the case.

In the earlier part of this book we emphasized the radical difference between the two opposed sexual types; the uterine and the orchitic on the one hand, and the clitorid and the phallic on the other. One of the most pronounced characteristics of the two latter types is that they cannot find any complete or lasting erotic satisfaction except in a more or less frequent change of partner. They soon tire of any one individual. Their passion is like burning straw: it is quickly extinguished, but is easily rekindled in another place.,It is for them that the saying holds good; that in love the first moments are the most delightful. Indeed, they experience these first moments often enough. Peaceful possession of the same person means nothing to them; it soon blunts all erotic pleasure. In the long run it may even lead to irritation and hatred towards a partner who is forced upon them, and whose attitude deprives them of the opportunity for fresh sexual adventure.

It is easy to see that the married state must weigh heavily upon those whose sexual desires are of this type. The satisfactions which marriage can bring are no longer available to them; indeed, the whole conjugal situation becomes a very painful one. There are many couples where the husband is so satiated as to have become practically impotent with his wife, although this is far from being the case with any other women. In such conditions neurosis soon appears, and before long becomes acute.A woman of this type will seek lovers; if necessary she will sacrifice her social position in order to possess them, or she will obtain a divorce for "incompatibility". The following observation is of interest in this connexion. A married woman of thirty, with children, fell a viction to an acute neurosis, which profoundly affected her life and caused various accidents, the origin of which was a mystery to those about her. With the help of psycho-analysis, the present writer was able to obtain the complete and unreserved confidence of this woman. She no longer loved her husband, though he on his part loved her greatly; all his endearments left her cold; she was reduced to tears and to despair by the idea that she was growing older, a prisoner to the married state, and would perhaps, "nevermore have an opportunity to belong to another man:" and thus "experience again" all the fresh and thrilling joys of a new love, leading up gradually to their culmination in complete possession.The thought of being definitely debarred from all this was more than the woman could bear, and she succumbed to neurosis. In fact she only recovered when she gained at least a certain measure of liberty for the purpose of a cure, rendered necessary by her failing health, a step which enabled her to realize her desire and take a lover (probably indeed several).

The German investigator Magnus Hirschfeld found that during a course of lectures dealing with the sexual life he was repeatedly asked one particular question – a question which, in a country where psycho-analysts had made so much progress, was expressed in its full natural frankness. "Although I am a happily married woman, I have an intense desire for another sexual partner. How do you explain this contradiction?" The lecturer replied there was no contradiction; the longing for another partner was the natural expression of primitive sexual desire, which has nothing to do with love in the strict sense. This explanation throws into vivid relief the confusion that arises in all discussions of this matter,so long as the fundamental legitimacy of the sexual acts has not been recognized. The conjugal neurosis is merely the form taken by sexual desire, when it is frustrated by being artificially confined to a certain conventional channel.

In man this neurosis is rarer, because he usually allows himself a grater freedom in extra-conjugal relations. But we often find that, just in so far as these relations are impossible or difficult, the husband too shows signs of being nervous, intolerant, irritable, curt, or ill-disposed; the wife, on her part, being worried and miserable. It often happens that her husband only becomes again the charming and lovable creature that he was when he has found a method of so ordering his life that he is able to satisfy his sexual desires, desires which have nothing to do with the family fireside.

This conjugal neurosis is at the bottom of innumerable divorces, especially in those households where there exists what Michelet has called "divorce in marriage" and such cases are legion.

(c) *Literary Neurosis.*—We may group together under this head all those neuroses of sexual origin where the patient, unable for one reason or another to find a cure in normal satisfaction, seeks a new and substitutive channel for his powerful desires, a channel which is indeed highly saturated with sexuality, but which is confined to some particular field of *phantasy* – often one that brings both paid and exaltation.

A very common type of this neurosis is found in certain persons of a religious disposition, whose mysticism is tinged with erotic sentiments, which are indeed sometimes amazingly concrete in their expression.The Song of Songs is a very ardent hymn of love. The Carmelite nuns consider themselves the betrothed of Jesus Christ. So also did Catherine of Siena, who enjoyed visions in the course of which. He placed a marriage ring upon her finger; it was she too who sucked milk from the breasts of the Virgin Mary. Mme Guyon had fits of suffocation, which necessitated the loosening of her clothing, and during which :she gave out a superabundance of grace so as to inflate the body of the Elect seated beside her". Marie Alacoque gives material expression to the mystery of the Sacred Heart by perceiving the bleeding heart of Jesus, and exchanging this holy organ with her own. Some other saints have been even more definitely sexual, and have been haunted by a desire for the prepuce of their God. It is needless to insist on these well-known neuroses, which, as we can clearly see, have originated in an intense, but at the same time intensely repressed, sexual exaltation.

Modern psychology admits that the sexual and the religious emotions have much in common. Psycho-analysis has brought further evidence, by showing that, under the influence of repression, the latter emotions may often serve as substitutes for the former. This explains, no doubt, why so many highly sexualized individuals show little inclination to become religious; the two activities being of the same kind, if one absor', all the energy available, little or nothing is left over for the other. And the opposite is also true, for religious paranoia may abolish sexual desire, though of course without prejudice to its reappearance in the guise of moral exaltation, in which a concentrated love, expressing itself quite often in definitely sexual terms, is directed to the Divinity himself (as with Saint Theresa).

Even lay minds are far from being altogether exempt from manifestations of this kind; though in their case the expressions are less frequent and less acute, because as a rule some more direct form of satisfaction eventually becomes available. Nevertheless the tendency of old maids, or of others who are suffering from lack of satisfaction, to write anonymous letters of an obscene kind has been often noted. Dr. Locard, director of the technical police laboratory of Lyons, tells us that anonymous letters "written in printed characters for purposes of disguise" are for the most part monuments of salaciousness. But the interesting point is that, when by chance their authors are discovered, they are often found to belong to families distinguished by their austere moral tone, where all ideas of the kind in question would be quite unknown. Dr. Locard reminds us in this connexion of the classic case of Mlle de Morell, in the *affaire* of La Ronciere le Noury. He says that "old maids, soured by age or social pressure, young men suffering from the continence forced upon them by their principles or their timidity, find expression in these letters (for which they imagine they will never be held responsible) for the secret, overflowing feelings of their strongly repressed desires. In practice one never finds that a document of this kind has been written by a prostitute, a roue, or even by a man or woman enjoying normal sexual life."

This author believes that we have here one of the best illustrations of the Freudian position. It does indeed afford a striking example of the imperious and unquenchable nature of the sexual urge, and shows that "repressions," whether imposed from within or from without, only serve to create unhappy, pathological individuals, who hate their own pretended virtue, and who throw it overboard as soon as they think it possible to do so without compromising their hypocritical conventions. They become abnormal, and therefore socially dangerous, because society has prohibited them from being normal and inoffensive.

We could give other examples of the secret but incessant working of repressed sexual ideas. Everyone possesses a hidden treasury of sexual words, fantasies and preferences, which he carefully conceals from everybody else; it affords a means of escape from a social condition in which human beings are enslaved to burdensome conventions – conventions which they defend without connection, merely in order to behave as others do. Sometimes a ray of light is thrown on this reserved territory, without the realization of the individual concerned. Delirium is often instructive in this respect. But examples can also be found in everyday life. A gathering of some dozen people were engaged in playing some "innocent little games" in which every member of the party anonymously wrote a word on a piece of paper.Every time the game was played there was found one more or less scatological expression; the handwriting clearly showed that this always came from the only young girl among those present, one whose temperament made it difficult for her to conform to the conventional standards of chastity. In the relations between lovers, too, we find the repressed feelings taking their revenge; often, either during actual embraces, or in correspondence, there is veritable flood of obscene, voluptuous or even scatological expressions; certain couples cannot derive the full enjoyment from each other until have indulged in exercises of this kind. One of the aspects of the loving conspiracy which unites two free beings consists in just this mutual breaking down of conventional "repression"; through this return to nature they experience much the same kind of relief as does the polar navigator when he wins through once again to the open sea ....

Sometimes a sexual neurosis will find expression in a more literary form. There are love poems innumerable. Some of them may be intensely religious, as was the case of the poet Sadi, whose verses, fiery with passion, are continually confounding the flesh and the spirit; and who, endowed as he was with a fierce consuming appetite, set out with equal ardour to introduce a carnal element into sacred love and to spiritualize the longings of the flesh; "My whole life is engulfed in Thee, and it is Thy whole life which moves in the blood of my heart.... " Bossuet (*Poesies Sacrees*) expresses the betrothal or union of his soul with his God in the following rather astonishing words, which are, however, of a kind often to be found in the mysticism of passion:

"Fuye, je n'en puis plus! D'un amant possédée,
Jalouse de mes fers,
Dans ses embrassements de plaisir inondee,
Moi-même je m'y perd."

A literary neurosis of this sort often underlies those distant adorations which recall the Platonic loves of the Middle Ages. There are many who are in love with actors or actresses whom they have never seen except in pictures. At the premature death of the film actor Rudolph Valentino, the Americans showed all the signs of a collective neurosis. At the lying-in-state of this "most beautiful man in the world" his feminine adorers were continually swooning. Such neurotics are not afraid of the ridiculous; many of the mourners carried onions hidden in their handkerchiefs with which to provoke rebellious tears. Ostentatious and provocative *mises en scene* of this kind are indeed among the characteristic signs of the neurosis in question. There are few neuroses which more easily reveal their sexual origin than those which thus take on a literary and mystic turn. Word and pen are themselves the best witnesses of this. "I have a need of tenderness and love which frightens me. This slender little body of mine contains inexhaustible riches which are suffocating me. On whom shall I bestow them? Who desires them?" This letter of the courtesan

Aimee Desclee, to the younger Dumas, was the reply of the times to the ardent cloistral exaltations of a Saint Theresa. But what is all this but the agonized cry of sexual torment which unsatisfied or repressed temperaments sometimes raise to heaven, a cry which makes the anchored tremble in his solitude?

There are some who go so far as to believe that repressed sexual needs, compelled to seek an outlet elsewhere, may find their "sublimation" in such appalling and catastrophic explosions as war. It is indeed difficult to deny that this latter institution has at certain moments appeared as though it were in some ways a more or less indispensable derivative of an intolerable social tension and malaise.The World War in 1914 brought to many a certain feeling of relief – in spite of the unknown disasters which fate might have in store for them. It put an end to that nervous strain which was the inevitable result of the lack of proper equilibrium in social conditions, and in its own terrible way it provided a single great channel of 'sublimation' for the hitherto frustrated energy. But we must be allowed to make a comment here. Those who need this sublimation are in lack of something; they require an object on which to direct their nervous energy; their lives have been rendered miserable by repression.They have become victims of their own submission to taboos, they are unable to escape from the all-devouring appetites of these Molochs, they are the slaves of our soul-destroying anti-sexual conventions. These are the people who turn hungrily to "sublimation," even in its most detestable and destructive form. It is they who let loose the catastrophe. If this is the case, such individuals ought to be regarded as peculiarly dangerous, both because of their obstinate and out of date insistence on primitive taboos, and because of their tendency to find such terrible substitutes for the natural functions of sex. Those, on the other hand, who are satisfied with the conditions under which they live – if by a happy combination of circumstances or by their own efforts, they have escaped the tyrannies of the taboo, and are thus able to live a full and happy life–have no need to seek any such far-fetched alternative outlet for their thwarted desires. The danger of sexual repression is that, in one way or another, it leads to an explosion, owing to the absence of an adequate safety valve.

(d) *Anglo-Saxon Neurosis.*—The psycho-analysts have carried out a series of very interesting investigations on the peoples of the West. Maeder, in particular, has studies the neuroses of the Anglo-Saxons; and indeed, as Laumonier has said, :of all peoples it is the English who should be among the first to arouse the curiosity of psycho-analysts, in virtue both of their conservatism and of their homogeneity." It is among the English, too, that we find modesty, or rather prudery, in its most striking development; and among them the Victorian era seems to have marked its climax. Here we are provided with ample material for studying the repression of the libido, both in its social and its individual forms. As R.L. Stevenson sadly remarked, there are many things an English author cannot say; in this respect he is far from enjoying the liberty of his French colleague. But this is not the place to study in detail the neurotic manifestations of the English, due to their intensely repressive education. We will only remark in passing that certain peculiar characteristics, such as those connected with flirting and with the extremer kind of feminism, seem in some of their aspects to be an outcome of the mania for sport. The psychoanalysts have dealt with all this, and we must refer the interested reader to their writings.

It is perhaps worth while, however, to say a few words about the American attitude in the same matter. The antisexual policy of North American society is perhaps even more inelastic than that of the Anglo-Saxons of the Old World, and, although this new race does not possess the ancient homogeneity of the British people, it is nevertheless one of the most profitable to study from the psycho-analytic point of view.

As we have already seen, the influence of Judeo-Christian doctrine has brought about a more or less general state of prohibition (there is scarcely any other suitable word, and this term is, as we know, customary in America) of all sexual relations outside marriage. It goes without saying that the neuroses due to sexual repression have every opportunity for a rich development in these conditions of permanent conflict between the libido and the exigencies of the law.The only remedy, one which was more or less forced upon society, lay in an increased facility both for marriage and divorce, thus permitting a sort of legal temporary union.

In the note that he made of his journey in the United States, Leandre Vaillat wrote: "The first thing to meet the eye on the table of our room in the hotel is an open Bible; the second a pair of bathing drawers.The former invites us to meditate on the Gospel for the day; the latter suggests that we should not forget our modesty in carrying out the duties of the toilet. We closed the Bible and threw the bathing drawers into the waste paper basket...." These Frenchmen are incorrigible! Nevertheless our traveller was justified in giving a place among his interesting notes to little matters of this kind, which many others would have rejected as of no importance. For they are of great significance for the psycho-analyst in the endeavour to understand the peculiar moral development of the American people, and the special mental attitude which this implies. From this ostentatious juxtaposition of the Holy Bible and the bathing drawers, psycho-analysis can draw two important conclusions with regard to the nature of the sexual neurosis; in the first place a proof of the close relation between the metaphysical taboo and the privative taboo on sex; in the second place a confirmation of the true obsessiveness of sexuality, an obsessiveness which manifests itself among the prohibitionists in an insistence on privation, just as it may manifest itself in others in the constant demand for satisfaction; though in the former case it reveals perhaps an even deeper and more persistent subjugation of the mind by sex. According to Judge Lindsey, the obsessiveness of sex is "one paramount evil in American civilization."

Is life better, healthier, or even longer, in a society so protected against itself that, except in the sacrosanct sphere of "business", the individuals are held in tutelage as though they are condemned to be for ever minors? If so, the system might be justified. But there is no escape from the inflexible laws of sexual neurosis. We may find an example of this in every case where public or private circumstances provide an opportunity; as at the death of Rudolph Valentino. North America strikes us by the gloominess of its moral outlook, from which escape is vainly sought in all kinds of artificial amusement. Coming to Europe, where sexual prohibitions have, in spite of everything, made some concessions to the claims of individual liberty, Americans confess that what impresses them most is our greater gaiety and cheerfulness; characteristics which are due to the relatively greater sexual liberty of the countries which have produced a Stendahl and a Casanova.

It is true that in the countries where sexual prohibitions flourish, there has been a clever attempt to compensate for the absence of sexual activities by an intensive development of sport—a necessity which has to a large extent been imposed upon these countries by sexual neurosis itself. In this way the nineteenth and twentieth centuries have given us an opportunity of studying a new method of substitution, as contrasted with the older methods of art and mysticism, which are co-eval with human though itself. This new method is no interesting that we may pause a moment to consider it.

Religious mysticism reigned without a rival in Western countries all through the Middle Ages and more recent times. It found its expression in triumphant Christianity. Then doubt began to arise, apparent already among the first "free thinkers" of the sixteenth century, and finally victorious in the eighteenth century. Freedom of thought has proved a formidable antagonist of faith; rationalism and materialism, not to speak of atheism, have become the garments in which much of human thought has been clothed. The first reforms introduced by these systems aimed at the toleration of free thought, thus assuring their own place in the sun, a place which would no longer be disputed, a place from which even religious proselytism has, as a matter of fact, been compelled to withdraw its claims.

But, though beaten in the field of metaphysics, this proselytism has not yet renounced its rights in the sphere of morals.The very persons who abandoned Judeo Christian metaphysics have remained enslaved to a corresponding system of morals, and above all to the essential feature of these morals, the antagonism to sex. Up to the time of the Freudian revolution, these morals were considered as a untouchable as were the metaphysics to an earlier generation; their justifiability was simply never called in question; the immorality of sex has been, and still is for many, a dogma, beyond all need of proof. Science and logic were for long denied the elementary right of showing that this view was wrong, wrong indeed on many points. The reactionaries redoubled their efforts to keep off the critical spirit from this field at least, and thus to preserve, if not the theory of sin itself, at least its consequences. Success here meant that the social aspects of human life could continue to be regulated in accordance with Judeo-Christian morals, which could be imposed even on those who had denied the metaphysics. It is this great effort, supported as it has been by considerable tactical skill, which is responsible for all that ethical propaganda, for all those legal reforms, which have characterized our civilization during the last hundred years, and which - to the astonishment and alarm of liberal minds - have led to the increasing domination of prudish busybodies and puritanical associations.

The question of substitution is one that also presents itself in this connexion. Casanova, master of love, would have had no time to lose over football; and record breaking would have had but few attractions for him. On the other hand such substitutes are essential to those societies which have declared war on sex. They have found them in the amazing development of sport, which empties the mind while fatiguing the muscles, which passes the time and arouses a certain superficial enthusiasm.And it is in the Anglo-Saxon societies, which have most whole-heartedly adopted the anti-sexual conventions, that sport has achieved its greatest triumphs. Neither have their women escaped; at any rate they have become active in entirely new directions, such as politics, business, medicine and law. In countries where they are assured a certain minimum of erotic liberty, women have no need of such substitutes, but remain faithful to the old tradition, which regarded love as the most important thing in life. This is doubtless the reason why in France, where women still enjoy great liberty, and prudery is less developed, we find that, if we except a small number of keen supporters with a well-wishing but by no means enthusiastic following, women themselves display only a very moderate degree of interest in feminism, a movement which has made such startling progress in all the more prohibitionistic societies.

But the result of all this effort has been very curious. It is true that, thanks to an education in sport which is at once enthusiastic and rational, the Americans hope in a few generations to produce the strongest and healthiest of human races. Nevertheless, we find their physiologists (Dr. Abraham Myerson, Head of the Department of Neurology in the Medical School of Boston; Dr. L.P. Clark, of New York, etc.) deploring the weakness of the human constitution in their country, and its inability to tolerate the conditions imposed by present-day civilization. Dr. Myerson has endeavoured to draw up a list of the causes responsible for this: "There is no doubt that our lives are too hurried for us to enjoy real pleasure or real culture; that we are over-stimulated; that our tastes are too luxurious; that we have too many pretences...." But also, we may be permitted to add, that we suffer from too many neuroses due to excessive prohibitions, which make life one long struggle for the individual against himself or against society. An American, in drawing the attention of Monsieur Paul Reynaud to "the nervous exhaustion, against which we find so many panaceas advertised on the bill boards," mentioned that a doctor of New Orleans had recently told him how surprised he was at the large number of men of forty or forty-five who had become impotent. The consequences of this rigorous prohibitionism are in accordance with the law of substitution: certain alternative channels must be found.Though sport may only be harmful to the intellectual development of the race, other substitutes may even endanger in physiological equilibrium; the report drawn up by the New York police, under the direction of their head, Mac Adoo, in 1927, concludes that the drug traffic in the United States is greater than that of any other country. The official insistence on chastity, and the serious neuroses that this brings in its train, are moreover from time to time punctuated by alarming half-insane explosions, in which sadism does not fail to play its part; as in the celebrated recent case of "Nelson the Gorilla," who had no less than eighteen violated and strangled girls to his credit, and in that of the complicated murder of a young girl, Marion Parker, at Los Angeles in 1927. Is not the key to all these mysteries to be found in outraged nature? Casanova lived till he was ninety....

The constant state of prohibition, of denunciation, of interference with private life, of strife, of public inquiry, which is characteristic of the American conception of sex, constitutes in itself a neurosis of very specific kind; a neurosis in which the mind is continually obsessed by sexual thoughts, the omnipotence of which is testified by the frantic efforts that are made to overcome them. As we know, the more serious the attach, the more strenuous is the defence. Quantitatively, the defence-neuroses have the same profound significance and value as the neuroses which give positive expression to the libido.

(e) *Prohibition Neurosis.*— Sexual prohibition in its collective form sometimes has unexpected results. Under the influence of the prohibitionistic attitude, certain European authorities have made considerable efforts to abolish prostitution in several ports of call in the Far East, and to place as many obstacles as possible in the way of sexual relations between foreigners and native women. They have succeeded to the extent that success is possible with measures of this particular kind.But the result is that at some of these ports the procurers are now offering "boys" to their visitors, in place of the "girls" who are too zealously guarded; Phryne proscribed has had to give place to Gnathon..... In the colonies of the Far East where sexual liberty has been much restricted, the resort to alcoholic drinks (not to speak of cocaine) has replaced the pleasures of sex – without any social gain in the exchange. In all these countries one is struck by a certain general atmosphere of gloom and boredom, which weighs upon the inhabitants and which can be dissipated neither by the excitements of sport nor by the deadening influence of whisky. One does not get this impression in China or Japan.

A remarkable instance of these collective neuroses, which are sometimes so serious as to lead to the actual disappearance of the race, is to be found in the Polynesian peoples of the Pacific archipelagoes, since the conquest and settlement of their islands by the Whities. It has made no difference which nation is the actual possessor in any given case (English, American, French, etc)., for everywhere the same causes have led to the same results. The Polynesian population is being decimated.We shall confine ourselves to quoting certain references without comment of our own.

According to the evidence of R.L. Stevension, 150 years of law and propaganda against the native habits and practices of Oceania have been much more efficacious than any artillery in bringing about the progressive disappearance of the native inhabitants.It is true that before the arrival of the whites these islanders were governed by taboos of their own, which were in no wise less absurd, tyrannical, or crippling than the superstitions of the West. But in most cases, at any rate, they still enjoyed great freedom in the moral sphere. It was here that they found their only real joy in life, expressed as this was in their costumes, in their songs and dances, and in sexual pleasure. The whites prohibited all this. "The Polynesian," writes R. L. Stevenson, "falls easily into despondency: bereavement, disappointment, the fear of novel visitations, the decay or proscription of ancient pleasures, easily incline him to be sad: and sadness detaches him from life. The melancholy of the Hawaiian and the emptiness of his new life are striking; and the remark is yet more apposite to the Marquesas... but in the lotus islands, with the decay of pleasures, life itself decays..... Upon the whole the problem seems to me to stand thus: where there have been fewest changes, important or unimportant, salutary or hurtful, there the race survives. Where there have been most, important or unimportant, salutary or hurtful, there it perishes... There may seem, a priori no comparison between the change from 'sour toddy' to bad gin, and that from then island kilt to a pair of European trousers. Yet I am far from persuaded that the one is any more harmful than the other; and the unaccustomed race will sometimes die of pin-pricks. We are here face to face with one of the difficulties of the missionary. In Polynesian islands he easily obtains pre-eminent authority; the king becomes his *maire du palais;* he can proscribe, he can command, and the temptation is ever, toward too much. Thus (by all accounts) the Catholics in Mangarava, thus (to my own knowledge) the Protestants in Hawaii, have rendered life in a more or less degree unlivable to their converts. And the mild, uncomplaining creatures (like children in a prison) yawn and await death... Experience begins to show us (at least in Polynesian islands) that change of habit is bloodier than bombardment...."

Elsewhere R.L. Stevenson has told us: "The mind of the female missionary tends to be continually busied about dress. She can be taught with extreme difficulty to think any costume decent but that to which she grew accustomed on Clapham Common." Even the use of tobacco, and of tattooing, which means so much to the native, is prohibited.Such peoples' minds are stuffed with Bible stories; in the true Anglo-Saxon manner they spend their lives with the Israelites of the Old and New Testament; hostile sects come into being, and the archipelago of the Paumotus is divided between Catholics and Mormons. The ancestral taboos have been succeeded by the taboos of the West, not a whit inferior in narrow-mindedness or incoherance. The Kind of the Gilbert Islands, who believes in keeping the Sabbath, refused to be photographed on that day. With a zeal that is natural and not difficult to understand, the neophytes show themselves even more rigorous than their masters; as in the case of Maka, who came from Hawaii to catechize the inhabitants of the Gilbert Islands, and who, according to Stevenson, "showed much severity in the repression of innocent pleasures".

Gauguin reports that in Tahiti, in the beginning, the missionaries "branded certain women with the sign of infamy, a threat of hell," by tattooing a Latin letter on the cheek. We need only call to mind the very free habits noted by the first navigators to New Cythera to realize what a deadly social revolution was here involved.In this twentieth century a French author is still able to write: The inhabitants of the Marquesas are dying out. This country, which as recently as 1850 had a population of thirty thousand, to-day has at most two or three thousand. The natives are dying of tuberculosis, of syphilis, and of the general lack of interest in life which is a result of the French administration."A congress of the Protestant missions held in Sydney in 1927 similarly came to the conclusion that, if the present mortality among the natives continued (in spite of the fact that they have all the advantages of Western hygiene), the race would be extinct in twenty years... The invasion of Oceania by the whites will thus have been anything but beneficial to the inhabitants themselves, who have led a miserable existence, harassed by the inevitable neuroses, which in the case of their own race are resulting in premature extinction – the consequence of an intensive campaign against the sexual life. The whites, however, are like people who have become inured to poison, a quantity which would be fatal to others does not suffice to kill them.But the contact of Western civilization with races leading more natural lives throws a startling light on the degree of habituation and resistance which is necessary before such deadly does can be tolerated tion in life itself, which we should be wrong to confuse with resignation.

The same difference can be observed in the behaviour of women who have sexual relations with men outside of marriage. In the West these relations constitute, especially from the Judeo-Christian point of view, the very essence of sin; even among those who have thrown off the yoke of Christian metaphysics, a sort of ethical atavism still ensures the persistence of this idea in some degree. Western woman tries to resist what she calls a "fall". For the sake of decency she will regard such conduct as shameful; with real or affected confusion she will say to the man who has just become her lover: "How you must despise me!" Nothing of all this is to be found in women of other races, unless their natural logic has been distorted by this particular ethical system. To give herself is for her a normal and healthy act, over which she makes no unnecessary delay; she accomplishes the act without embarrassment; she neither regrets it nor blushes for it; the pleasure consummated, she feels herself the equal of her partner, happy in a joy that they have shared, and proud of having been able to procure this joy. Such was once the state of mind in Tahiti. It is still to be found in certain countries, and should serve as a precious guide of what we can achieve by a healthy attitude to physiological facts. Here there is no neurotic trouble to disturb the mind; indeed we experience a certain pleasure and relief in the mere contemplation of such conditions.

To these normal and, we may add, happy peoples the Western races have been generous enough to bring the two terrible gifts of syphilis, which had been hitherto unknown, and sexual neurosis. The earliest travellers were delighted at the charming state of affairs that they discovered: Tahiti was baptized the New Cythera, and Cook wept on the deck of his ship when he was obliged to leave the island.But presently there came the educators, obsessed by the superiority of Western ethics; it never even occurred to them to make an impartial comparison between the two moral codes, since they considered that their own had been given them by divine "revelation". For this anomaly of simple happiness obtained by merely following the laws of nature, these pedagogues substituted (by force or persuasion) the whole system of their Western ethics, including the Judeo-Christian doctrine of sin and the nervous disorders that result therefrom. When they came up against strongly organized cultures., they produced little impression, and there resulted little change; this was the case in China and Japan. But small defenceless groups, such as those in the Polynesian archipelagoes, were almost entirely at their mercy, and the result, as we know, has been decisive and deplorable.

Countries which enjoy sexual liberty are free of sexual neurosis; we may even say that they are free of the *crime passionel* so common in the West; but this is a matter which we shall study in another place. As we have said, travellers are astonished at the happy life of these countries; the foundation of this happiness lies in the ease with which the sexual act can be accomplished and the absence of moral associations in regard to it. We may even state the matter in the form of a general law to the effect that the happiness of a society is in direct proportion to the rights enjoyed by the inhabitants to indulge in sexual acts a law which we shall do well to bear in mind, if we wish to understand the true meaning of human life.

Individual Types that are Exempt from Sexual Neurosis as a Result of their Deliberate Rejection of Repression.— Morals, as a code for governing conduct, have no meaning without that psychological aspect of morality that we call conscience; morals without conscience would be just as absurd as laws that are in manifest contradiction to the established habits of the people concerned. But what is conscience? Freud defines it as "the inner perception of objections to definite wish impulses that exist in us; but the emphasis is put upon the fact that this rejection does not have to depend on anything else, that it is sure of itself." From this we can see at once that in order to retain its mastery, or more strictly speaking in order to continue its existence at all, conscience must refuse to discuss the reasons why certain desires have to be repudiated. It must insist in regarding these reasons, even when they are not understood, as no less cogent than those which underlie taboo; which, it will be remembered, were treated as indisputable,were as a matter of fact never called in question, and were in many cases really beyond all understanding.

Ethical principles can thus only live in virtue of a very general consensus of opinion. Whence can they obtain the necessary strength for this? From two sources only: either the social state is such that no one thinks or dares to discuss the principles in question, in which case it matters little whether the principles are reasonable or not (just as with taboo); or else the principles themselves are so logical and reasonable that everybody will agree to them, even in a society which has arrived at a mental level where everything can be, and is, subject to discussion. But if one of these conditions is lacking, if, for example, an ethical principle, which has neither reason, logic nor scientific evidence upon its side, happens to come across a society, which is accustomed to weight its values and submit them to a critical examination, it is not likely to survive for long. People will treat it as we to-day treat so many taboos that seemed indisputable to primitive man, but which do not make us hesitate even for an instant, so childish do they now appear.

This is what has been happening for some time to the ethical principles connected with sex. They have been studied closely; and in the face of this pitiless examination they have put up but a poor show of resistance. When we ask of them the scientific and logical reasons for their existence, they can only reply to us in terms of taboo – a miserable line of defence in this modern world. At the very best they will find ranged against them the growing army of rational thinkers, who will deny that they have any value, or will at any rate demand a thorough and complete revision of the foundations upon which they stand.

From now onwards, ethical principles must take into account a large new class of individual, who, intellectually acute and in no wise neurotic, have on their own initiative submitted the traditional morality of sex to a severe and critical examination, have not been satisfied with this simple answer of "taboo", and continue to demand arguments stated in logical and scientific terms. If such arguments are not forthcoming, they will consider these moral principles as no more justified than the taboos that are already overthrown. Their own principles will make them hostile, or at least indifferent, to the old forms of censorship and repression; once they are truly convinced, they may even work for the destruction of these barriers or repression, which they will look upon as nothing more than fraud or trickery. They will arrange to live their lives without these artificial obstacles; both their principles and their conduct will be in contradiction with the present rules of sex. And this will not be in consequence of neurosis, but as a result of deliberate reflection. Psycho-analysts will have still another reason for calling attention to the fact that many persons who indulge in homosexuality, onanism, etc., are not necessarily or especially neurotic; they will understand better why it is that these liberties with the present ethical code are often taken by persons of high intellectual standing; it is just because these persons are capable of realizing the falsity of the prevalent ethical principles, principles which less active minds continue to take for granted, and therefore to approve. In truth, a very simple phenomenon; analogous moreover to one with which we are already familiar in modern times. There are to-day many people who have been brought up in a particular religious faith, but who at a certain age submitted this faith to a critical examination and thereupon rejected its precepts, which played no part in the remainder of their lives.

Chapter-9

The Mechanistic Theory of Sexuality in its Relation to Morals

Chapter 9

Inadequacy of the Ethical Aspects of Psycho-analysis. — When we study the work of Professor Freud - so truly remarkable and so essential for our present purpose - we are forced at the end to the following conclusion: that, having started from the treatment of neurotic patients, he has remained throughout, above all other things, a student of medicine, and that, although a psychologist of genius, he has only become so, as it were, secondarily and incidentally (by this we mean that his doctrine, known under the name of psycho-analysis, has been erected entirely on the foundation of his clinical observations); and finally, that he has taken but little interest in the problems of the ethical philosopher, since he has not drawn from his data the logical conclusions which moral science has the right to expect.

Freud observed among his nervous patients — even among those whose trouble did not seem to have a sexual origin — an acute conflict between sexual desire and the various privations caused by taboo; and this led him to a closer examination of this continually recurring source of trouble. As a result he concluded that even among those whom the terrible struggle had not reduced to such straits as to require the attention of a specialist, the mental conflict was still present, though in a less acute form, as a consequence either of a more easy-going temperament or of a greater strength of the censorship produced by education. This *should* have led Freud to certain *practical* conclusions opposed to the morals of taboo. It should have led him to recommend a much greater liberty in the exercise of the sexual sense, as a means of remedying this tendency to neurosis. But the theoretical conclusions of psycho-analysis, as we shall see, are far from being as clear upon this matter as they might be.

Criterion of Normal and Abnormal Sexual States. —

Disease is an abnormal condition. It is easy to recognize abnormal states in the purely physiological sphere: as a rule the patient is only too glad to call in the doctor to talk about them. But as soon as we pass from physiological to psychological conditions the distinction is much more difficult, except of course in obvious disturbances such as mania or delirium.

Nevertheless, there is a thread to guide us through this labyrinth, the same moreover which serves us in the case of physiology. A condition is normal if it is in harmony with the laws of nature, if, instead of contradicting these laws, it makes use of them, even though it be in a brutal or cynical way. A condition is abnormal if it is based upon a denial, a reversal, or a misunderstanding, of these laws. A patient is ill if his physiological or psychological functions are contrary to organic laws. On the other hand, he is not necessarily diseased because he behaves in a way that is contrary to a *social convention*: in this case we must first determine whether the convention itself is in harmony or disharmony with nature. In the latter event, we must surely realize that he who denies the convention, far from being ill, is nearer to psycho-physiological truth than those who criticize him because he does not observe the convention.

Applying this criterion to the laws of sex, our problems immediately become much clearer. In an earlier chapter of this book we drew attention to the essential difference between the function of reproduction on the one hand and the sexual sense upon the other — both of them legitimate, and both imperious in their demands. We dwelt upon their purely physiological, natural, and a-moral character. We saw that they were objective mechanisms of the same kind as respiration and digestion; no more complicated than these, until the human brain began to twist and torture their meaning and surround them with all sorts of artificial conventions. In the light of these considerations we must now ask how we are to distinguish between health and disease, between the normal and the abnormal.

A mind that was not dominated by thousands of years of anti-sexual taboo would have no difficulty in answering this question, and in making the necessary distinctions without resort to any superfluous psychiatrical complications. Such a person would say :

(a) That the exercise of the sexual organ for the avowed purpose of procuring sexual pleasure, and ultimately also for the purpose of reproduction, is natural, normal, proper, legitimate, and indeed necessitated by the demands of our constitution.

(b) That failure to exercise these organs, as a consequence either of voluntary abstention or of external circumstance (chastity, legal prohibition, etc.), is, on the contrary, an artificial, abnormal, unhealthy, and unpleasant state.

(c) That sexual pleasure, the immediate aim of sexual activity, is obtained through an appropriate mechanism. This mechanism presents certain variations; but, so far as the general principle is concerned, and except for possible differences in the degree of pleasure obtained, it is independent of the quality (and, above all, of the moral value) of the methods or the partners employed for setting it in action; it can function just as well without a partner (as in onanism), or with any kind of partner (as in homosexuality or incest).

These laws are indisputable, since they represent physiological conclusions. They are also sufficient, since they permit of the complete and satisfactory realization of the normal aims of sexuality. All else is a matter of intellectual and aesthetic appreciation, or of social convention, and has nothing to do with the physiology or logic of the sexual mechanism. This much established, there can be no doubt that the person who conforms to these laws and applies them to his own life without allowing himself to be deterred by any mere conventions must be regarded as normal. He is not a pathological case. If the word pathological has any meaning, the abnormal and the pathological are those who set themselves up against these laws: those who, under the influence of artificial conventions (only too often accepted quite uncritically), oppose the natural working of these laws, either in themselves or others.

The Errors of Psychiatry in the Field of Sex. — It is here that we come across the great error of this relatively new science, which is still in its infancy and burdened with a heritage of many centuries of false ideas: the science of psychiatry, which proposes to study the disorders of the mind. A very worthy science, so long as it keeps strictly to its role, confining its attention to those who are really ill, and not endeavouring to classify as such those who are most certainly not ill. A doctor, when he is called in to see a patient, should not a *priori* jump to the conclusion, merely on the strength of a report from the patient or his family, that he is necessarily in the presence of a pathological case. There exist *malades imaginaires,* whose relatives, blind to the real condition of affairs, foster the patients' delusions concerning their condition. The first duty of the doctor is to make sure whether a patient is really ill or not, and, in the latter case, not to treat him as a patient, but by all the means in his power to enlighten him as to his true condition.

Unfortunately, psychiatry has completely failed in this most elementary duty. It has unquestioningly accepted society's pronouncement to the effect that a given individual is ill, and has eagerly set out to "cure" him. As between the natural, physiological and scientific conception of the sexual act (as we have already described it), and the artificial conception adopted by society on the basis of taboo and of an arbitrary (though constantly changing) standard of moral values, psychiatry has not hesitated for an instant; nor has it ever been in doubt as to the relative approval it should bestow upon the normal man, who lives in conformity with the natural conception of sex, and the abnormal man, who of his own accord or through necessity refuses to adopt it, and endeavours to oppose his own physiological functions. Influenced by a thousand obscure and unavowed motives, psychiatry has sided with the social conventions, and has therefore inevitably changed the natural roles, reversed the usual terminology of medicine, and looked upon those who do not conform to the conventional rules as being abnormal and therefore pathological.

In this field psychiatry had, and still has, a great task to perform. It should refuse to bow down before the diagnosis of society, as it had done, but should, on the contrary, start by examining the accuracy of this diagnosis. It should say: where there is a simple application of the laws of nature there is no disease; and the best proof of this is that the unnatural conventions of society have eventually resulted in the sexual neuroses which oppress "civilized" peoples. There would be no question of neurosis, repression (a word which itself indicates an artificial pressure against natural acts), or disease, if natural laws had not been transgressed. In a word, the so-called "abnormals" are not abnormal when judged according to the *laws of nature.* They are only abnormal when judged according to *social conventions,* which is by no means the same thing. It is indeed so far from being the same that the physician will find himself compelled to reverse his diagnosis, and to admit that the case of illness are really to be found among those who, through observing — willingly or otherwise — the dictates of society, have so far removed themselves from the laws of nature that they have utterly lost sight of them, misunderstood them, and denied them, and have ended by achieving their own downfall by neurosis. For it is not possible to deny natural laws with impunity. Conversely, medical science will have to recognize that those who have deliberately infringed the rules of abstinence, and have treated their own sexual desires with tolerance and freedom, are, as individuals, much the happier and better and balanced, both physiologically and psychologically: they have saved themselves the torture of denying nature; they have allowed nature to enjoy her rights. To such people the life dictated by convention, in which artificial scruples and prohibitions are continually tormenting both body and mind, seems no better than a dark and narrow prison, in which they themselves would very soon have succumbed to illness or to death.

It would seem therefore that current sexual ethics has been guilty of a complete reversal of values. Moreover, the happiness, and perhaps the very existence of humanity, confined as it is more and more in the stifling atmosphere of this prison, imperatively demand a full exposure of the true nature and consequences of this reversal.

It is easy to see the general objections that will be raised by the psychiatrists: those who have less resistance, it will be said, are ill without knowing it, and it is just because they are diseased and abnormal that they construct their theory of sexual liberty and live up to it. This is a very specious objection; but we cannot be deceived by it for a moment. We believe that in our earlier chapters we have adequately shown that such an argument ignores all the teachings of the psycho-physiological analysis of the individual *as he is,* and not as our conventional education would like him to appear. As between nature and convention, psychiatry always sides with convention, and brands the natural as "the abnormal." Starting from this disloyalty to its own scientific premises, psychiatry soon becomes blind to all logical conclusions.

It is here that we are made to realize the full significance of the data collected by the psycho-analysts, as well as of those further observations recorded at the beginning of this book on the sexual manifestations of children and races who have not been the victims of an intense repression. The decisive importance of these observations, which at this point serve us in good stead, consists in showing that *many sexual manifestations which the anti-sexual moralists and psychiatrists regard as pathological are really in strict conformity with nature. The Greeks, the Romans and many civilizations of the East and Far East have shown themselves superior in so far as they have not committed this grave error, an error which has poisoned the whole sexual ethics of modern Western culture.* This allows us also to reply to the complaints of those who pretend that such observers as Freud or Lindsey have a tendency to look at everything from the sexual point of view, and thus to misinterpret the facts. In truth, these authors are guilty of no misinterpretation, but only of greater experience and acuter observation. But there is misinterpretation, and of a terrible kind, in the refusal to look at nature just because her manifestations have the impertinence not to fit into the frame of preconceived commandments.

The General Consequences of these Errors. — There are some diseases of which the causes are well known. What does the physician do in these cases? He explains the cause, with a view to preventing their recurrence. If he is treating an alcoholic or an opium addict, he shows the patient that alcohol or opium is at the basis of the trouble, and he forbids the further use of these substances. If he is treating a diabetic, he prepares a regime, in which everything which would prolong or renew the trouble is carefully excluded. Nothing could be more logical than this; but when it is a question of treating the sexual neuroses, we immediately come across one of the many striking illogicalities which are so frequently met with in the sphere of sex; for we find that here the doctors are in the habit of adopting an exactly opposite procedure.

The sexual neuroses are produced by repression and by the whole mental attitude which regards the sexual acts with disfavour and circumsribes them with prohibitions. They represent, in fact, nature's revenge on man for the adoption of this attitude: a revenge of the same kind as she would take on anyone who attempted to deprive himself of food and drink. The whole present system of sexual prohibition results in physical ill, in moral discomfiture, and in social complication. This being the case, the natural course would be to demand a revision of the system of sexual morality which has had such painful and such dangerous consequences. The evil should be attacked at its root, and when the causes have been abolished, the neurosis should itself disappear.

But the psychiatrists, far from adopting such a course, do the very opposite: they attack nature and do all they can to retain and foster the disease. In their eyes nature is wrong and is itself abnormal. They assume that our artificial conventions must be retained at whatsoever cost, and they therefore persist in regarding as diseased those who in reality merely have the courage to be themselves, and to live according to the light of nature. It is here, we may be sure, that the all-powerful taboo has *ab ovo* crushed the whole spirit of scientific inquiry and rational thought. We are indeed face to face with one more demonstration of the difficulty which the human mind has in seeing its own errors, especially when these errors lie at the roots of powerful and passionately defended dogmas.

We are now in a position to see how wrong in principle are the psychiatrists who insist on looking upon the sources of sexual desire (the mightiest of our instinctive forces) as though they were dealing with the causes of a disease or an anomaly. They insist on assuming the existence of a conflict between sexual desire and a supposed reality which is in contradiction with this desire. The desire is supposed to be abnormal, while the pseudo-reality—composed, as we know to our cost, of sexual anaesthesia, impotence, abstinence, chastity and conspiracies of silence—is looked upon as normal. They then proceed to examine the internal secretions — the importance of which we freely admit — in the hope of finding toxic factors which will explain the presence of desires which are recognized as very powerful, but which are nevertheless always held to be abnormal. Their interpretation is in fact a complete reversal of the truth.

It is true there is a conflict, a conflict indeed of so acute a nature that it leads to a neurosis. But if the conflict is between the normal and the abnormal, we must realize that it is the sexual desire itself which is normal, and its suppression or prohibition which is abnormal; the source of the evil must be sought in our own conventional taboos and not in nature.

Extension of Psychiatric Errors to the So-called Sexual Aberrations. — In the next chapter we propose to examine the various sexual acts, which, in the language of psychiatrists, are usually called "aberrations." We must, however, realize, once and for all, that this term, like the corresponding word "perversion," is only an unstatisfactory linguistic expression of the general error committed by the psychiatrists in their interpretation of sexual phenomena.

The traditional view of psychiatry is that all sexual acts other than coitus between persons of the opposite sex are "aberrations," a category which , therefore, includes such important manifestations as onanism and homosexuality.It should scarcely be necessary to show that such classification is only possible in virtue of a total lack of scientific discrimination between the function of reproduction and the sense of sexual pleasure. There is thus an all-important error at the very start. For the view in question condemns all exercise of the sense *when unaccompanied by the function* — a position which implies a total misunderstanding of the autonomy of the sense of sexual pleasure, as expounded in an earlier chapter of this book. The confusion in question is quite blatant, as when for instance Dr. Paul says: "among persons especially liable to the diseases of love and to the deformations of the corresponding instinct, are those who, instead of considering love as a means, look upon it as an end, as a source of pleasure." This is precisely the doctrine of the prohibitionists, who look upon love as nothing but a means of reproduction.

We should point out at once that these theories are often stated in such a grotesquely exaggerated form that their weakness and absurdity immediately become apparent. Their upholders tend to see degeneration in everything; thus they will even regard "a disposition towards poetry or music" as an indication of "a profound hereditary affection of the nervous system"! In Lombroso we find a tendency to look upon originality as itself a manifestation, or at least as an important sign of mental anomaly.He forgets, for example, that the social unit of the family is after all only one particular form of the human group, and that other groups can be both scientifically conceived and actually shown to exist; and having done this, he regards the absence of attachment to the family (which, incidentally, he confuses with the capacity for "affection") as a proof, or at least an indication, of mental unbalance. Systems of this kind lead the alienists and Lombroso in particular, to open the doors of their asylums astonishingly wide. If we follow those theories, we shall soon be finding "half insane" people everywhere, which is equivalent to finding them nowhere, and is detrimental to the establishment of a more scientific criterion; for, amazing as it is, even Platonic love meets with no mercy at the hands of these experts, who classify it as a special aberration under the title of "erotomania"!

It is possible to provide the clinician with certain *very rare* cases as clearly pathological as the gastro-enteritis or scarlet fever: the nymphomaniacs, for instance, belong to this category, as do also the true paranoiacs, who may commit very definite acts of persecution in the erotic sphere, just as other paranoiacs, may be guilty of homicide or suicide under the influence of revenge, melancholia or mysticism; the erotic manifestations of maniacal excitement similarly fall within this group. But apart from cases of this kind, a careful examination of the so-called aberrations immediately reveals the fact that they are of such universal occurrence, and are indeed, as we feel tempted to say, so natural, that if we insist on retaining this point of view we must at least admit that these supposed "abnormalities" are just as widespread the "normal" phenomena of sex.

Let us take a rapid glance at two of the most frequently mentioned of these supposed aberrations.

Onanism was openly practised in many ancient communities. In one or other of its very numerous forms, either individually or *d deux*, it is prevalent throughout modern society. Indeed, we shall be perfectly safe in asserting that, on account of the ease and security of the practice, there are far more cases of onanism than of coitus.The embarrassment manifested by the upholders of taboo in trying to understand and explain how it is that onanism, regarded by them as an "unnatural" act, is nevertheless just as frequent as the essentially normal act, quite as commonplace as coitus itself, provides an amusing and instructive spectacle of the blindness suffered by the human mind as a result of its enslavement to convention. After having made a profession of faith in the strictest prohibitionistic terms, and after having exhibited a total ignorance of the distinction between sexual sense and sexual function, Dr. P. Garnier, in his monograph upon the subject, feels compelled to write on the matter with a certain melancholy as follows:"When we bear in mind that at certain periods and among certain people onanism had become so habitual as to be regarded as commonplace, even in those manifestations of it which are looked upon to-day as shameful, degrading or illegal, we may be tempted to wonder whether at bottom it is not merely a more hypocritical attitude of modern civilization which makes us look upon this practice as a guilty and pathological perversion. . . ." Left in the lurch both by history and present fact, by logic, physiology and social science, the upholders of taboo find themselves compelled to pronounce a solemn curse, without being able to put forward any grounds for doing so; and in this they are of course acting in the best traditions of taboo.

History tells in the homosexuality too has always existed in human societies. Many children are at first homosexual, often as a consequence of not understanding the differences between the sexes. Greek and Roman antiquity, not to speak of Sodom, accorded an important place to homosexuality, and in practice recognized it as legitimate. "Homosexuality became so general in some communities that it was considered a disgrace if a young man did not have a male lover." In China, the book *Tsin-pi-mei* speaks of pederasty with brothers, father and grandfather. To a superficial observer, homosexuality might appear to be relatively less developed in modern societies, so far at least as men are concerned; a deeper study shows that this is not the case. We may refer the reader to what Freud had said on this point in the first of his *Three Contributions to the Theory of Sex* apart from this, we may confine ourselves to a quotation from a contemporary publication, reserved and conservative in tone, which says that "formerly only veiled and passing allusions were made to this subject, but since 1914, the date in which Baron de Charlus appeared in the works of Marcel Proust, the subject of inversion has been treated in contemporary literature with amazing effrontery.'

History also, as we have already indicated, shows the falsity of the theory which would regard all such phenomena as aberrations. Indeed, if we insist upon looking at them as aberrations, the exceptions would be so numerous as altogether to overwhelm and annihilate the rule. We should have to regard as abnormal whole populations of the ancient world, who had but little interest in this kind of sexual restriction. Onanism alone is so widespread that, if it is a morbid aberration, almost the whole of humanity would have to be shut up in asylums. . . .

We must insist on settling this point: we must decide whether, just to please our psychiatrists, we are going to look upon everybody, or very nearly everybody, as mentally deranged; whether we are going to believe that we are, one and all of us, descended from demented societies—since our ancestors undoubtedly indulged widely in sexual practices which modern society regards as symptomatic of dementia. Common sense of course rebels against any such interpretation. "Everyday experience has shown that most of these transgressions, at least the milder ones, are seldom wanting as components in the sexual life of normals *who look upon them in exactly the same way as they do upon other intimacies*." These are words of good sense; if our taboo had had a little more respect for private life, it is probable that we should not to-day be so wildly at sea in all our ethical ideas on sex; there would be no need to make the formidable efforts that are now necessary to reduce our topsy-turvy theories to some sort of order—and illustration of the truth that it is essential that the rights of the individual should be preserved in every scheme of social co-operation, if this scheme is really going to work.

On the other hand, if sexual practices such as onanism of inversion were really abnormal aberrations, it is almost certain that the subject won presents these symptoms would reveal other pathological characteristics of a general nature. But this is not the case.Freud tells us that "homosexuality is found also among persons whose capabilities are not disturbed, who on the contrary are distinguished by especially high intellectual development and ethical culture." Exactly the same is true of onanism.

But what are the findings of the psychiatrists themselves? "In spite of the backwardness of pathological anatomy in the field of psychiatry," writes Pierre-Kahn in 1927, "the gradual development of our knowledge points to the conclusion that there are no psychic troubles without cerebral lesions." Wise words this time, expressed with a caution indicating the truly scientific spirit. But now we must choose. If the patient is not really ill, it is because his supposed aberrations are nothing more than normal variations of the sexual sense, which, like the other senses, exhibit all sorts of individual preferences and peculiarities; in fact these variations, which it has been customary to look upon as aberrations, are physiologically normal. It is only often they had been deliberately branded with a moral stigma that the theory which regards them as unnatural and degenerate was invented for the express purpose of justifying the stigma. The trouble to which the psychiatrists have gone to explain the normal in terms of the abnormal, nature in terms of convention, health in terms of mental disease, is scarcely to be believed. To get an idea of the extent of their efforts, the reader must study the works dealing with the sexual psychoses; he will find that this solemn science is capable of giving much quiet amusement to the philosophically minded. The distinctive method of its system is that every time it comes across a natural act that is contrary to the prevailing conventions, it brands this act as a symptom of mental derangement of abnormality. All the consequences of this act, as natural as the act itself but of course no less unconventional, are likewise classed as morbid.

A particularly striking achievement of this kind is the definition of a group of persons who have been labelled "conscious degenerates, " among whom are included certain persons who are hostile to the idea of sexual repression, and who, "far from endeavouring to keep away the harmful obsession, welcome it and cherish it: with whom the will not only fails in its function of exercising the supreme moral control, but itself a victim to the morbid and perverted process, uses its power for the purpose of co-ordinating the other faculties, with view to the complete execution of the abnormal act so ardently desired."

In a word, this system does not ask whether the disharmony between an individual and our social conventions can be explained on the ground that the conventions are open to objection and are in fact objected to; still less does it pause to consider whether the objection itself may not be a sign of a healthy tendency on the part of such an individual to obey the laws of nature. No, it is much more convenient to look upon him as a pathological case and to use all the ingenuities of dialectic to explain how it is that he may at the same time be in the possession of all his faculties: may indeed often exhibit the signs of an unusually brilliant intellect. The system clearly reeks of social conservatism, a quality that may be necessary in little groups, struggling painfully for their existence: but one which affords but tottering support in an age of free inquiry, in which many people, unlike the docile psychiatrist, insist on carefully examining the acts in question, together with their *raison d'etre*, before joining in whole-hearted condemnation of those who practise them.

But psychiatry has gone even further than this in its object and unconditional surrender to taboo. Without any attempt at verification it has accepted at their face value many of the prejudices and superstitions which have resulted from taboo. There exists a whole group of neuroses based upon fantastic and utterly unscientific notions; quite a considerable portion of humanity lives and has its being in a world that is peopled by illusory and imaginary entities –gods, prophets, saints, angels, devils, demons, ghosts – with whom they have daily converse, whom they call upon for help or counsel, whom they bribe or curse or worship, for whose sake they are ready to ruin both themselves and their families. Here, then, there is a formidable neurosis, which (unlike the manifestations of sex) is incapable of explanation in terms of normal, natural, easily verifiable, healthy processes. It is a neurosis that has sprung fully armed from its parent, the human brain. A triumph of artifact, it yet eludes the probing analysis of the psychiatrists, and almost entirely escapes their disapproval, pitiless as this may be in other directions.... So discreet a choice shows the measure of confidence that we may have in the pronouncements of this science!

The Attitude of Psycho-analysis to the Errors of Psychiatry. — It is unfortunate that psycho-analysis has not taken up a more definite attitude in dealing with this conflict, but has, on the contrary, shown a regrettable tendency to follow in the old false paths. The key to the whole conflict lies, as we know, first in the distinction between the function of reproduction and the sexual sense, and secondly in the fact that, so far as the activities of the sexual sense are concerned, one mechanism is as good as another, provided the desired satisfaction is attained. But a mechanism is in its very nature a moral, and we obtain a totally wrong conception of it if we place it in the category of moral values. Every time that psycho-analysis, in its pathological and therapeutic discussions, uses the word "perversions" to designate certain sexual manifestations of whatsoever kind, it contradicts the whole spirit of its own conclusions and discoveries, and is guilty of the old errors of the psychiatrists.

This is all the more astonishing in that, in one of the more recent developments of his doctrine, Professor Freud himself has been led to identify the libido (i.e. the sum total of the sexual desires) with the whole tendency towards life, in opposition to the "ego instincts", which tend ultimately towards death, i.e. (to employ what is doubtless a better expression of the same idea) tend to abandon the complicated, short-lived, unstable equilibrium that constitutes human life, and to reduce it once again to its chemical and material elements. It is true that this view is still open to criticism, but that does not alter the fact that, according to this theory, libido is an essential manifestation of the vital force.And if this is so, we are led to the conclusion that the sexual desires are so potent, just because they are essential factors of life, of health – in a word, of nature. And how are we to reconcile their healthy intensity with the view that regards their powerful urge as pathological, their incessant demands as aberrations, and the people who obey these demands as crazy or perverted? Life consists in living according to nature; and those who attempt to find the meaning of life in the feeble, fleeting, changeable conventions of human society, at the mercy of every new fashion in social organization or metaphysical superstition, will never understand the true significance of life.

Furthermore, Freud has propounded a theory of the sexual object, a theory elaborated with all the skill and care that are characteristic of his scientific work. But, as we should expect, he is compelled by his experience of sexuality as revealed to him by psycho-analysis, to admit that the "object" is in its very nature variable, and at its best possesses but a secondary importance. The great psycho-analyst could, indeed, scarcely have come to any other conclusion as regards a point so fundamental.He has written: "A point which seems to me of basic significance is that, in many circumstances and for a surprising number of individuals, the nature and value of the sexual object plays a secondary role. This compels us to the conclusion that the object itself is not the essential and constant element of the sexual tendency." Let us bear in mind these weighty words; we shall have need of them a little later, when we ourselves attempt to put forward a positive theory of sexuality.

As a result of his well-known and detailed study of infantile sexuality, Freud comes to the conclusion that "the sexuality of the perversions is nothing else that infantile sexuality, magnified and decomposed into its various specific elements'. But, having said this, the master psycho-analyst soon found himself the object of violent reproaches from those who followed the traditional view of sex. "you consider therefore," it was said, "that the child is by very definition, a perverse being! And indeed you cannot deny this, since you have yourself in another place called the child a 'polymorphous prevert.'" The reproach is here quite justified, and this is due to the fact that Freud, in spite of his observations which threw so much light upon the subject, felt himself obliged to retain the terms "perverse" and "perversion". Having decided to keep them, he was compelled to apply them to the child, since they are the conventional terms applied to certain acts which are carried out by the child. We know that this is not what he should have said. He ought to have said: "the fact that these acts are carried *out naturally* by the child compels us to the view that such acts are not "perversions": the term in question is one which has been wrongly attached to these acts when they were performed by the adult." To say, under these circumstances, that "the child naively asserts his rights to carry out *abnormal* practices and shows at every moment that the way of purity is as yet totally unknown to him " is clearly to employ a faulty terminology.

We know, of course, what Freud means by the "fixation" of a sexual tendency (the fact of a "component instinct" failing to pass beyond a certain phase of development, which should normally have been outgrown) and by "regression" (the return to an earlier phase of development). But who does not see that these earlier phases are nearer to the infantile condition, nearer to the state of nature? It is true that, from the point of view of taboo, these fixations and regressions are reprehensible; but from the point of view of physiology they are no more than a return to a state more natural than that which an artificial sexual education has failed to establish as a permanent condition.

The Essentially Artificial Character of Censorship and Repression.—This much granted, it will perhaps not seem very surprising if we raise an objection to the manner in which psycho-analysts have represented their fundamental theory of repression. The possibility of this objection has not escaped them, but, owing probably to the purely medical origins of their science, they have failed to realize its true importance. Psycho-analysis, a method of treatment for patients whose condition is due to an education in contradiction with the principles of nature, has observed here and there a weakening of the habitual resistance due to censorship and repression. But it regards these instances of weakened resistance as blemishes which should be cured. It adopts the vocabulary of taboo: it speaks of "sexual perversion," when it observes that repression has diminished and that the natural needs are reasserting themselves; it provides excellent treatment for those who are neurotic, but, instead of admitting that they are the victims of a conflict between taboo and nature, it accepts all too easy the view that they are abnormal just because they are in rebellion against taboo; and as an inevitable consequence of this, it tends to think that the normal are to be found among those who successfully carry out the *tour de force* that is necessary to defy nature in the way that convention demands.

But if we once admit that sexual desire is legitimate, we are forced to regard these pseudo-abnormals, as normals as representatives of a sincere and natural humanity. There is certainly conflict (to employ Freud's term) between the *libido* and the *ego*. But we should realize that the *ego* in question is not the normal being which nature has created and placed upon this earth; it is, on the contrary, an artificially-moulded being, guided in-all the more deliberate aspects of its behaviour by taboo-like and illogical conventions, conventions the toxic influence of which has sapped its vitality and spirit, even though it still continues to defend them.

Psycho-analysis has noted the correspondence between the mental processes of the neurotic and the child. "In the neurotic," Freud tells us, "we always find a good many remains of infantile mental characteristics; either because he has been unable to outgrow the psycho-sexual conditions of childhood, or because he has returned to these conditions (i.e. because there has been either an arrest of development or a regression)". Doubtless; but it should be added that nature is on the side of the child, and artificial convention on the side of the average adult.The arrest in development which is here in question does not take place if the organism is allowed to continue in the course of its *natural* growth and expansion; it is an arrest in its social development; or, better expressed, it is a refusal to conform to certain rules in force at a particular moment in a particular society governed by a definitely anti-sexual system of ethics; it is a case of inability to transgress the natural law of favour of convention. Regression is only the return of an insufficiently trained animal to the behaviour that is natural to that animal.

The Normal Weakening of Censorship and Repression. —Further, a diminution in resistance to the claims of instinct may follow from two very normal causes, which are in no sense pathological.

As regards the first cause, we must remember that, in those civilizations which do not devote all their forces to combating the instincts of sex, these instincts are regarded as natural, normal, and legitimate. This type of civilization is, beyond all doubt, more healthy than the anti-sexual type; in it censorship and repression will not be the principal methods of education. The individual will not experience the effects of these mechanisms, or will at least experience them to a much smaller (sometimes an insignificant) extent. Resistance to instinct will not manifest itself, and will not bring neurosis in its train. Ignorance of the Judeo-Christian dogma of sin is one of the most favourable conditions for this type of society, where, so far as his sexual life is concerned, the individual enjoys an almost perfect mental equilibrium (absence of nervousness, anxiety, and unjustifiable shame). In such societies phycho-analysis would be quite unnecessary because it would find scarcely any patients needing cure. Psycho-analysis is a remedy for societies which suffer from a morbid hostility to sex.

The second cause is one that is to be found even in the heart of societies of this latter type. Even in these societies the prevailing anti-sexual views have always met with a certain degree of opposition.The dogma of sin, and all the consequences, psychological, ethical, and social, that ensue are not necessarily admitted by everyone without a struggle, a struggle that has sometimes led to a direct refusal to admit the doctrine in all its implications.In minds that are thoroughly impregnated with the spirit of religion, such a refusal has led to the creation of mixed systems grafted on the main body of animistic or even Christian doctrine, the incompatibility of the elements embodied in these systems sometimes giving them a very weird appearance; as in Mormonism or the sexual fantasies of the monk Rasputin. In other cases the refusal has been more whole-hearted, because it was based on rationalistic or materialistic principles, and has therefore taken the form of a logical and reasoned protest. In such cases, the anti-sexual prejudices have been deliberately condemned as unreasonable and unscientific; a process which has led to the creation of "libertines", who have rebelled both against the doctrines of animism themselves and against the sexual consequences of these doctrines. But in such "libertines", and in the rationalists who are not far behind them, there takes place a deliberate and voluntary rejection of censorship and repression, since these processes are looked upon as abnormal and undesirable; if therefore, in these cases, resistance to the claims of instinct has but little strength, this is not due to a pathological condition, but is the result of a deliberate and conscious act of will.

This, incidentally, is the reason why dreams do not necessarily always have a sexual meaning; a point which psycho-analysis does not contest. There are dreams which are inspired by vanity, by questions of business, of profession, of money. Certain persons, who are terrified by bulls or thunder, have periodical nightmares, of more or less the same content, dealing as they always do with these same objects of terror. But more than this: there are purely sexual dreams, which may even go as far as orgasm and nocturnal pollution, and which take no trouble to veil their meaning with circumlocutions or symbols but portray quite crudely the underlying erotic wishes. Now, if we admit that certain persons, as the result either of education or of deliberately adopted principle, have rejected censorship and repression, and in the waking state meet their libidinal desires without resistance, fear, or shame, it follows that these persons should have no dreams, or else at the most only voluptuous dreams, since in them the sexual resistance having been deliberately and permanently abolished, there should be no need to resort to round about or hypocritical expressions. It is difficult, therefore, to exaggerate the importance of dreams; for there exist cases where the characteristic dream process of veiled and incomplete expression should have no interest for minds which have already achieved complete freedom.

Its Bearing on Psycho-analysis.—The abandonment of the false theory of "sexual perversion" enables us to reply to certain objections that have been raised against psycho-analysis by its opponents; to reply, indeed, much more effectively than the psycho-analysts themselves have done, hampered as they are by their inadequate ethical formulations. It has been said that Freud has constructed his system on the basis of observations made on his own patients, and that in consequence his experience has been gained through abnormal and perverted cases in whom the sexual manifestations were unusually pronounced. He has therefore, it is maintained, built up his theory on exceptions, and the theory does not hold good for the majority of persons.

This criticism is fundamentally unsound. Except for certain

acute cases, which fall outside the territory of psycho-analysis altogether, the "sexual pervert" has no real existence, nor any proper place in the nomenclature of disease. Those who are improperly called perverts are persons with whom, for one reason or another, repression has not been able to establish itself with sufficient force, or by whom it may even have been deliberately rejected. But these are not pathological cases; they are, on the contrary, people who have remained in much closer touch with nature, truth, and health than those who, willing or otherwise, have succumbed to repression. It is they who, far more than others, have a true understanding of the meaning and value of sexual acts for the total physiological economy.Everything considered, deliberate chastity can be much more justifiably considered as a morbid symptom than can the ordinary manifestations of the sexual life, even when they are exuberant.

In the interests of psycho-analysis itself, we cannot therefore follow psycho-analysts in their division of sexuality into two classes; normal sexuality (i.e.that part which is tolerated by our conventional morality; and which has the officially sanctioned aim of reproduction), and abnormal sexuality or "perversion", Freud has, of course, employed figurative expressions to establish a theory in support of this distinction. These expressions are useful so long as they help him to explain the actually existing conflict which our conventions bring about; but we must not allow them to lead us into fundamental errors of principle.

Nor is there any reason to congratulate ourselves on the fact that neurosis is a sort of compromise between libido and the ego as educated by convention, a *pis aller* which still expressed, though in a milder form, the acute conflict between these two uncompromising adversaries. On the contrary, we must regard it as a strong condemnation of our whole artificial system of morality that we should be reduced to consider neurosis as a desirable alternative to the worse catastrophies that this system could, and would otherwise, produce. Why can we not see that what is really necessary is to reform the system itself, false as it is in its very essence, and not, while tolerating the fundamental cause of the trouble, to content ourselves with attacking neurosis, which is merely one of its effects? This policy of resignation and submission cannot be the final outcome of psycho-analytic therapy; timidity of this kind would be fatal to permanent success.

A similar change in point of view is required in another matter also. Adopting, as it would seem, the standpoint of conventional morality. Freud is pained and astonished to find his patients attached to their particular modes of pleasure, is disappointed to discover that they have immersed themselves in their disease in much the same way as in former times people retired to a monastery as a refuge from the blows of fate. Elsewhere, too, he states: "when we undertake to cure a patient of his symptoms, he opposes against us a vigorous and tenacious *resistance* throughout the entire course of the treatment...." and he adds: "One hardly ever meets with a patient who does not attempt to make a reservation in some department of his thoughts, in order to guard them against intrusion by the analyst..."

Doubtless; but the point is that there is no disease, and therefore no "patient", where a sense or function is allowed to develop naturally. "Disease" is here nothing but a conventional term, erroneously applied to a natural manifestation. Therefore it is not the so-called patient who is in need of cure; it is the term that should be changed. It is the whole system, which subjects to moral condemnation certain a moral but natural manifestations, that is false. There is no real disease here, and it is for this reason that we find the patient clinging so desperately to his condition; he feels that at bottom it is the obstacles opposed to these desires that are abnormal. He regards the conception of taboo as a collective human malady. It was really not worth while to show, as psycho-analysis has done, that this whole institution of taboo is in conflict with all the strongest and most spontaneous forces of nature, it, at the end, we are ourselves to take up arms against these latter and to range ourselves on the side of false, dangerous, and intolerant conventions. Psycho-analysis and the whole process of interpreting "symptoms" and "symbols" go astray, if they allow themselves to become docile instruments of the conventional errors, instead of proclaiming the rights of those great but hitherto misunderstood forces of the mind, which they themselves have sobrilliantly revealed.

Consequently, when Freud writes: "the preponderance of the sexual components of the impulse over the social components is the determining factor of the neurosis," we are in a position to complete his statement as follows: "and thus neurosis is the consequence of a conflict between the natural tendencies and the taboos which prohibit them and endeavour to make the artificial prevail against the natural." And this lead us to quote what the master psycho-analyst says a little further on: "We may say that hysteria is a caricature of an artistic creation, a compulsion neurosis a caricature of a religion, and a paranoiac delusion a caricature of a philosophic system." But since we ourselves are little convinced of the infallibility and superiority of the human intelligence, since we are conscious of all its faults and deficiencies, of its frequent inability to attain its object, of its uncertainties and formidable errors, we should like to add, as a counterpart to the Freudian suggestion : "we may say that a work of art is a rationalized hysteria, that a religion is a deliberately and authoritatively accepted compulsion neurosis, and that a philosophical system is a well-constructed paranoia."

The Difficulties Experienced by Psycho-analysis in Separating the Normal from the Abnormal. —It will be noted that Freud experiences a very natural difficulty when he has to draw a distinction between the normal and the abnormal, a difficulty which is a direct consequence of his uncritical adoption of these terms. In a chapter of his *Introductory Lectures* which he devotes to the sexual life of man, he has considerable doubts about "those perverts who have, so to speak, cut out sexual differentiations from their programme" (i.e. the inverts), first of all beacuse they are so very numerous (if we count both the open and the latent homosexuals), and secondly beacuse "they behave towards their sexual objects in more or less the same manner as the normal behave towards theirs."Then he hesitates again about another category: "there follows a whole series of abnormals whose sexual activity departs more and more *from what a reasonable man would consider desirable."* We have put these last words in italics because they show the whole weakness of the system; where are we to place the arbitrary line which shall delimit the group of "reasonable" men? The distinction is a purely subjective one; the judgement of the prohibitionistic missionary in Somerset Maugham's *Rain,* for instance, would be seperated by a deep gulf from that of the rationalistic thinker. It is once again the story of the heap of sand: it is impossible to say when it begins. The mechanistic theory of the sexual acts provides the only means of escape from this uncertainty, offering as it does a sure and satisfactory criterion. Without it all is arbitrary, and progress in the critical apprieciation of sexual ethics becomes impossible.

Freud himself admits that certain sexual acts, which are usually looked upon as curious or disgusting, "represents a real sexual activity of the individuals in question" an "play in their lives the same role that normal sexual satisfaction plays in ours; to obtain their own peculiar satisfaction, such individuals will make the same, often very great, sacrifices that we make." And further on: "To take refuge behind the statement that we are here concerned with rare cases, with pure curiosities, is to expose oneself to the likelihood of being very quickly deceived. The phenomena in question are, on the contrary, extremely frequent and "widespread...."; so much so, indeed, that "these perverse attitudes have existed in all known periods, among; all peoples among primitives, as well as among the most highly civilized; they have, moreover, sometimes enjoyed toleration and general recognition."

It could scarcely be possible to express better the fact that these so-called anomalies are not anomalies at all. It is clear from this, too, that confusion will continue to reign in all these ethical questions, which Freud himself has left untouched, until the sexual acts are definitely classified according to the strict and automatic rules of the mechanistic theory. We cannot help regretting, oncé again, that the great psycho-analyst should have continued to use the words "perverse" and perversion" in a strictly psychological treatment of the subject.

We must point out too how difficult it is to disciminate, as Freud attempts to do, between those perversions which are in a certain sense legitimate and those which are not. He says: "To the extent that the perverse actions only enter into the sexual life as preparatory or reinforcing measures, which lead up eventually to the normal sexual act, it would be unjust to describe them as perversions." It will surely be admitted that this concession is far from being easy to understand. A given action must surely be perverse or not. Nevertheless, this qualification shows us how Freud's observations on the psychology of sex compelled him to protest against the very conception of "perversion" which he himself employs, but which, in all probability, does not satisfy him. Unfortunately, like all half-measures of this kind, the somewhat vague and uncertain compromise that he proposes is not likely to prove really satisfactory to anyone.

But what is Freud's conclusion? That in the sexual sphere "we meet with special difficulties, which indeed begin to appear insoluble from the moment that we attempt to establish a definite distinction between simple variations, still within the bounds of normal physiology, and morbid symptoms."

It may seem that we are very lacking in modesty to suggest that our own solution provides the real key to the problems which the master has pronounced to be so complex. Nevertheless, we cannot avoid the impression that we have really brought scientific order into this confusion, and that a distinction that we have previously made is of great importance heer. It may, as Freud has said, be impossible to distinguish between variations and aberrations in the sexual sphere. But this is perhaps because we are attempting to make a distinction which corresponds to nothing in nature. If, however, we look for the distinction elsewhere, between functions and sense, between reproduction and pleasure; and if we reject both the arbitrary condemnations and the no less arbitrary approvals of social convention, then a more useful criterion emerger of itself, and it becomes possible to accord to each manifestation its true ethical value.

Criticism of Psycho-analytic Terminology (from the Ethical Point of View). — We quote here a few examples of the (from our present point of view) objectionable terminology to be found in Freud's work, a terminology which he has been led to use just because he has not recognized the full import of the distinction between reproduction and pleasure.

A *normal* sexual object can be found only, it is supposed, in a member of the opposite sex. Such an object is therefore contrasted with *abnormal* objects. But we know that, for the sexual sense, every mechanical procedure is normal, no matter what processes or persons are involved.

A *normal* instinct is supposed to be one which leads the individual to a person of the opposite sex. But we know that this so-called normal object-choice is only necessary for the function of reproduction, and has nothing to do with the instict (if we must employ this rather unsatisfactory word) of sexual pleasure, which demands nothing more than its mechanical satisfaction.

The nature of *normal* sexual satisfaction is no easier to understand. The function of reproduction can scarcely be carried out except by coitus; but pleasure may be completely attained by any other method, sometimes indeed even more completely; for in some individuals coitus is less satisfactory from this point of view that are certain other procedures.

The *normal* sexual aim is supposed to be "a contact of the

genital regions in coitus, sexual deturgescence, followed for a time by the disappearance of the corresponding instinct of desire." But we know that the aim of the sexual sense is perfectly attained, even though the specific pleasure may have occurred without coitus or even contact.

To say that the sexual instinct at the time of puberty "puts itself in the service of reproduction" and "becomes, so to speak, altruistic," has no meaning for us. We do not say that taste puts itself at the service of the stomach to aid the function of nutrition; in reality we know that function and sense are here entirely independent. We know too that, nine times out of ten, sexual pleasure pursues its own end, and is not at all concerned with reproduction, is indifferent to it, and, in many individuals, is even compatible with a strong conscious desire to avoid reproduction. The most that we can say is that the particular method of coitus offers certain great advantages from the point of view of satisfaction (a contact of mucous membranes, odour, possession of the partner, mutual pleasure, etc.), and therefore constitutes a very favourite choice; but even this is not true of all individuals.

These differences of terminology are important: it is not merely a question of words. This is immediately evident on reading Freud's conclusion at the end of his review of "sexual deviations" in his *First Contribution:* "In studying the perversions we see therefore that the sexual instinct has to fight against certain obstacles of a psychological kind, among which modesty and disgust are the most conspicuous. It would seem as though these latter were forces destined to keep the sexual instinct within the limits which are usually described as normal ...."

This view, though stated as if it were intended to be final, is far from satisfactory. It has the great disadvantage of seeming to give still further support to that distinction between the normal and the abnormal which has brought so much confusion into sexual questions, and which we ourselves have been obliged to abandon. It is true that this confusion is customary in psychiatry; but we should surely have expected psycho-analysis to rectify rather than to perpetuate mistakes of this description. Freud's view, as just expressed, leads him moreover to add a few lines later on: "This should make us expcet that the sexual instinct itself is not a simple entity, but is composed of various elements, which become dissociated in cases of perversion." This complication, which is far from easy to understand, is spared us if we reduce the manifestations of sex to their simple elements as revealed in the corresponding nervous mechanisms.

Finally, we cannot possibly approve of Freud when he says: "Having recognized how widespread are the tendencies to perversion, we have found ourselves compelled to admit that the disposition towards perversion is really the general and original disposition of the sexual instinct, which only becomes normal as a result of organic modifications and psychical inhibitions which occur in the course of development." To state the problem in this way is to say in effect that our general and original nature is artificial, while the artificial conventions so carefully erected by taboo are really natural. We ourselves have reached exactly opposite conclusions. The word "normal" in the above quotation has no meaning unless it signifies "conventional" or "agreeable to convention." We admit that there occurs a process of modification which results in a conventional state; but this process is detrimental to the natural condition which preceded it. And we have surely good grounds for wondering how it is that the artificial can have been regarded as *normal* by the psycho-analysts, who, above all others, have understood the true nature and importance of the neuroses which this condition, through its concomitant repressions, has produced.

Certain Further Criticisms of Psycho-analysis.— The indifference of psycho-analysts to moral implications had had some curious results. Psycho-analysis itself has been denounced as a cause of mental trouble, of having aggravated rather than relieved the patient's condition.

There is indeed some truth in this accusation. Psycho-analysis stopped with only half its task accomplished; it was an imperfect remedy that it provided for the patient. It began by telling him: "Yes, you are ill, and I will try to cure you...." In this way it discovered the great urgency of the sexual needs, but it omitted to give these needs the proper place in the natural development of the individual, and, through mental inertia or fear of its own conclusions, continued to regard the needs themselves as abnormal.

A great weakness, which has allowed the enemies of psycho-analysis to say that it was both incomplete and superfluous! Psycho-analysts have been told : "Your doctrines cannot serve as the basis of a new morality." And this is true, as long as psycho-analysis is regarded as a cure for those who have become ill as a result of conventional morality. The basis of a new and scientific sexual morality is beyond the sphere of psycho-analysis as thus conceived; it consists in the revision of sexual moral values, in the reclassification of these values in a reversal of the categories of "healthy" and "diseased."

This is not a matter of academic interest only. Because of its own timidity, psycho-analysis has real grounds for fearing that it is not an adequate or profitable form of therapy. It leaves its patients in the lurch. It enlightens them about themselves and their behaviour; but at the end it leaves them still with their neurosis, because the true cure has not been attempted. Where there is no disease, the physician's efforts are inevitably wasted. But a doctor is false to all his promises if he does not tell his patient that he is not ill, if he does not provide him with an enlightened view of the so-called morbid acts, and if he does not realize that much of what social convention looks upon as morbid is perfectly healthy from the point of view of nature. Thus psycho-analysis has correctly *understood* the urgency of sexual needs, it has *perceived* the possibilities of a cure through the reasonable satisfaction of these needs, but it has failed to realize the necessity for a revision of the ridiculous way in which our present conventions look upon the manifestations of sex.

It seems unnecessary, therefore, to follow psycho-analysis in its recent accessory ventures into the uncertain field of metaphysics, where it contrasts life and death, associating libido with the former, and stern reality with the latter. We enter here on the unprofitable paths of mysticism. Sexuality and sexual behaviour are facts, and facts which can sometimes be terribly deceptive. Their roots lie deep in the physiology of organic beings; they form one of the essential substrata of these beings. They demand obedience, just as do the other senses and the other functions. The individual experiences them as intense needs, and, in opposing these needs, humanity is committing suicide. What is the useof metaphysics in the face of these realities — realities that are far stronger than any words? The great philosophical systems seldom escape the temptation of conquetting with mysticism. But this latter, wrongly understood or confusedly applied, leads men back to dogma, when their real needs is for action.

Logical Doubts of Psycho-analysis Concerning the So-called Perversions. — We can scarcely doubt that, with his usual perspicacity and profound knowledge of the phenomena of sex, the Viennese professor must regard with suspicion the psychiatric and moral theory of perversion. He has not given us any clear statement of these suspicions. Nevertheless, certain of his words make us realize that they are there. He speaks in places of the "so-called perverts." He uses, at least occasionally, the expression "deviations with relation to the sexual object," which, being strictly objective, is infinitely preferable to the terms "perversion" or "aberration." He adds that "there is little justification for attaching to the term perversion a sense of blame." Finally, he does not hesitate to pronounce that "in view of the frequency of perversion, we are forced to admit that the disposition to these tendencies is not something rare and exceptional, but is an integral part of the normal constitution...." Here then he comes very near to abandoning the word and the concept of "perversion" and to adopting the position that we ourselves have taken.

This should justify us in refusing to follow Freud, when he says (at the conclusion of the passages just cited) that infantile sexuality evolves in such a way as to develop "into perversion, into neurosis, or into normal sexual life." Of these three terms one is superfluous. Infantile sexuality is free or hampered, complete or incomplete in its development, at liberty to unfold naturally or trammelled by repression. In the first case, we have the normal sexual life, which should be regarded as such, no matter what the particular activities in which it manifests itself; since these activities merely concern the detailed mechanism employed, and are, in truth, still normal, even when they are traditionally regarded as perverse. In the second case we have the neurosis which results from, and bears witness to, repression or restriction, and this no matter what may be the particular tendencies repressed. These are the only two alternatives —which amounts to saying that at bottom there is only nature (the instinctive exercise of the sexual sense) or convention (the taboo of this exercise).

Freud and the Psychiatrical Theory of Degeneration. — The inadequate theory of the degeneration, with which psychiatrists hope to reply to all objections, is, on the other hand, one against which Freud himself has been constrained to rebel, and which he has replaced by a new tentative system of his own. According to the principles of sexual taboo, any individual who exhibits sexual tendencies that are not strictly confined to the goal of reproduction must be considered abnormal. "It has in fact become customary to designate all morbid manifestations not of traumatic or infectious origin as degenerative. Indeed, Magnan's classification, of degenerates makes it possible that the highest general configuration of nervous accomplishment need not exclude the application of the concept of degeneration. Under the circumstances, it is a question what use and what new content the judgement of 'degeneration' still possesses." Let us add that psychiatry has been kind enough to invent a new term for those patients who are obviously not lacking in intelligence (and who may even possess genius); it calls them "superior degenerates," hoping thus to satisfy everybody.

It is now easy to reply to Freud's question. When the psychiatrists find themselves confronted with a case which displays neither trauma nor infection, they still refuse to regard their patient as a normal individual. They consider him abnormal, because he does not conform to the conventional pattern decreed by taboo. But since this so-called anomaly must, from the scientific point of view, be supposed to have a cause, they are forced at all costs to invent such a cause, and do so with the help of the empty theory of degeneration, which does not mean, and never has meant, anything. If it had a meaning, it should — etymologically — be somewhat as follows: The degenerate is a person who, instead of blindly following the dictates of taboo as regards what is and what is not permitted, in open defiance of the ancient traditions of the human race, dares to behave without reference to these dictates. Degeneration would thus consist in the fact of refusing to obey rules that we know to be conventional rather than natural. Such a definition, however, falls into the old error of the psychiatrists, and the word "degeneration" itself, as Freud himself has realized, would only be worthy of the physicians portrayed by Moliere.

The Mechanistic Theory of Sexuality in its Relation to Morals. — The foregoing critical examination will permit us to embark on a very necessary but very delicate undertaking: that of deciding what theory of sex we ourselves shall adopt, as being logically and scientifically sound enough to be of use in determining the relation between sex and morality.

We were compelled to admit with Freud, that "the neuroses are products, not of sexuality itself, but of the conflict between sex and the ego." Indeed, it is scarcely possible to do otherwise, in view of the fact that the ego is a complex resultant of education, is in practice enslaved to taboo and is hampered in all its actions by the restrictions which taboo imposes. The above phrase is indeed comparable to saying: "The diseases of the stomach are products, not of hunger or of the need of food, but of a conflict between hunger and the lack of food." For both hunger and sex, are injunctions of nature: that which opposes them is unnatural prohibition. The true *ego*—not that of which psycho-analysis speaks, but that with which we are born and in virtue of which we are *ourselves*—this ego, far from being in conflict with sex, is inseparable from sex; and it is when we try to separate it, to make it declare war on sex, that it begins to suffer and to lose touch with nature. Further we ought not to say, as Freud does, that the ego "seeks, at each stage of its development, to put itself in harmony with its sexual organization, to adopt itself to this organization." It is born in complete harmony with sexuality, a fact which finds expression in the infantile manifestations of sex. But when we endeavour to transfrom the ego, it seeks, and is obliged to seek, the least harmful and painful of the possible alternatives with which it is presented when it is constrained and harried by social convention into giving up its natural harmony with sex.

But *any* such alternative to a full recognition of the rights of sex (the recognition for which we have been pleading here) is bound to be painful and unsatisfactory; it is bound in some sense, even to be pathological. On the other hand, once we have recognized the elementary rights of sex, we are in a position to lay down the following rules with regard to the relations between a sexual act and its object (and therefore also with regard to the ultimate evaluation of such an act before the bar of an enlightened and reasonable moral code):

(i) *A sexual object is not essential or indispensable for the full satisfaction of the sexual sense. For this purpose, any one mechanical process may be as good as any other, whether this process involves the use of an object or not.*

(ii) *If an object be employed, the nature of this object may vary from one case to another, and is never essential. The important element lies in the mechanical process at work, and this may quite well function without an object (as in solitary onanism).*

(iii) *It is purely as a consequence of the obsessive (perhaps atavistic) influence of certain limitations imposed by sexual taboo that certain of the available mechanisms are prohibited or disapproved while others are tolerated.*

(iv) *As a consequence of this taboo there has arisen an artificial but very persistent belief that the mechanisms approved by convention are ethically superior, or even that they alone are justifiable. In this way there has grown up for example the belief in the greater justifiability of intersexual coitus, and, within this sphere itself (implying an even narrower field of choice, but one that is very characteristic of taboo) of coitus between a man and woman who have been united by certain conventional rites (marriage).*

In a word, the object is secondary, and the mechanism alone is of prime importance: all our investigations point to this conclusion.

The concept of sexual mechanism enables us to introduce considerable simplifications into the theory of sex. For instance, there is no need any more to ask, with Freud, whether the anal and oral mucous membrances can be considered as "possessing the value of the genital zone." First of all, he should have said "sexual zone" to avoid that very confusion between genital and sexual against which psycho-analysis itself has so often protested. In the second place, we have to admit that one mechanical process is as good as another, provided it is equally effective. There are perhaps qualitative differences between the various possible mechanical processes, but they are fundamentally alike in their real nature. This being so, if the anal, oral and sexual mucous membranes are all equal suited to play their part in the mechanical process, they are all of equal value, and it is no more necessary to delimit these specific zones than it is to compare their relative efficacy. They are of equal value, and, except for certain qualitative differences, might have just the same worth as a purely muscular process in which a mucous membrane played no part; but should we say as regards the use of the hands that there is a perhensile zone "which possesses the value of a genital zone"? In reality, all this amounts to nothing more than that the anal and oral zones behave like the genital zone; a comparison which, of no great value from the anatomical point of view, only becomes useful if we consider the behaviour of the zones from the strictly mechanistic standpoint. This behaviour derives its value from the fact that the cavities in question have all more or less the same form; but we know very well that in onanism the prehensile members show themselves quite capable of creating an artificial cavity which serves the same mechanical purpose. Therefore we cannot say with Freud that there exists a "secondary genital apparatus"' there are many forms of apparatus, all capable of stimulating, more or less successfully, the organs of the sexual sense, and, by appropriate contact and movement, of producing this specific pleasure in varying intensity and completeness. We must not even exclude vision, which plays so important a role in the case of the *voyeur* and exhibitionist, and is ultimately reducible, from the point of view of physiology, to an indirect sense of touch.

Conclusion. — We satisfy our hunger and our thirst, and fortunately the human mind is so constituted that it has not pronounced any taboos on the public or private gratifications of these natural acts. But quite the opposite holds of the sexual acts. Notwithstanding their imperious character, their conformity to nature, and their evident biological necessity, sexual ethical systems have, in the face of all logical and scientific evidence, prohibited them, persecuted them, vilified them and regarded them as immoral and superfluous. This attitude has produced its inevitable consequences. Repression resulted in neurosis. This is not surprising, though the absence of these effects would have been astonishing enough. And this neurosis, latent, chronic, or acute, according to variations in temperament and circumstance, has reacted on the whole individual and social life of modern civilization.

When members of this civilization find themselves in a society where, owing to primitive conditions of existence, or some other reason, sexual life is less restricted and neurosis is unknown, they breathe more freely and are thrown into a state of wonder and delight as though they had recovered their Paradise Lost; this was the case with those who discovered Tahiti (New Cythera) or those who visited Laos, Bali, or certain parts of Africa. No more neurosis! Is such a thing possible? As in Jules Verne's *Dr. Ox,* they get a vision of the healthy life — that is, life without neurosis —on leaving behind them their conventional environment, all saturated as it is with harmful emanations. The neurosis due to sexual prohibition weighs heavily on the whole of modern civlization; it reinforces the already numerous ills due to mental overwork, defective hygiene and social fatigue. It is in vain that our worried and harassed contemporaries try to find a means of escape in artificial excitements or the inanities of sport; they remain slaves to neurosis, and, as we shall try to show elsewhere, it is this which probably accounts in large part for the diminished fertility of the Western races, who are the most affected by the sexual prohibitions.

To have revealed the origin of neurosis, as Freud has done, is excellent. To have proved this origin, by bringing to light the causative emotion, usually misunderstood if not actually forgotten and relegated to the unconscious, was no less valuable. The creation for this purpose of the method of psycho-analysis, designed to evoke the pathogenetic factors of the neurosis, both proximate and remote, from the associations of the patient himself, was an admirable piece of work. And finally, by the catharsis of the rediscovered memories and emotions, to diminish the neurosis and attempt a cure, this was only a development of the natural task of the physician.

But psycho-analysis ought not to remain a mere therapeutic tool in the service of an out-of-date system of conventions. Clearly, it should also serve as a point of departure for the revision and reform of this system, with a view to the better and understanding and organization of the sexual life. Otherwise, the full significance of its discoveries will have been lost.